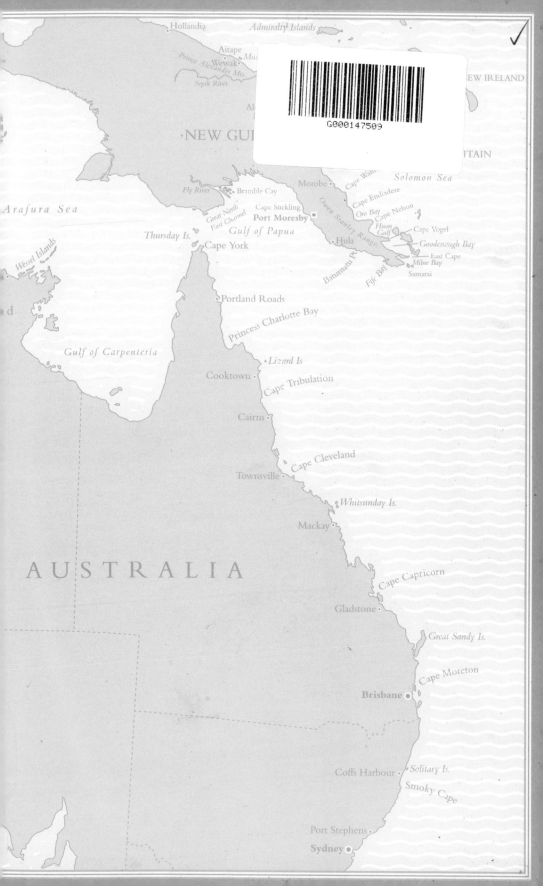

THE MIEGUNYAH PRESS

This is number sixty-one in the
second numbered series of the
Miegunyah Volumes
made possible by the
Miegunyah Fund
established by bequests
under the wills of
Sir Russell and Lady Grimwade.

'Miegunyah' was the home of
Mab and Russell Grimwade
from 1911 to 1955.

A MERCIFUL JOURNEY

A MERCIFUL JOURNEY

Recollections of a World War II Patrol Boat Man

MARSDEN HORDERN

THE
MIEGUNYAH
PRESS

THE MIEGUNYAH PRESS
An imprint of Melbourne University Publishing Ltd (MUP Ltd)
187 Grattan Street, Carlton, Victoria 3053, Australia
mup-info@unimelb.edu.au
www.mup.com.au

First published 2005
Text © Marsden Hordern 2005
Illustrations from Marsden Hordern's personal collection
Design and typography © Melbourne University Publishing
Ltd 2005

National Library of Australia Cataloguing-in-Publication entry

Hordern, Marsden C. (Marsden Carr), 1922– .
    A merciful journey: recollections of a world war II patrol
    boat man.

    Bibliography.
    Includes index.
    ISBN 0 522 85165 7.

    1. Hordern, Marsden C. (Marsden Carr), 1922—
    Correspondence. 2. World War, 1939–1945—Naval opera-
    tions, Australian. 3. World War, 1939–1945—Naval
    operations, Australian—Anecdotes. I. Title.

940.545994

For my mother who kept all my letters

There's something in a flying horse,
There's something in a huge balloon;
But through the clouds I'll never float
Until I have a little Boat...

Rocking and roaring like a sea;
The noise of danger's in your ears,
And ye have all a thousand fears
Both for my little Boat and me!

'PETER BELL'
WILLIAM WORDSWORTH, 1819

CONTENTS

ACKNOWLEDGEMENTS

My principal debt is to my mother, Iris Mary Hordern. When I was a child she urged me to keep a diary, and when I left home she insisted that I write every Sunday to let her know how the world was treating me. She kept all my letters and after her death I found them here in a box in the attic. They sharpened and corrected the recollections of many of the incidents recorded in these memoirs.

Commander A. I. Chapman RAN (Ret'd), my captain in HMAS *Abraham Crijnssen* in 1942, supplied the details of her unusual commissioning into the RAN and the photograph of her leaving on convoy escort duty. The account of His Majesty's Australian Motor Launch *814*'s operations in 1943 was greatly improved by 'Chips' Wood, her First Lieutenant at that time, who read and commented on the relevant chapters.

Other people helped me too. Captain J. J. Doyle AM, RAN (Ret'd), a former RAN Hydrographer, prepared the maps, conversion tables and illustrations, and gave many faded and yellowing photographs a restored appearance. Josephine Tait, Archivist of Knox Grammar School, assisted my research for Chapter Two, and the late John Iremonger, sometime publisher of Hale and Iremonger, Melbourne University Press, and Allen and Unwin, tutored and encouraged me to continue.

In 1989 when my friend our family doctor Angus Cottee pronounced that there 'were two more books' in me yet, I was doubtful. That he has been proved right is evidence of his continuing care, and I thank him for that.

I was most fortunate to have the editorial assistance of Clare Coney. The meticulous care she brought to the grooming of the manuscript was equalled only by the tact and tolerance she showed when she pulled me into line.

My special thanks are also due to the late Lieutenant F. O. Monk, my mentor on the second expedition up the Sepik River. In 1945 he led a dangerous patrol through that part of New Guinea, discovered the Indian prisoners held there by the Japanese, and gave me the Japanese general's pass reproduced in this book.

And for the third time I cannot express the thanks I owe to Lesley my wife for typing one of my manuscripts, reducing its bulk, and greatly improving it as she went along.

'Rivenhall'
Warrawee, NSW
Christmas Day, 2004

PREFACE

Like fingers of doom, the three chimneys of Battersea Power Station leapt out of the fog, flashing under the wing of Piper Cub G-AKAA. Sick with fright, I shoved the throttle forward, eased back on the stick as far as I dared, and climbed into the darkening sky. Now at least we knew where we were, and that was some relief.

Late autumn was known to be a time for fogs in the Thames Valley, but the forecast for 6 November 1949 had been promising, and I had left Elstree Aerodrome with Richard Rumbold on a return flight to Lympne in Kent in clear weather. A former RAF bomber pilot and aviation writer, Richard had flown the Cub on the outward journey while I navigated. We had got lost somewhere over the hop-fields of Kent but with good visibility it had been a simple matter to pick out a railway line, follow it to the next station, zoom down to read its name—Headcorn Junction—and fix our position.

Now we were lost again, but in much more dangerous conditions. We had left Lympne on the return journey late in the afternoon and I was at the controls. I had never flown at night; we had no radio or landing lights and, as we approached the sprawling suburbs of south-east London, the fog rolled in obscuring the ground. In desperation we began dropping lower through the overcast to identify a landmark and this often fatal practice nearly proved so for us when Battersea Power Station's chimneys dramatically revealed themselves.

Still unable to see the ground sufficiently to estimate our drift and correct our course for Elstree, we flew on blindly into the gathering night until Richard tapped me on the shoulder and pointed under the wing to a double line of orange lights. It was an aerodrome and, determined not to miss it, I began to circle the control tower, narrowly missing a Swiss Air Constellation coming in to land. When at last a green Verey light arched into the air, I touched down thankfully on the grass beside the runway of what turned out to be Northolt Airport. I had only learned to fly a Tiger Moth eleven months before and, unfamiliar with a high-wing monoplane, I was tense and nervous.

We landed badly, bouncing heavily along the ground and, as we rolled to a stop, a rabbit, illuminated by the runway's lights, sat up in front of us and scratched its ear. This broke the tension. Laughing uncontrollably, we shook hands, and Richard confided to me that it had been his most frightening experience in the air.[1]

We had been saved by a miracle, or—to use my father's expression —a 'journeying mercy'. He found them continually in everyday life. Bestowed by a kindly Providence to lighten life's load, they ranged from discovering a flat tyre while at a service station or finding an electrician in the congregation at Evensong when the power failed, to unexpected deliverance from real dangers and disasters. As a child I had dismissed them as just lucky breaks but now, reviewing my long and happy life, I see many of my escapes from trouble as my father would have seen them.

Most of the incidents mentioned in this book were recorded in diaries, journals, log books, letters and reports. Others, however, not recorded at the time, are told as I remember them, and may be partly fictional for, as T. H. Huxley aptly observed, 'Autobiographies are essentially works of fiction, whatever biographies may be.'

1 | MILK AND HONEY

My mother's voice quavered on the phone. 'I don't want you to think, Lesley', she began nervously, 'that Marsden was named for that *dreadful wicked* man. That had nothing to do with it.'

My wife was surprised. During her seven years as a member of the Hordern family she had imbibed much of its lore, and it was firmly imprinted on her mind that I had indeed been named for the Reverend Samuel Marsden. She had frequently been told that at the time of my birth in 1922 my father, Hugh Hordern, himself a member of the cloth, was reading *The Life and Labours of the Reverend Samuel Marsden* by the Reverend J. B. Marsden and had been so impressed by its lauding of the parson's achievements as chief chaplain of the colony, as a magistrate and in the New Zealand mission field, that he had settled on the name 'Marsden' for his newly arrived fourth child.

But Australian historiography was maturing; we were beginning to take a harder look at our legendary figures, and in 1961, when the Australian Broadcasting Commission produced a television serial, *The Outcasts*, based on the colony's early years, its portrayal of Marsden as a 'flogging parson', notorious for his harsh discipline and irascible and violent magisterial behaviour, had greatly diminished my parents' reverence for that godly man. We had lent our eighteenth-century cot as a prop for the series and, as the *Australian Women's Weekly* was about to interview me on the Hordern/Marsden relationship, my mother was anxious to play it down.

My mother went on to tell Lesley that, in fact, my name reflected a connection between the Marsden and Hordern families. In 1841, my father's great-uncle Anthony had married Harriet Marsden—daughter of a Samuel Marsden from Windsor, and reputedly a cousin of the Reverend Samuel—and, although the relationship between Harriet and my parents seemed too remote to justify such commemoration, Lesley had to be satisfied with that.

With hindsight, my parents might also have queried the suitability of the second name 'Carr' which they gave to their four sons, it having been the maiden name of my great-grandmother Rebecca, wife of John Hordern. Their son, my grandfather Edward Hordern, who also bore 'Carr' as a second name, was often referred to as 'E. Carr Hordern' to distinguish him from his uncle and cousin, both of them 'Edward', and as time went on our branch of the family was sometimes known as 'the Carr Horderns'. At the time of his marriage to Rebecca in 1845, John Hordern must have known that her father, John Carr, had been deported to Sydney for theft, but this unsavoury knowledge had been concealed from succeeding generations. When my brothers and I were born there was still a stigma attached to convict ancestry, and it seems unlikely that my father would have chosen to perpetuate the name of this great-grandfather if he had known the true story.

Despite these nominal handicaps, I grew up in a secure and happy environment, enjoying the benefits of two quite separate facets of Sydney life. From the Horderns there was the comfort of wealth, for while we ourselves were not rich, our background was secure. My Australian forebears, Anthony and Ann Hordern, had arrived in Sydney in 1825 with four children, one of whom was my great-grandfather, John. Their means were slender, they had little education and no political influence, but they were industrious and business-like and, through the shop-keeping activities begun by Ann and fostered by her in the next generation, they prospered. By the third generation the family had become a force in the Sydney retail world; Anthony and Sam Hordern were rapidly developing their father's store, Anthony Hordern & Sons, which was to become one of the largest 'emporiums' in the British Empire, their cousins Edward and Cecil Hordern had sizeable shops in George Street, and my grandfather, Edward Carr, and his two brothers, John and Alfred, had established Hordern Brothers in Pitt Street.

Although not reaching the stature of their cousins' emporium, Hordern Brothers did well, and in 1906 Edward Carr bought a large house in Centennial Avenue, Chatswood. He named it 'Chislehurst', for his wife's home town in Kent, and there he and my grandmother, Frances Lillie, raised their four sons and two daughters. To my family, accustomed to spartan rectories of the rural or inner-city parishes in which we grew up, this ornate mansion, set in about fifteen acres of gardens and paddocks, with an orchard, stables, cows, horses, glasshouse, aviary, tennis court and croquet lawn, seemed very grand, and while we visited it only by invitation, the very fact of its existence fortified us. There was also security in knowing that while my father had a limited clergy stipend, so that we seldom had expensive new possessions or much money to spend and were accustomed to wear hand-me-down clothes, in the matter of education, health and holidays, my grandfather saw to it that we did not want. We were, as St Paul put it so neatly to the Corinthians, 'as having nothing and yet possessing all things'.

We also benefited indirectly from a certain renown attached to our name. This emanated mainly from the achievements of my grandfather's cousin, Samuel Hordern, who had made Anthony Hordern & Sons a household name in Australia, but my grandfather was also highly respected in the city as managing director of Hordern Brothers.

My heritage from my maternal forebears, the Whites, was of a different character and perhaps more valuable to me. Here was no sustaining material wealth; my mother's father, Walter David White, whom we called 'Bompie'—a childish corruption of 'Pappy'—was a journalist and poet, and lived in a small cottage in Chatswood, where he kept a few laying hens and a much-loved Australian terrier. He had no car or servants, and the outhouse was in the backyard. But he was a reader and a thinker, and by gentle instruction gave me an appreciation of literature and art and an interest in history which has greatly enhanced my life.

My father, Frederick Hugh Hordern, was the fourth son of Edward Carr and Frances Lillie. During the family's early years my grandfather, as overseas buyer for Hordern Brothers, travelled continually between Australia and England, and the family lived there for several long periods. During one of these my father and two of his brothers attended Eastbourne College, and after their return home continued their education at SCEGS, North Sydney. On leaving school my father began work as a salesman in Hordern Brothers, where it was assumed that with his elder brothers, Edward ('Ward') and Stewart, and his twin, Maurice, he would carry on the family business and enjoy the comfortable lifestyle it provided. But Divine intervention overruled my grandfather's plans for Hugh. As a schoolboy, while attending church at Wentworth Falls, he had met the parish locum tenens, the Reverend George Alexander Chambers, whose 'fair complexion ... round face and curly hair' had earned him the descriptor 'cherubic'. They struck a common chord which sounded sweetly for the rest of their lives. Soon after my father had left school, Chambers, then vice-principal of Moore Theological College in Sydney and later to become the first bishop of Central Tanganyika, called on him in Hordern Brothers and spoke to him so persuasively that my father abandoned all thought of a business career and opted for Holy Orders.

My grandfather opposed the idea strongly, painting a discouraging picture of the drawbacks of clerical life. He made it clear to my father that if he became a clergyman he would have to make do with his stipend, which would be derisory compared to that of a director of a large retail store, and that he would have no permanent home or even be able to choose where he would live. This was a stern judgement, but my father had an ally in his mother, Frances Lillie, who loved and actively supported her church, and most probably had influenced his decision. A gentle and cultured woman, she was also determined, and in the end my grandfather, yielding to pressure, agreed that Hugh should have his way. He also softened sufficiently to ensure that Hugh did not suffer the extreme poverty he had threatened.

In 1909 my father attended Moore Theological College in Sydney under Canon Nathaniel Jones and completed the ordinary course of studies in 1911. He then entered St John's Hall at the University of Durham in England, where he graduated L.Th. Returning to Sydney, he was ordained in 1915 and appointed curate of the Holy Trinity Church, Dulwich Hill, under the rectorship of his former mentor, G. A. Chambers. Over the next few years he helped Chambers establish Trinity Grammar School, and claimed to have taken its first class of about six boys, seated around the rectory dining table.

In 1914 he and my mother, Iris Mary White, were married. This was the result of another significant schoolboy meeting. Some five years before at a fete held at the waterfront home of his cousin Cecil Hordern, in Kirribilli, he had seen my mother, herself a schoolgirl, serving on the cake stall, and had fallen in love. A prolonged courtship and lengthy engagement followed, but on my father's return from Durham there was to be no further delay and they were married on 14 November. The wedding was held at St Paul's Church of England, Chatswood, with a reception for eighty guests at 'Chislehurst'.

At the end of my father's curacy with George Chambers he and Iris, now the parents of two small girls, Mary and Noel, moved to Tasmania. He had been appointed curate of the historic St George's Church at Battery Point in Hobart under the Reverend Donald Baker who, like Chambers, was to wear a mitre in later life. Renting a two-storied house on The Esplanade, they were soon caught up in the social life of Hobart, and made enduring friendships there.

Photographs, documents and letters from these Tasmanian years show them to have been very happy. They also record the beginnings of my father's colourful driving career. He now owned a Harley-Davidson motorcycle fitted with a sidecar to accommodate my mother and the girls, and in their travels around Hobart he several times fell foul of the law. After his death I found among his papers a traffic summons, endorsed 'keep this—very precious'. Attached to it was a newspaper cutting reporting that he had been fined five pounds for riding his machine at speed down one of Hobart's principal streets and, in making a right-angled turn, had 'not kept close to the left-hand kerb as practicable'. This latter description sounds a familiar note with those who saw him driving around Warrawee in his retirement years, straddling or even passing inside a 'silent cop'. On another occasion in Hobart, according to family legend, when riding at night without lights, he had hit a cow which was also travelling on the street without lights. This insouciant attitude to the rules of the road persisted throughout his life, earning from his colleagues of the cloth the nickname 'Jehu'—'for he driveth furiously' (II Kings, ix, 20). When he finally gave up his licence and I transferred its distinctive number plate 'HH123' to my wife's car, she was several times greeted with the earnest comment, 'I'm so glad to see that the Reverend Hordern has given up driving!'

In 1918 the family returned to Sydney where my father was appointed curate of Rose Bay and Vaucluse, and from 1920 to 1922 was curate-in-charge of the Conventional District of Rose Bay and North Bondi. With the family's numbers increased to five by the arrival of my brother Hugh in 1920, they had moved into a cottage in Newcastle Street, Rose Bay, which they named 'Narara' after my maternal grandfather's house. The Harley-Davidson had given way to a Ford car, more suited to the transport of their growing family.

With total disregard for my father's clerical obligations, I was born at 'Narara' on the morning of Sunday, 26 March 1922, and news of my imminent arrival that morning threw Matins into confusion. The church warden, Dr F. G. N. Stephens, who was also our doctor, was called away with a nurse to attend the birth and my anxious father, having chosen the shortest possible hymns and lessons, delivered a sketchy sermon and hasty benediction and raced home to greet me.

When I was six months old my father became rector of the parish of Prospect and Seven Hills, 28 kilometres west of Sydney. This parish breathed Australian history and the spirit of its pioneering families—

the Lawsons, Icelys, Howards, Horwoods, Pearces, Archdalls and many more. In 1789 the First Fleet diarist Captain Watkin Tench, pushing westward, had climbed a hill and descried a range of blue mountains. His vantage point, 'Tench's Prospect Hill', was later simply named 'Prospect'. In 1791, favourably impressed by Tench's report on the country, Governor Phillip settled twelve families on small farms in the vicinity, and in 1841 when St Bartholomew's 'Church on the Hill' was opened, it became the mother church of a large parish incorporating Seven Hills, Blacktown, Toongabbie, Wentworthville, Parklea, Girraween, Bungarribee and Pendle Hill.

Here, for the next five years, assisted by two catechists, W. A. Parrott and Eric Gidley, my father ministered to his flock in a world which was as close as I have ever come to finding heaven on earth. My first recollections of life there are of hills and valleys, clear running creeks, farms, old country homesteads, horses, cows, sheep, pigs, poultry, fields of standing wheat and ripening corn. In 1923 in his publication *A Delectable Parish*, William Freame painted an evocative picture of the family's new environment:

> Comparatively slow may be the features of life in Prospect and Seven Hills, where the stores close their doors during the dinner hour, but it is ... this repose that lends to the district one of its charms. To its environs approach the cultivated fields and green meadows bisected by long winding red roads, along which the Rector rides his favourite horse as he does the rounds of his extensive parish.

The handsome two-storied Victorian rectory adjoining the church was approached from the road by a carriageway which ran under arches of climbing roses and past the stables to the house, and from its upstairs balconies and the square iron-railed tower on the roof we had extensive views over the countryside towards Castle Hill, Toongabbie and Prospect. Around the house were several acres of paddocks occupied by horses and cows, pig pens, sheds and other farm buildings.

St Andrew's Church, erected in 1880, was younger than many of its parishioners. Simple country people, they lived close to the soil, and at Harvest Festival decorated the church with an abundance which was in itself an act of worship, festooning nave, chancel and pulpit with sheaves of corn and wheat, pumpkins, potatoes and marrows, apples, pears and other manifestations of earthly bounty.

For many of them, Sunday service was the social event of the week, and about an hour before the service commenced they would start arriving, all in Sunday best, on foot, horseback, in sulkies or occasionally by car. The horse-owners would water their animals at the trough near the Parish Hall, ease their girths or unharness them from the sulkies and tether them under trees in the churchyard, while the dogs which had trotted along behind, settled down in a patch of shade.

One warm afternoon, when the little church was nearly full, one of these dogs came in. Evensong was in full flight; we had had the usual prayers, the Magnificat, the collect asking for our darkness to be lightened, and to be defended from all perils and dangers of the night. We had sung a hymn or two, and father in his freshly laundered cassock and surplice was in the pulpit when a large brown dog walked through the western doors and up the aisle. After an anxious search and a lot of sniffing he found his master and, settling beside him with a satisfied grunt, began to snore loudly. My father, inured to the snores of parishioners, paid no attention. But I watched fascinated as a brown riding boot emerged from the end of the pew, paused heel-down for a moment in mid-air, then plunged into the dog's belly. It fled down the aisle with a shriek and my father, bringing his sermon to a close, announced the collection hymn. His flock filed out, collected their various animals and headed for home.

In October 1924 the family was increased to seven by the arrival of my brother John. This placed a further strain on a household which, like many others of the time, relied for its maintenance on intensive manual labour. The rectory had no electricity, and therefore no washing machines, refrigerators, or other such appliances which we now cannot easily live without, and while at dusk the house glowed softly with candle and lamp light—a romantic sight—the candles and lamps had to be lit, trimmed or filled regularly. For domestic use we had rainwater caught from the roof and stored in iron tanks, and if this failed in long dry spells we could draw clear water in a bucket from a well close to the kitchen door. But there was no running hot water. For the communal bath, buckets of hot water had to be carried upstairs from the kitchen, where it was heated in a boiler on the fuel stove. In winter we had wood fires in all the principal rooms and these were always needing replenishment. There were no septic tanks; two separate outhouses stood well away from the house, and all the bedrooms were equipped with chamber pots which had to be emptied each morning.

Fortunately my mother was spared these gruelling and unpleasant chores. Grandfather Edward Carr provided funds for domestic help which would have been quite beyond my father's means and our staff increased in number as the household grew. Many of these were young Britishers who were coming out in numbers at that time—perhaps as a result of the First World War and the 'flu epidemic which followed it—in search of a new life. The exception was Elizabeth Sherwood, the first and most notable member of our workforce, who came to us from Blacktown at the age of twenty-six. She was to remain with the family for over half a century and become intimately associated with all our lives. A cook and maid of all work, she had no set routine of days or hours of duty; every couple of weeks her father would drive over in his sulky to take her home for the weekend, but before she left she would bake extra cakes and prepare pots of stews or curries so that we would not starve in her absence. Her sister Violet also joined us as a housemaid and to help with the washing—an onerous ritual performed on Mondays in the laundry equipped with a wood-fired copper, large tubs and a mangle.

Minnie Godfrey, a general help who hailed from London Bridge, could turn her hand to almost anything, but for us children her greatest asset was her glass eye. She used this to great advantage when there was strife in the nursery; she would take it out and, holding it in her hand, fix us with the other while she regaled us with colourful stories of her childhood in the London slums. She never came to terms with Australian fauna and to the delight of the nursery always referred to wombats as 'wombums'.

Our nanny, Gertrude, a buxom, fair-haired woman who wore lace-up boots, had also come from the 'old country'. With a smile and kind word for everyone, she was a great favourite in our home and in the parish, and her engagement to the 'elderly' Mr Lovegrove and their susbsequent marriage in St Andrew's was a big event for us. My sisters Mary and Noel attended her as flower girls and church and parish hall were lavishly decorated by her many friends. When she left us I felt bereft, but as the Lovegroves lived just down the road towards the station I occasionally went to stay in their little cottage. Roses bloomed in their front garden and I slept in a small white-washed room at the back of the house. After the evening meal 'Nanny' would hear my prayers, tuck me into bed, read to me and kiss me good night. She always left the candle burning and when there was a draught I would watch its flickering shadows playing on the roof timbers.

Among the governesses we had from time to time were the Misses May Button and Lucy Winchcombe. Miss Button, member of a respected pioneering family, lived at home in Parramatta and had to be collected daily in the sulky from the Seven Hills station. Miss Winchcombe lived with us, occupying a room which, because of its distinctively purple-patterned wallpaper and curtains, was always known as 'the mauve room'. My final childhood memory of the female staff who passed across the stage during our years at Seven Hills is of two housemaids, Char and Dorothy, recalled only for their uniforms and starched white caps.

The outdoor maintenance of the rectory was under the super-vision of Mr Main, a gently spoken Englishman of about thirty, who sometimes took baffling initiatives. His most notable effort—an attempt to 'please the rector'—was to brighten the appearance of the prized Ford by daubing it with some strong blue paint he had found in the stables. On learning of this my parents immediately organised a working bee of children and staff, all rubbing furiously at the car's blotched surface with kerosene-soaked rags, but it was too late. The paint had nearly dried, and although some yielded to reveal the original sober green underneath, elsewhere it simply ran in streaks, and thereafter our blue and green striped vehicle was a distinctive sight in the district.

My father was in his element at Seven Hills. A simple and practical man, he took pleasure in physical activity and manual tasks, and through his interest in country affairs, related comfortably to his flock. He was also well qualified to train the outdoor men, most of them newly arrived from England and ignorant of Australian farm matters. These included removing the night soil, milking the cows, feeding the pigs and poultry, cutting the wood, tending the vegetable garden and pruning the climbing roses.

To carry him on his extensive parish rounds he now, in addition to the Ford, had a sulky more suited to travelling along rough and dusty roads, and he also rode occasionally. For this he kept six or seven horses and a couple of ponies, most of which were pastured by generous parishioners, among them the Holts, Pearces and Horwoods. Every few weeks the horses in use would be put out to spell and others brought in. These, being fresh, would need careful handling, but my father was a good horseman and managed them well. We particularly admired his handling of Black Bess, a spirited animal who was a fractious mount and had the disconcerting habit of cantering and rearing in the sulky. By contrast, Brownie, our favourite, was one of the dearest, gentlest creatures I have known.

When out of his cassock and surplice my father was great fun—often more like a big brother than a parent. He was an enthusiastic builder of bonfires and billy carts. Wherever he went there was a child in tow and whatever he was doing became a game. When milking, he had a favourite trick of lining us up and squirting the milk straight into our open mouths, but as his aim was uncertain we would return to the house with smeared faces and stained shirts.

Under Mr Main's guidance he became an enthusiastic bee-keeper and extracted the honey in the stables, ringed by an admiring group of children. He used a double-frame slinger and whichever child turned the handle would be rewarded with a piece of honeycomb. At robbing times there was always a dish of it on the breakfast table with our own milk, cream, butter, eggs, and bread baked in the kitchen oven.

Even when my father was not there, life at the rectory was never dull. We had each other for company, and my elder brother and sisters shared their lessons with others from the neighbourhood who became close friends. And animals were part of our very existence. When a cow calved, the calf would be declared the property of the next birthday child, and when it was sold the money would be held in trust for that child except for a few pennies kept to spend on some treat, or put into a money box. The Commonwealth Savings Bank issued these free—a tin replica of its head office building with a slot in the top big enough to take a penny, which in theory could never be retrieved except by the bank. But we soon learnt that by poking the blade of a kitchen knife into the slot, turning it parallel to the ground and shaking the box until a coin landed on the blade and slid out of the slot, we could get cash in hand.

Morning prayers after breakfast were a daily ritual conducted by my father in the dining room with most of the household present. On Sunday evenings the family gathered around my mother at the piano and made its own music singing hymns. We were all taught to play the piano or violin, but in later years none of us persevered with this part of our education.

About 1927 we discovered the wonders of wireless. Now the proud owners of a crystal set equipped with earphones, we learnt how to 'hear the man talking' by applying a thin wire prod to a crystal and manipulating it until the sound was clear and free of static. Accustomed to sharing in the nursery, we soon found that two of us could listen at once if each held one earphone and plugged the other ear with a finger to block off surrounding noises.

Although I was still too young to have any formal education, the rectory nursery was itself a school, and in it I learnt some of life's important lessons and acquired some valuable maxims. One of these came as the result of a birthday party, the pièce de résistance of which was an ice-cream cake—a rare treat ordered from Hordern Brothers' Florentine Restaurant in Sydney. In all its curly creamy delight, it had been packed in dry ice and sent by steam train to Seven Hills Railway Station. Five small Horderns and three friends sat expectantly around the nursery table. Enter the cake, already beginning to melt, and the birthday child was told to serve it quickly. But our anticipation turned to disbelief, and then shock, as the cake, instead of being divided into eight equal portions, was sliced into seven minute slivers, leaving one hefty wedge on the platter for the birthday child. The nursery erupted in outrage. Hearing the noise my mother arrived to calm the storm and reapportioned the cake. She then used the occasion to teach us a dictum we never forgot: 'You cut and I choose'. Since that day, when-ever something is to be shared among our close-knit circle, that prin-ciple has prevailed.

When I was about five and no longer the baby in the house, but still too young to join Miss Button's class in the parish hall, I began to accompany my father on his rounds. On weekdays he went visiting the sick and bereaved, and baptised infants, and on Sundays would generally conduct four or five services in halls or little bush churches in outlying parts of the parish. Sometimes we had to travel quite long distances. Always warmly received and offered refreshments or a meal, my father would discuss the weather, crops and animals with his parishioners as he ate and, if he was taking a service and the weather was fine, I would be put to sleep on the seat of the sulky in the shade of a tree, with the horse munching contentedly at its nose-bag.

From these excursions two particular memories remain. We were trotting along a deserted dusty road on a hot spring morning with the song of magpies in the air when my father took his watch from his pocket, looked at it, and pulled the horse over into a patch of shade under a tree. Taking off his hat, he told me to remove mine and bow my head. For a long time, it seemed, father, son, and grateful horse remained there with the country silence broken only by birdsongs and the rustle of the breeze in the boughs above our heads. Then he checked his watch again, replaced his hat, and we trotted off. As we went on he explained to me that it was eleven o'clock on the morning of 11 November, which he said was called Armistice Day. He told me of his undergraduate friends from Durham University who had been killed in the Great War, the significance of their sacrifice, and the blessings of peace. Nearly eighty years have passed since that pregnant morning pause on a Seven Hills country road, but at eleven a.m. on 11 November each year, I am there in that sulky again.

And another dear memory. It had been a long hot Sunday and we had left the rectory early with Brownie between the shafts to attend a number of services. The last Evensong was done. Brownie's halter was replaced by her bridle, and a weary father and son climbed into the sulky and set off on the long journey home. Night fell, out came the stars, and lying back on the seat before dropping off to sleep I watched the spidery shadows of the wheel-spokes, thrown by the candles in the sulky lamps, revolving on the bushes beside the road. Suddenly the sulky stopped and I was jerked awake: Brownie was standing with her head over the rectory gate looking at her stable, while my father, the reins fallen from his hands, was dead to the world. Brownie was a wonderful horse.

The year 1928 saw great changes for our family. The Church Missionary Society in Australia had accepted the financial responsibility of supporting a bishop and staff in Tanganyika (now Tanzania); George Chambers had been appointed the first Bishop of Central Tanganyika and he wanted my father to become his 'organising secretary'—a roving commission to raise funds for the work in Africa. My father, accepting the challenge, may have welcomed the prospect of life on the open road. But for me it was a wrench to be leaving our milk-and-honey existence at Seven Hills. The rectory was the only home I had known and I gave it a sad farewell. On the afternoon before we left I walked around its rooms and garden for the last time; near the kitchen door, I climbed under the tank stand and, making sure that no one was looking, kissed the wall.

The next morning a new chapter in my life began. In it I was to receive formal education and discipline in a world about to be gripped by the Great Depression and moving inexorably towards the world's most terrible war.

2 | BEING PREPARED

In April 1929 we moved from Seven Hills to Wahroonga, where we rented a Federation-style bungalow called 'Ingledene' on the corner of Neringah Avenue and Lane Cove Road, now the Pacific Highway. Although much smaller than the rectory, it was a pleasant house, and its large rambling garden became our own private world. After we left, the house was demolished and replaced by a red brick reservoir.

Exchanging the Seven Hills countryside for suburbia brought a new way of life for us, although in the 1920s some features of Wahroonga were still familiar to country eyes. Many of its houses sat in large gardens surrounded by paddocks and bush and, while some of the major roads were sealed and partially lit by electric light, others were little more than narrow dirt tracks through the gumtrees. I once saw a baker's cart bogged in Redleaf Avenue.

But there was much to marvel at. Milk no longer came from a cow, but a tap at the rear of the milkman's cart. The milkman would collect our billies from outside the kitchen door, fill them from the cart, return them and walk on to the next house, his horse keeping pace beside him. And bread, no longer baked in a fuel oven, could be bought from the bakery just a block away; a service station now stands on that site and the paddock where its horses grazed is a public car park.

We now had water piped to taps in the house and garden, and this made possible another marvel—the water closet in the bathroom. An outhouse enclosing the more familiar arrangement with a pan remained in the garden, however, for use by the domestic staff. Its pan was removed and replaced weekly by council workers who arrived in a large malodorous truck. We called them 'dunny-cart men'.

Gas and electricity facilitated other tasks which at Seven Hills had been performed by housemaids, laundresses and outdoor men, and of our former numerous household helpers only Lizzie remained. Gas heaters over the kitchen sink and bath allowed us the luxury of hot showers and water for washing up, and instead of the wood-burning kitchen range which demanded constant vigilance there was a gas stove capable of producing instantaneous heat. The flick of a switch could flood a dark room with electric light, and in cold weather an electric radiator supplied warmth without anyone having to cut and carry wood, or remove ash next morning. As yet we had no electric refrigeration, but the ice chest which cooled our butter, milk and meat was a vast improvement on the metal safes shrouded with damp cloths which we had known at Seven Hills. The block of ice housed in its top compartment was delivered regularly by the 'ice man'.

But our most valued labour-saving device was the Universal Washing Machine. Standing on four iron legs, it had a gear box and levers to control the agitator and wringer. Eliminating the back-breaking routine of pummelling heavy wet clothes with a stick in a wood-fired copper and feeding them laboriously through the mangle, the Universal was a boon to our large family. And it became something of a household god. When I moved into my father's home fifty years later I found it under the house, carefully preserved, together with its sales docket, instruction book and correspondence about subsequent repairs. The Sydney Museum of Applied Arts and Sciences, to whom I gave it, were surprised and grateful for 'so much authentic documentation'.

This was typical of my mother's archival zeal; she had a passion for recording the provenance of books, pictures and other household items, and for saving correspondence and newspaper cuttings. Many of the pictures we found in the house had information about their origin and cost written on the back, and in the attic were meticulously bundled letters, tagged with pieces of discoloured cardboard bearing such cautionary messages as 'Keep this—valuable', or 'Letters from the boys at the war—do not destroy'. For better or worse I have inherited her penchant for preservation, and it is largely on my own collection of documents that these memoirs are based.

Electricity brought other changes to our lives. We no longer had to squabble for possession of the crystal set's headpieces but could listen to the wireless as a family, gathered around its loudspeaker. And we could travel into Sydney quickly and easily for, instead of the infrequent steam-train service we had known at Seven Hills, electric trains ran every quarter of an hour from nearby Hornsby to Milsons Point Station, meeting a ferry which landed the passengers a few minutes later at Circular Quay.

The move also affected the structure of our family. Having been accustomed for so long to the continued presence of our father in the home, we now had to adjust to his absence for lengthy periods. His deputation work took him to Anglican parishes in many parts of New South Wales where, aided by two projectors—one electrical and the other fuelled by kerosene—he would stage slide shows, projecting pictures of mission work in Tanganyika onto a white sheet hung on the wall of the church or parish hall.

On these journeys he sometimes took Bompie, who delighted in revisiting some of the towns he had known as an inspector in the Child Welfare Department. They usually stayed in rectories or were billeted with parishioners and, if accommodation was limited, sometimes had to share a double bed. Once they slept in a church, using the communion kneelers as mattresses.

These marvellous jaunts were not without their afflictions. A devoted husband and parent, my father was constantly sending letters and postcards home assuring my mother of his constancy: 'My darling

Idy, I am missing you so much and hate being away from you …' There were also times when he found the work unrewarding and depressing. Writing from the New South Wales far south coast, where his reception had been cool and attendance minimal, he complained to my mother, 'These are a Godless people …'

The move to 'Ingledene' also saw the demise of our schoolroom group: Mary and Noel were enrolled at Abbotsleigh, the Church of England girls' school across the road from 'Ingledene', and Hugh and I entered the Presbyterian Knox Grammar School at Wahroonga. My parents came in for some criticism for this, my father receiving an anonymous note: 'Hugh, you call yourself an Anglican and send your boys to Knox!'. But the fledgling Knox was closer to home and well regarded. It also—and this was vital—offered half fees to the sons of clergy.

Today one of the nation's notable schools, Knox Grammar was then still in its infancy, having been founded five years before. The headmaster, Neil MacNeil, was a stern disciplinarian. The product of a strict Presbyterian upbringing, and with distinguished war and academic records, he preached patriotism, duty, robust physical activity, and the development of an independent mind. Most of the masters and boys feared and respected him.

The school's first buildings were erected on the former estate of Sir Charles McKellar which fronted Lane Cove Road. It had been bought in 1923 by the trustees of the Presbyterian Church for £12,000 but, perhaps mindful of the story of Egypt's seven lean years, they only paid Sir Charles £2000 down and borrowed the balance from him for seven years at 6 per cent interest. This was prudent: in 1923 the world was moving towards the Great Depression which would see unemployment soar to around 30 per cent in Australia, and some schools like Knox hung on by the skin of their teeth.

In 1927 the Church bought Dr George Armstrong's mansion in Billyard Avenue, Wahroonga, for a preparatory school. Armstrong, a member of the pioneering Victorian squatter family, had donated

£4000 towards the purchase of the house and its six and a half acres and, in recognition of this, the Church gave the junior school Mrs Armstrong's maiden name: it became 'Ewan House'.[1]

On 1 May 1929, now aged seven, with a handful of other small boys, I received my first lessons there from C. J. Harvey-Maple in the little gatekeeper's lodge—later to be sadly disfigured by insensitive additions. It guarded the gates of the carriageway which swept past a large Italianate fountain and up to the house's imposing front door. All that elegance has now succumbed to an age with very different disciplines and values, and I often wonder what happened to Dr Armstrong's fabulous fountain.

My days at Knox were undistinguished and only twice did I achieve any notable success. One was in coming first in a sack race at the sports, for which I won a bronze medal emblazoned with the Knox insignia. The other, when I received a handsomely bound copy of *Hans Andersen's Fairy Tales* for 'general excellence', was glorious for me—not because I was pronounced generally excellent, but because I received it from the hand of Rear-Admiral E. R. G. R. Evans, CB, DSO, RN. 'Evans of the *Broke*' was a living legend. A distinguished author and adventurer, he had been Scott's close companion in the Antarctic and was one of the Royal Navy's most decorated officers and a hero of the Empire.

But Evans was also one of those mavericks who delight in embarrassing the establishment, and while the headmaster might have congratulated himself for having induced such an eminent person to appear at the school, Evans's opening remarks must have caused him some disquiet:

It is always an honour for a man or woman to be invited to present prizes at a big school [but] ... I wonder what the headmaster of the Public School from which I was expelled would have said had I told him on the day that I was thrown out into the world, branded as an exile, that the day would come when my name would stand high enough for this invitation to be extended to me?

My first expulsion was for constantly playing truant and for fighting for pennies in the London meat market in school hours ...

At his next school, Evans, coveting another boy's chameleon, had armed himself with his father's loaded revolver and demanded it, at gunpoint. The chameleon was ultimately retrieved, 'chastisement proportional to the offence' meted out, and Evans was lectured by the headmaster:

Look here, Evans Minor, we like you at this school and don't want to expel you. You are always top of your class, but you don't work and you set a bad example. If, instead of expelling you, I make you a prefect, will you promise to look after the other boys and stop being a pirate, for that is what you are?

This anecdote occasioned some awkward laughter, but Evans made his point. Responsibility, he told us, had so reformed him that he had won 'that coveted prize amongst boys of our beloved Empire—a cadetship in His Majesty's navy'. He then went on to extol the virtues of the Boy Scout movement which, by encouraging self-reliance, had 'obliterated more than fifty per cent ... of the naughty boys of today. All we wanted was permission to roam and play pirates.'[2]

Coming from so great a man, this recommendation of the scouting movement inspired me, and when Knox formed its own group soon afterwards I quickly joined, proud to wear on my shirt the patch '1st Wahroonga, Ewan House'. And so began a happy period of roaming and playing pirates, during which I acquired some basic survival techniques and, under the keen tutelage of our teacher and scoutmaster, C. R. A. Riley, learned to recite the ten Scout Laws.

1. A Scout's honour is to be trusted—If a Scout says 'On my honour it is so', that means that it is so, just as if he had taken a most solemn oath.

2. A Scout is loyal to the King, his officers, his parents, his employers, and to those under him. He must stick to them through thick and thin against anyone who is their enemy, or who even talks badly of them.

3. A Scout's duty is to be useful and to help others … and he must try his best to do at least one good turn to somebody every day.

4. A Scout is a friend to all, and a brother to every other Scout, no matter to what social class the other belongs.

5. A Scout is courteous. That is, he is polite to all—but especially to women and children, and old people and invalids, cripples, etc. And he must not take any reward for being helpful and courteous.

6. A Scout is a friend to animals. He should save them as far as possible from pain and should not kill any animal unnecessarily, for it is one of God's creatures …

7. A Scout obeys orders of his parents, Patrol Leader, or Scoutmaster without question.

8. A Scout smiles and whistles under all difficulties … Scouts never grouse at hardships, nor whine at each other, nor swear when put out, but go on whistling and smiling.

9. A Scout is thrifty. That is, he saves every penny he can and puts it into the bank so that he may have money to keep himself when out of work, and thus not make himself a burden to others; or that he may have money to give away to others when they need it.

10. A Scout is clean in thought, word and deed. That is, he looks down upon a silly youth who talks dirt, and he does not let himself give way to temptation either to talk it or to think, or to do anything dirty. A Scout is pure, clean-minded and manly.

Today this wording seems quaint and, to some, its philosophy outdated. Riley summarised these laws for us in a little jingle that still runs through my mind whenever I see a scout or guide:

Trusty, loyal and helpful, brotherly, courteous, kind.
Obedient, smiling and thrifty, pure as the rustling wind.

1935 was a momentous year for Australian scouting: an international Jamboree was to be held at Frankston in Victoria. Over 30,000 scouts were expected, and Lord Baden-Powell, hero of African colonial wars and scouting's founding father, was to attend. This was an experience not to be missed and my cousin, Hunter Hordern, Hugh and I, joined the Knox contingent attending it. Hunter's father, Stewart Hordern, donated a Union Jack, and my mother an Australian Commonwealth flag, but the honour of carrying these at the head of the Knox troop in the Grand Parade had to be earned: the Union Jack was to be carried by the scout who submitted the most informative essay on its composition and history, and the Australian flag, by the one submitting the best essay on 'The History of Scouting'. No Horderns qualified for these honours.

For the information of those attending the Jamboree and to encourage them to keep a journal, each boy was issued with *The 1935 Australian Scout Diary—Jamboree Issue*. Tailored to fit in a scout's pocket, it had as frontispiece an imposing portrait of Baden-Powell, the 78-year-old World Chief Scout—'CCMG, CCVO, KCB, FRGS, LLD, and DCL'—who was 'illustrious in the arts of peace and war, a model of chivalry, a pattern of courage and of courtesy, a visionary, who has brought noble dreams to noble fulfilment, a practical idealist, Soldier and sportsman, writer and sculptor ...'[3] This was heady stuff for an eleven-year-old son of a rectory and, determined to put Baden-Powell's gift (for so I saw it) to good use, and in compliance with my mother's urgings, I earnestly filled all available space with reports on each day's activities. These were mainly banalities such as, 'got up, had a shower, had breakfast' and ended almost invariably with 'slept well', but while this little book does not make gripping reading I treasure it because it introduced me to the pleasurable occupation of keeping a journal. I now have a collection of notebooks of various qualities and shapes, some written (illegally) on active service while below decks in steamy tropical waters, with perspiration smudging the ink as I wrote, some in lonely hotel rooms while on European business trips, some at the end of a long and happy day's driving through the Australian countryside. These journals chart my life's voyage.

In addition to refining our scouting techniques, the Jamboree developed our consciousness of being part of the British Empire and, in the arena at Frankston, we were treated to long dissertations on the subject by Sir Wilson Dugan, Sir Philip Game and other dignitaries. We paraded before Baden-Powell twice, and while it seems from my records that his words affected me less than the fact that there were scorpions in my tent—perhaps a sensible apportioning of priorities— the knowledge that he had travelled so far to address us induced a glow of self-importance and pride in being British. This was heightened by receiving a 'personal' message from King George V, which ended in a wishing us a happy Christmas.

That his message reached us some weeks after Christmas did not cause us to question the depth of the King's interest in our activities. We were proud to have it, and accepted his greetings in the spirit in which no doubt they were meant.

Among my confused recordings of showers, scorpions and speeches, one incident remains clear. Baden-Powell, astride a magnificent white horse, was inspecting us. As he approached 1st Wahroonga, Ewan House Troop, we froze to attention. He stopped to speak to a scout about four places to my left, leaving me confronting the charger's sleek rump and flowing tail and, while a stilted exchange was going on up front, the boy next to me whispered, 'Dare you to get a hair from its tail!' This was a challenge and, a true scout, I seized the opportunity to display initiative in a challenging situation. Knowing that a firm but gentle hand was a good approach with horses, I put my hand on its flank. Seeing no reaction, I began to slide my hand gently towards the tail, intending to pluck a hair in one sharp tug. But when my hand had almost reached its goal, my nerve failed. Blessed—or maybe cursed— with an active imagination, I have always tortured myself with Technicolor visions of the possible consequences of seemingly innocuous actions and 'What ifs?'. What, I asked myself, if the horse suddenly reared, throwing and perhaps killing the old man? I could see the

This is a cMessage *to*

YOU

from His Majesty the King

✦ ✦ ✦

"I send you, Boy Scouts of Australia, my warm thanks for your loyal and affectionate greetings on the occasion of the first Australian Jamboree.

"I watch with interest and pleasure the uninterrupted growth of the Boy Scouts and Girl Guides movements in all our Overseas Dominions, Colonies, and Protectorates, and I trust that the spirit of brotherhood which it spreads among you will continue to unite you as members of our great Commonwealth in the years to come. By keeping up this comradeship you will be making a real contribution to the well-being of the Empire and peace and prosperity of the World.

"I wish you all a very happy Christmas and New Year."

(Signed) GEORGE, R.I.

Presented to each participant in the Australian Jamboree, 1934-35, at Frankston, Victoria

Baden Powell

King George V's belated Christmas message to his Empire's scouts

splendid animal bolting into the distance and the lifeless body on the parade ground surrounded by crowds of shocked boys. And as I hesitated, Baden-Powell nudged his horse into action, the tail gave a farewell flick, and they moved off. I had failed to attain glory, but was left with a powerful memory of the time I *almost* took a hair from the tail of Baden-Powell's horse.

While at Seven Hills I had hardly been conscious of the extended family of Horderns and Whites who were my grandparents, uncles, aunts and cousins, but the move to Sydney's North Shore brought me increasingly into contact with them. Three of my father's brothers lived on the upper North Shore while his sister Edytha, married to Dr Geoffrey Aitkens, lived at Westmead, and 'Chislehurst' was the focus of the family. Edward Carr and Frances Lillie did not have wide-ranging interests; apart from my grandfather's attention to his business, they lived for their family, their home and the church. With eighteen grandchildren living in or around Sydney, they found interest in promoting our well-being and enjoyed gathering us under their roof for special occasions. At Christmas, with my father now released from his demanding round of services, we became part of the traditional 'Chislehurst' party where our family—and that of my Aunt Edytha—being the 'poorer' cousins, were privileged to join our grandparents for dinner. Other family groups dined at their homes but arrived soon afterwards for the distribution of gifts in the billiard room. The presents covered the wide spectrum of childish wants, but had one common characteristic—with few exceptions they had been bought at Hordern Brothers, where the family got a hefty discount.

Sometimes, when it was thought that my mother needed a rest, Hugh and I would be packed off to stay at 'Chislehurst' for a few days. After 'Ingledene', we found the house, with its formal billiard and reception rooms and discreet uniformed servants, rather daunting, and we spent most of our time outside. There was a large garden to explore, and beyond it a fringe of bushland with a creek. A croquet lawn offered entertainment, there were horses for us to ride, and all the domestic animals—cows and poultry—common to large North Shore properties of that time.

Apart from the servants, the 'Chislehurst' household consisted of my grandfather, Grannie, and her sister, Auntie Clara Dryland, who had come out from England early in my grandparents' marriage to be her companion. A petite and elegant woman, Clara Dryland equalled her sister in the gentle arts. They both spoke French, sang, painted, embroidered, played the piano and organ, chess, draughts and croquet. But Auntie Clara was dependent on her brother-in-law's support, and her consciousness of this slightly inferior status was reflected in her manner. Although always treated as a family member, she remained slightly in the background, never volunteering a critical or provocative comment, but always wearing a sweet and seemingly fixed smile. Only once did I see that smile fade. Auntie was teaching us croquet. The lawn was set up with its hoops and marks, and we had collected our mallets from the wooden chest on the verandah. Auntie had gone over the rules with us, and the game had begun. But I was having trouble directing my ball; it kept shooting out at an angle, and soon I found myself in an impossible position far from the next hoop. I glanced at Auntie. She had her back to me and was showing one of my cousins how to hold her mallet. Cautiously, with one eye on Auntie's back, I dribbled the ball with my foot until it was right in front of the hoop. Then, calling 'My go!', I prepared to drive it through. But as Auntie turned to watch, her smile froze. Moving close to me, she whispered softly, 'Put the ball back where it was, darling, we don't do that here. We call that cheating.' She had taught me another of life's lessons.

Life at 'Chislehurst' was very ordered by contrast with the hurly-burly of 'Ingledene'. At nine o'clock on weekdays, John, the uniformed Cockney chauffeur, would bring the Hudson Six from the stables to the front door and bear my grandfather away to Hordern Brothers in the city. Grandfather returned at about five and on winter nights, before the dinner gong sounded, we would all settle in the billiard room in front of the fire while he read the *London Illustrated News*, the *Graphic*, or the *Sydney Morning Herald*, whispering the words to himself as he ran a finger along under the print. At dinner in the spacious dining room, hung with heavy Victorian oils, Grandfather, seated between Grannie and Auntie at the head of the large table, would regale us with stories of the day's happenings in Hordern Brothers while we ate silently. Then we would all return to the billiard room to read or play chess until bedtime.

My grandfather had not had an easy childhood. While he was quite young, his alcoholic father had committed suicide by cutting his throat with a Bengal razor, leaving his sons in far worse circumstances than those of their many Sydney cousins—the children of Anthony II and Edward Hordern—and they envied them accordingly. Tertius and Sam, sons of their uncle Anthony Hordern II, in particular, represented to my grandfather all that he had been deprived of, and he strove to emulate them. In his youth he had worked on Sam's property at Greenwich Park near Goulburn, and from this experience he developed a love of country life; in the early 1900s he bought a 640-acre retreat at Colo Vale near Bowral in the Southern Highlands, where Sam now had his splendid estate, 'Retford Park'. My grandfather called this property 'Wensleydale' after the Wensleydale sheep he had imported from the Lake District hoping that the cold climate of the Southern Highlands of New South Wales would suit them, but the venture failed. His other aim in buying the property, however—to provide a holiday home for his growing family—was a great success.

Like 'Chislehurst', 'Wensleydale' was a roomy Victorian homestead with a billiard room and large living areas downstairs, most of them with marbled fireplaces. Upstairs, the bedrooms opened through French doors on to pillared verandahs overlooking the paddocks and countryside.

During school holidays we and some of our cousins—often accompanied by friends—would be packed off to 'Wensleydale' to be cared for by the resident married couple. These were happy days; sometimes there were five or six children there together, and the house throbbed with life. We acquired some of the country skills—riding, shooting, fencing, ploughing and burning off. We made bonfires to celebrate Empire Day, swam in dams and creeks, caught yabbies, fed pigs and calves, milked cows, churned butter and—although it now pains me to reflect on it—hunted almost any wild thing that moved.

Mostly we trapped rabbits, selling their skins to the Sydney merchants Hoffnungs. They were sold by the pound, and we soon learned a simple trick to augment our takings: when skinning the rabbit, the pelt was generally cut at the neck and the skin turned inside out and dried in the sun on a hoop of fencing wire. But with a little care the rabbit's ears could be left attached to the pelt and tucked inside, out of sight, thus slightly increasing its weight and our profit.

Soon after we moved to Wahroonga I found a special friend in my maternal grandfather, Walter White. This was a different relationship from that with my Hordern grandfather. While we were accustomed to visit Edward Carr at 'Chislehurst' or 'Wensleydale', Bompie would stay with us, for there was no spare room for grandchildren in his small cottage, and while he could not endow us with financial blessings, he enriched us with the product of his fertile mind and wide experience of life.

Born into a poor Bristol family, he had begun work at the age of twelve, selling newspapers on the streets to help support his family, before joining the *Bristol Mercury and Daily Post* as a cadet journalist, and at the end of a seven-year apprenticeship he had proudly become a Fellow of the Royal Institute of Journalists. As a child he was a boy chorister, first at St John's Church, Bedminster, and then at St Mary's, Redcliffe—described by Queen Elizabeth I as 'the fairest church in England'—and the musical education he had received there, together with a knowledge of literature and art gained through his journalistic training, gave him wide cultural interests.

When in his twenties, he worked for two years in South Africa, and through his reminiscences of that country we became familiar with the stories of the battles of Isandlwana and Rorke's Drift. We never tired of hearing about Lieutenants Chard and Bromhead and the Zulu king Cetewayo, who was reputedly 'a very big man'. 'How big, Bompie?' we would ask, and be told that the king had 'a thigh as thick as an Englishman's waist'. I grieved to hear that the proud king, defeated at Ulundi and shipped off to England to lay his head at the Great White Queen's feet, had been so overwhelmed at his first sight of the sea that his eyes had filled with tears and, raising his arm towards the ocean, had called out 'The land moves!'. That nearly made me cry too.

At the end of his time in South Africa, my grandfather prepared to book his passage back to England. The night before he was to pay his fare he hid the money in a sock in a drawer in his lodging and went out to dinner, but returned to find the room ransacked and his money gone. Shocked and penniless, he recommenced the laborious business of saving a fare home.

In those days Cape Town was a maritime crossroads of the world, and on Sundays my grandfather would go down to the docks and look wistfully at the ships leaving for home. One afternoon, while admiring a tall-masted ocean flyer, he fell into conversation with one of her mates leaning over the taffrail, pipe in mouth. On hearing that my grandfather was planning to return to Bristol the sailor, whose voice had a West Country burr, removed his pipe, hawked, spat into the water and said, 'A young fellow like you should be running east, not west.' He then went on to extol the virtues of Australia: it had a climate like South Africa's; there was room to move; emigrants were flocking there, and there was gold for the taking. Even horses' hooves, he told my grandfather, had turned up golden nuggets.

Bompie pondered this advice and, when he next could afford to book a passage, it was east, for Australia. He never saw England, or any of his family again, and I owe my happy existence to a Cape Town thief who, nearly a century and a quarter ago, caused my grandfather much distress.

On arrival in Sydney Bompie joined the staff of the *Sydney Morning Herald*; later, as an early member of the Labor movement, he became sub-editor of the *Labor Daily*. He was also at various times secretary to the 1895 Royal Commission on Fisheries, Senior Inspector in the Child Welfare Department of New South Wales and a frequent contributor of prose and verse to English, American and Australian journals.

In Sydney he met and married Mary Hodge—a descendant of the American pioneers, Captain John and Helena Underhill, who had landed in Boston in 1630. When Mary died from cervical cancer, leaving him with three young children, he was devastated. She became the subject of some of his most moving poems.

I began to know him well in about 1930. Then seventy-three, he had remarried and was living at 'Narara', a small cottage on the corner of Sutherland and Whitton roads, Chatswood, not far from 'Chisle-hurst'. Neither remains, although 'Narara' proved the more resilient. 'Chislehurst', resumed by the State Government in the 1950s, soon fell to the jack-hammers, but 'Narara' survived until 1996, when it was engulfed by a housing estate.

I never tired of Grandfather White's company. Devoted to my mother, he spent a lot of time with us at 'Ingledene', although his second wife seldom accompanied him. He often took us to the art gallery where, planted in front of Alphonse de Neuville's dramatic *Defence of Rorke's Drift*, painted in 1880, he would recount the story of that glorious battle. Then we would pass on to Evariste Luminais's *The Sons of Clovis II*; hearing his story of the young rebel princes, and looking on their broken feet and pale pain-wracked faces propped against red cushions, I would envisage myself suffering a similar cruel drifting death, and a lump would rise in my throat. Some twenty-five years later I took my children to see those pictures and was shocked to find them gone. A reply to my letter of protest, promising their return, calmed my outrage, and now when I visit the Art Gallery of New South Wales I always salute the *Defence of Rorke's Drift* and *The Sons of Clovis II*.

Bompie occasionally went with us to 'Wensleydale'. There he would tell us about Hume and Hovell and the other explorers who had opened up southern New South Wales, and on starry nights, standing under the sky's vast black canopy, would point out the brilliant constellations of the southern sky and tell us how they had got their names.

On 8 June 1930 the family was further increased by the arrival of my youngest brother Ian, born in my parents' bedroom at 'Ingledene'. His arrival, and that of the trained nurse engaged to look after him, increased the household to ten and put further strain on our accommodation. To ease this, Hugh, John and I were moved from our bedroom to a sleep-out verandah at the back of the bungalow.

Shortly after we had moved to Wahroonga my mother received a neighbourly call from Mrs W. C. Adams, who lived in a large house on the corner of Ada Avenue and Lane Cove Road—now incorporated into Abbotsleigh girls' school. The Adams's six children were of much the same age as we, and had a similar capacity for unruly behaviour. Margaret Hypatia Adams—noted for being the first woman to drive a motor car from Sydney to Melbourne, in 1912—was given to good works, and for many years served with distinction as the Girl Guide District Commissioner for the Ku-ring-gai area.

Like many large families in that area, the Adamses kept a cow, milked by Jessie—a fun-loving Aboriginal girl. When Ian was born, Mrs Adams offered to supply us with milk; my mother accepted gratefully, and we all throve on it. It became my job to collect it each morning, and I was often in the cowyard before Jessie had finished milking. One dark, cold winter's morning, after a night of heavy rain, I crossed Lane Cove Road with the billycan and, on reaching the cowyard, had to pick my way through slush and cow pats. Jessie, who had not finished milking, greeted me with a grin and a flash of white teeth. She was milking with her bare feet in the bucket to keep them warm.

These were the middle years of the Great Depression, when thousands of men were tramping the road looking for work. They carried their swags and often slept out under the stars. Many were professional men who had known better days. One morning a tall man carrying a stick and a bundle over his shoulder knocked at the front door. When my mother opened it, he said in a well-modulated voice, 'Good morning, madam. I expect that you have no work to offer, but could you give me something to eat?' Leading him through to the back verandah, my mother made a pot of tea, set it on a tray with a jug of milk, bowl of sugar and two thick slices of bread and dripping, and told me to take it to him. 'Thank you, sonny', he said, and I went back into the house. But, puzzled that this man, who—despite his unkempt appearance—looked and talked like my parents' friends, should be eating bread and dripping on the back verandah, I went to the window, eased back the curtain and watched him. There was something almost ceremonial about the way he approached that simple meal. First he poured a cup of tea, added several large spoonfuls of sugar, and began sipping it slowly. Then, peeling the crusts from the bread, he munched the centres, washing them down with a second cup of heavily sugared tea. Finally, taking up the crusts and wiping every vestige of dripping from the plate, he chewed them very deliberately, as if to make them last longer. Then, returning the tray to my mother, he thanked her, and went off down Lane Cove Road.

This was the first time I had seen anyone beg for food; it shocked me and, as my week's penny pocket money was still unspent, I decided to give it to him. Running down the street, I caught up with him at the next corner. He was trudging along with his head bent. 'Excuse me!' I called out. He stopped and turned. His eyes were red, and tears were running down his distorted face. Terrified, I threw the penny on the ground, turned, and bolted for home; as I fled I heard him calling, 'Come back, little boy, I won't hurt you!' That is my memory of the Great Depression.

In progressing to Knox's senior school I entered another world where school life was far more regimented and formal than it had been in the 'Prep'. Many of the older boys were larger than some of the masters, had men's voices, and often sported incipient beards. One morning, when I was standing below the clock tower, one of them approached, smiling, and asked, 'What's your name?' I told him. 'So is mine. Hello, little cousin!' he said, and off he went. It was Peter Hordern who, I learned later, lived with his grandfather, Alfred Hordern, at 'The Highlands' in Waitara. On leaving Knox, Peter joined the Royal Air Force, and was killed piloting a bomber over Norway in April 1940. He was one of the first Knox boys to die for his country in battle, and one of twenty-six boys I knew at school who never lived to see the tomorrow they had fought for. Today, when I stand before the school's War Memorial gates, run my eye down the list and read

St Paul's injunction to the Corinthians, 'Quit you like men, be strong', I linger on Peter's name, see again his amiable smile, and hear him saying, 'Hello, little cousin!'

In 1934, having completed his work for Bishop Chambers, my father was appointed rector of St Peter's Church, in the industrial Cooks River area, adjacent to Botany Bay. As this was a long way from Knox, Grandfather Hordern agreed to my becoming a boarder, and I, now nearly twelve, was thrust into the harsh environment typical of boys' boarding schools at that time. The hours of study, work and play were rigidly controlled, the food was spare and unimaginative, and discipline inflexible. Caning by masters and prefects—often for quite minor misdemeanours—was accepted by most educationalists, parents and pupil-victims alike, but for the victims it was a punishment to be dreaded. Two, four or six lashes on a bent bottom left weals which developed into blue bruises with lingering flecks of red, and the pain of sitting on a classroom bench remained for days. Sometimes the end of the supple cane whipped round and struck the hip bone. Those wounds were the worst: their bruises—initiation scars of puberty— lasted longer and were flaunted for weeks under the communal cold shower. A popular remedy was the 'water treatment': to take your pants off and sit in a basin of cold water was supposed to ease the agony. But the ease lasted only as long as you sat in the basin and after that the pain returned with a new force. It was a harsh world, but the world waiting to receive the schoolboys of the 1930s was much harsher and some were better prepared for it by their boarding school experiences.

Apart from these discomforts, Knox senior school was not an unhappy place. Our exuberant energies and fertile imaginations found outlets in the cadet corps, choir, model aeroplane club, debating society, organised sport and other activities of this nature, and through them I made many lifelong friends.

At St Peter's, we again experienced a change of lifestyle. After the verdancy of Wahroonga our surroundings were drab, and the pungent emanations from nearby tanneries offended noses accustomed to the fragrance of the frangipani and roses at 'Ingledene'. But there were compensations: as well as the churchyard and its historic cemetery, the rectory grounds took in a large garden, a separate cottage—occupied by the outside man who doubled as verger—and a paddock occupied by a brewery's draught horses. This became a wonderful playground.

The rectory accommodated our household of nine without any undue sense of crowding, except for its limited plumbing. With only one bathroom for eight people (Lizzie again had an outside lavatory) my parents imposed strict controls on its use. Dallying was not encouraged, and it was laid down that during the morning rush hour those leaving it had to call loudly, 'Bathroom's empty!'

One great benefit for me at Cooks River was its proximity to Mascot Aerodrome—just an easy bike ride away along Ricketty Street. Since joining the Knox model aeroplane club I had become engrossed in aviation, and on long weekends and school holidays I went there whenever possible. At that time it was little more than a paddock, and its hangars simply large sheds. But in them were De Havilland Puss Moths, Hornets, Percival Gulls, Stinsons, Fairchilds and Fokkers—names that I would recite to myself like an incantation. Some of these aircraft were owned by legendary aviators—Kingsford-Smith, Ulm, Scotty Allen, Jimmy Melrose, Ernie Clarke and Jean Batten. They were my heroes; I assiduously collected their autographs and glowed with pride when they occasionally let me help push their machines onto the tarmac. I dreamed of being an aviator, but it was to be ten years before I would know the thrill of soaring skyward, looping, spinning, and side-slipping down over tall trees into a country paddock.

Since my parents' Tasmanian days they had kept in contact with their friends there; some had visited us and were constantly inviting us to return the call. The cost of such an excursion was beyond my father's means but not those of grandfather Hordern. Already, in 1926, he had sent the whole family to Hobart in the steamer *Riverina*. While at St Peter's we went again, this time in the *Zeelandia*—later to become a twisted wreck on the bottom of Darwin Harbour. These were the first of the many ocean voyages I enjoyed over the next fifty years.

As life at Seven Hills and 'Wensleydale' had introduced me to the pleasures of the country, so my mother's brother, Dr Norman White, and his daughters, Dai and Bobby, now taught me the delights of boats and sailing. From this grew my love of the sea. A graduate in dentistry from Edinburgh and the North Western University in Chicago, my uncle had set up his surgery in a two-storied house, 'Greycliff', which he had built opposite Pymble station. A keen sportsman, he drove an open Armstrong Siddeley tourer with a sphinx on the radiator and owned a beach house at Newport, north of Sydney. But for me his greatest asset was his 32-foot gaff-rigged cutter *Temptress*, in which he often took me cruising. After a day's sail we would haul into one of his favourite anchorages—Refuge Bay or The Basin—and, after rigging the riding light and hoisting it on the backstay, would go below to prepare the evening meal. I loved those nights. The glow from the lamps in the cabin bathed the table, bookshelf and barometer with a soft light. There was no radio: our music was the slap of wavelets against the hull or, if the wind was fresh, the slatting of halyards on the mast. After dinner we would talk and read ourselves to sleep. At day-break I would make him a cup of tea, and we would row ashore for a swim and, if we were in Refuge Bay, a shower under the waterfall tumbling from its rocky ledge onto the beach. Then back to the *Temptress* for toast, bacon and eggs, and up sail and off as the wind served, for a tramp offshore or a quieter cruise in Pittwater before another sweet night in a landlocked cove. Sometimes Dai or Bobby would join us. Both girls were splendid sailors; they taught me to manage their VJ—knowledge that later served me well in a more serious world where anyone who knew how to sail, shoot or fly was in demand.[4]

In 1937 my father became rector of St Paul's, Cleveland Street, Sydney, the beautiful Blacket church which is now the Sydney Greek Orthodox Cathedral.[5] This was an important appointment and his induction a great moment for us. The church was packed with parishioners, family and friends. There was the Bishop Coadjutor, C. V. Pilcher, the Moderator of the Presbyterian Church, and numerous other clergy, their varied robes glowing brilliantly in the sombre setting.

Until then I had never thought much about symbolism in the church, but that night it came home to me. My most moving memory of the service is the singing of the hymn which opens,

We love the place O God
Wherein thine honour dwells
The joy of thine abode
All earthly joy excels.

That was an appropriate salute to Blacket's splendid building. Then we began on a spiritual safari as the clergy perambulated around the church. Moving down the southern wall and crossing the centre aisle to the font, they halted and, after the organ's preparatory chord, we sang,

We love the sacred font
For there the Holy Dove
Pours out, as He is wont
The effluence from above.

On they went across to the northern aisle, up towards the chancel and right on to the lectern, then to the altar beneath the magnificent five-light eastern window and down again to the prayer desk, and at each halt we sang the appropriate verse. Finally, they confronted the choir:

We love to sing below
For mercies freely given;
But oh! we long to know
The triumph song of heaven.

The sentiment was moving; but at the age of fifteen I was in no hurry to hear that heavenly song.

One other clear impression I have of that service is of a very pretty choir girl with golden hair flowing beneath her mortar board. Later, when I had also joined the choir and we had become better acquainted, we went into Blacket's secluded little northern porch to examine a stained-glass window showing a saint with a big sword and the admonition, 'Stand Fast in the Faith'. Then I had my own induction: she kissed me hard on the lips and, so far from standing fast, I was walking on air.

Our home was not the original St Paul's rectory. After the church had been built, its grounds, which had stretched as far as Regent Street and on which the first rectory had stood, had been resumed for the extension of the railway from Redfern to Central Railway Station. Our rectory looked eastward over Prince Alfred Park and westward over a former valley in the bush to another Blacket building, Sydney University. On the ground floor, the sitting and dining rooms, with open fireplaces, and my father's study, which gave onto a verandah overlooking the church, were roomy, and from the back door an entrance passage connected with the kitchen, laundry, pantry and a northern verandah with a bathroom and lavatory. All the bedrooms were on the upper floor, two of them with balconies looking east and west. It lacked Blacket's style, but suited us well. Here, at least, there was more than one bathroom and, to my great delight, for the first time I had my own bedroom.

But there were always comparisons to be made with previous homes, and while we now enjoyed a spacious house, it was the first I had known with no real garden and very little room to play. In the front only a narrow lawn separated the rectory from Cleveland Street, with its noisy traffic and trams rattling by the front door. There was no buffer between us and the world beyond the rectory, and our move to Redfern brought us forcibly into contact with it. Although living in the industrial area of Cooks River had to some extent conditioned us to environmental change, at Redfern this difference was even more pronounced. We were now in an inner-city slum parish in which poverty and hopelessness were endemic. My father was continually distressed by the plight of some of his parishioners, particularly the 'down and outers' who drank methylated spirits laced with boot polish, but could do little to help them.

Church life at St Paul's was an education in many other ways. From time to time, when my father was preaching elsewhere, visiting clergy would occupy his pulpit, and to one of these, Arthur Killworth, I owe a debt of gratitude I cannot repay. A classical scholar and renowned preacher, Killworth must have been well over eighty when he preached the sermon on St Paul's journey to Rome which so influenced me. It was probably late in January, near the Feast of St Paul, and the church was uncomfortably hot. Some of the congregation were fanning themselves and everyone longed for the service to end. But Killworth's subject was dear to his heart and he would not be hurried. After talking of St Paul's wanderings, he took us on a tour of Imperial Rome and, as he dwelt on its glories, a light came into the old man's eyes. Roman roads, architecture, laws, literature and language, he impressed on us, were part of our inheritance, and unless we read Edward Gibbon's *Decline and Fall of the Roman Empire* we would go to our deathbeds deprived. And if we could not read it all, we must not miss his account of the fall of Constantinople. These words stayed with me. Rummaging through the crowded shelves of a second-hand bookshop in England twenty-five years later, I found a three-volume edition of Gibbon's great work, published in 1869 by Frederick Warne and containing 2400 pages of very small print, and bought it for ten shillings and sixpence. Since then I have read it twice from cover to cover and still turn to it for the joy of Gibbon's scholarship, imagery and prose. And every time I open that book I fall further into Arthur Killworth's debt.

At Knox my scholastic progress had been mediocre, my principal pleasure lying in writing occasional poems for the *Knox Grammarian* or the children's section of the *Sydney Morning Herald*.[6] This would not get me to university, however, and my mother believed that my verbosity fitted me for the bar. To study Law at Sydney University then one needed the Matriculation Certificate, and so when I was fifteen I was removed from Knox and sent as a boarder to Malvern Grammar School at Hunters Hill, whose headmaster, the Reverend Alfred James Rolfe, a classical scholar and mathematician, had a reputation for getting unpromising pupils through.

The atmosphere at Malvern was much freer than at Knox. Prefects and seniors were not allowed to assault their juniors with a stick and there was no caning for trivial misdemeanours. We boarded at 'Cambridge', a handsome old sandstone house which had a large garden running down to a swimming pool on the Parramatta River. The food was good; we were allowed to keep a dog, and bicycles, and go for walks and rides after school. And we could go home at weekends. Sometimes in fine weather I rode to Redfern on my bike.

Under Rolfe's guidance my scholastic performance improved, and with his gift for teaching the classics, Spencer, Milton, Cicero, Horace and Virgil soon became my friends. But mathematics, which I had not enjoyed at Knox, remained my bugbear, and once, while I was wrestling with the binomial theorem, Rolfe expressed amazement that I could not understand a simple mathematical law. Stung, I waited until the end of the lesson, then dashed off a short poem, which commenced:

> God give me eyes that I may see
> The laws that Thou hast made for me,
> And grant me sense to understand
> The marvels of Thy gracious hand ...

This saved me from further reproach. Entitling it 'A Schoolboy's Prayer', Rolfe not only recited it at Speech Day but had it printed and included in all the prizes awarded that year. My mother was intensely proud.

Bompie often stayed with us at St Paul's, and when I was home we would visit museums, art galleries and other places of interest in the city. His activities and associations were wide and varied and he was never dull company. Arriving home one weekend, I was delighted to find him at the rectory, and readily accepted his invitation to a meeting in the Australian Railwaymen's Union Hall, just across the road from us in Cleveland Street. The Spanish Civil War was then at its height, Communism had become an emotive issue in Australia, and that night there was to be a newsreel showing some of the horrors of the war and an address to raise funds for the comrades' cause. It promised to be well attended, and as we crossed Cleveland Street, although it was still early, we could see a crowd pushing to get in.

Bompie was, as always, impeccably dressed. I never saw him without a suit, a waistcoat, gold chain, fob watch and trilby hat. A connoisseur of opals, he wore a large stone mounted in a gold ring, and to the comrades in the porch of the Australian Railwaymen's Union Hall that night he would have looked a 'toff'. The table in the foyer was guarded by several burly bouncers and, as we passed it, a hefty fellow in braces and collarless shirt fastened at the throat with a stud accosted him, demanding, 'What's yer name?' 'Good evening, friend,' Bompie replied urbanely. 'Walter David White, Justice of the Peace. Would you show this to the meeting's chairman?' and, taking a faded card from his purse, he gave it to the man, who disappeared with it into the crowded hall. About five minutes later he returned with the chairman, who drew my grandfather aside and they talked earnestly for some minutes. Then he led us through the crush and noisy chatter onto the stage, where, calling for quiet, he introduced us as 'one of the fathers of the Australian Labor Party, Mr Walter David White, JP, and his grandson'. This was received with enthusiastic clapping. Bompie responded briefly. I don't remember what he said but when he finished they clapped him even harder. I felt proud, standing there beside him, but uncertain, too, about what my other grandfather, a capitalist and a big employer of labour, would think of my presence in the Australian Railwaymen's Union Hall that night.

About this time, St Paul's celebrated its eightieth anniversary. In such a young country as Australia this was an important civic, religious and historical event, and my father worked hard on its planning. The Archbishop of Sydney, the Most Reverend H. W. K. Mowll, had agreed to preach, and organisations such as the St John's Ambulance and the

Boys' Brigade were to attend. The first lesson was to be read by the Honourable William John McKell, state Labor member for Redfern and a parishioner, and my father and I called at his terrace house in South Dowling Street to discuss it with him. A genial McKell opened the door and led us through to the kitchen at the back of the house. Dressed in clothes similar to those worn by the bouncer at the Australian Railwaymen's Union meeting, he made tea while he and my father discussed the arrangements. I liked him but, still conditioned by the conservatism of my early years, was surprised by his informality.

On the big night the church was packed, and the future Governor-General of Australia appeared in a very different light. Immaculate in a dark jacket and striped trousers, he read the lesson in a commanding voice. But his manner and expression remained as pleasant and un-affected as they had been in his Dowling Street kitchen.

By now, most of us children were in our teens and beginning to take part in the running of the family. Our parents were not strict discipli-narians and, despite their devotion, left much of our upbringing to others. My father was never a stern parent; always young at heart, he was more our loved companion than head of the household. His pleasures were in simple things; from necessity he had become com-petent at making do and delighted in teaching us the skills by which he kept the house in good repair, showing great ingenuity in fixing apparently irredeemable pieces of furniture or machines with a piece of string or wire and a few nails. On his death I was touched to find in the attic of his home a Heath-Robinsonian device for coping with a leaking roof: on a chair underneath the leak he had propped at a slight angle an enamel basin, and from this had led an old piece of guttering to the nearest window, whence it shed its contents on the garden below. Often he joined in our romps. Once, when we visited my uncle Norman White for dental treatment *en famille*, my aunt, investigating a disturbance in the waiting room, found a muddle of nephews tossing her cushions around the room and in their midst as rowdy as any, her brother-in-law, Hugh. This was not the material from which canons and archdeacons were chosen, and it is not surprising that, while many of his contemporaries and juniors advanced in the hierarchy of the church, he remained a simple, and much-loved, parish priest.

Faced with the daunting task of being virtual sole parent to her unruly brood, my mother took refuge in her undoubted ill health, which required her to rest frequently. At Seven Hills she was fortunate to have various governesses or nannies to take us boys 'off her hands', but with our move to Wahroonga much of our care fell to my sister, Noel. Of the two girls, she was the more practical, competent in household skills and needlework, and now it was she—although still a schoolgirl herself—who saw to it that we got to school on time, correctly dressed.

In these circumstances, lacking strong direction from above, we grew up with an unusually heightened sense of responsibility for ourselves and for the direction of family affairs, and became accustomed to pronounce freely on such matters. Our parents came to rely on our advice and with time the balance of authority within the family was reversed. In my teens, however, I sometimes abused this authority, and the hectoring tone of some letters I wrote from boarding school shames me. We had developed quite a menagerie at the rectory—a dog called Rex, a white cockatoo and an aviary with smaller birds—and, returning home for a long weekend, I had been shocked to find them neglected. In my next letter I laid down the law:

> If you keep a cocky you must look after him, sometimes he is not fed until I arrive … Please see that the lovebirds have <u>water and food</u> (Please tell Ian to do this). Tell him to go into the aviary and see if they have <u>water and food</u>. Also, John noticed that Rex was walking a funny way with his back legs. He might be getting a tick and it is paralizing his back legs.

Fortunately for my character, my gentle mother would not allow such arrogance and I received a sharp reply: 'We were so pleased to have your letter yesterday but I don't like the way you wrote ... you must never again ... write like that ...'

When I was about sixteen my appendix was removed and, as my mother had been unwell for some time, my grandparents decided we would both benefit from a sea voyage and sent us on a cruise to Fiji in RMS *Strathnaver*. This was my first glimpse of a world beyond Australia, and the memory of Fiji's exotic charm remains with me still. On Easter Day in Suva we attended a service in a thatched open-sided church; as we walked towards it along a road flanked with hibiscus and frangipani, a huge Fijian with a head of fuzzy hair, bare-footed, and wearing a gay floral lap-lap, gave us the greeting used on the first Easter morning, 'He is risen', and my mother made the traditional reply, 'He is risen indeed.' This incident touched me more than anything else on the cruise.

In about 1937, my father bought an eleven-acre property, 'Green Gables', at Wentworth Falls in the Blue Mountains. Now we had a country retreat of our own where my mother could escape Sydney's midsummer humidity. From its wide verandah we had extensive views stretching away eastward to Sydney and at night the scene sparkled with thousands of tiny lights. The comfortable old bungalow, surrounded by pines, oaks, silver birches and other mature trees, had a large garden and a courtyard with a well of sweet water. The land sloped away steeply and a stream ran through it into a valley which at night was full of glow-worms. Even in the driest seasons the stream still ran strongly, and we dammed it to make a small swimming pool, but the water was too cold for comfort and we seldom swam in it.

Now, instead of spending school holidays at 'Wensleydale', we went to 'Green Gables' and the house was usually full of friends and relations bent on pleasure; with them we arranged picnics, bonfires, excursions to scenic spots in the Blue Mountains and long bush walks. For Christmas 1938 my grandfather Hordern gave me a horse named Bill which he had kept at 'Chislehurst', and after Christmas dinner there I set off on Bill for Wentworth Falls. The first night I reached Westmead and slept gratefully at my Aunt Edytha's home on the corner of Hawkesbury Road and the Great Western Highway. As it promised to be a hot day, we were off again at five o'clock next morning, jogging steadily westward. About noon I took a spell on the bank of the Nepean River at Penrith, then, pushing on up the steep gravel road over Lennox Bridge without seeing a soul, we rejoined the Great Western Highway and went on to Warriewood, where I tethered the horse to a tree and slept beside him. Again we were on the road at dawn, and about midday a weary boy and horse came to rest under the lofty pines of 'Green Gables'.

On Sunday 3 September, 1939, my family, together with millions of other Australians, gathered around wireless sets to hear Neville Chamberlain, Prime Minister of Great Britain, announce in what I thought was a quavering voice that Britain and Germany were at war. Shortly afterwards the Australian Prime Minister, R. G. Menzies, came on air to tell us that, in consequence of Chamberlain's announcement, we too were at war with Germany. A long cruel night was descending on the world and my unclouded childhood was over.

3 | WAR

1939 was an exciting year for me and most of my friends. Too young to comprehend the true consequences of World War I, we had been bitterly disappointed by Chamberlain's pact with Hitler in 1938. War was now certain, however, and, reared on the glory and achievements of the British Empire, we burned to fight for it.

But first we had to finish school. In a tumult of emotions we struggled through our final term and, as soon as the Leaving Certificate exam was over, I went camping at Newport with my Malvern friends, John Small, Guy Roberts and John Thomas. During the days that followed, as we swam and wandered along the beach, or sat around the campfire, we talked and dreamed of nothing but joining the RAAF. Already we saw ourselves as fighter pilots in Hawker Hurricanes or Supermarine Spitfires, swooping out of the sun with guns blazing on to a flight of Heinkels or Dorniers. As soon as we returned to Sydney, Small, Roberts and I went to the RAAF recruiting depot at Woolloomooloo to enlist as air crew.

But this was not as easy as we had imagined. They would accept us as ground crew immediately, we were told, but if we wanted to fly we might have to wait some months before being sent to Canada or Rhodesia to train under the newly established Empire Air Training Scheme. Undeterred, we persisted, and having been deemed sufficiently educated to study navigation, air gunnery, bomb aiming and other aeronautical mysteries, were approved for air crew. Sent for a medical test, again we passed with no problems.

Then came the snag. As we were under eighteen, we must have parental consent to fight overseas. Assuming this was just another formality to be undergone, we returned home in high spirits, clutching the necessary documents. And, indeed, my friends' parents signed without demur. But my mother read the form twice, in silence, and with a troubled face. Then, handing it back to me, she said, 'Marsden, I will not sign this, nor will your father.' Shocked, I offered the traditional protest that the other boys' mothers had signed: to which she gave the equally trite response that she was not the other boys' mother. She did not share my passion for aviation and distrusted aeroplanes. Boats, however, were another matter. Her loved brother, Norman, had a yacht, and to her the sea was a safer environment. 'I did not rear you to be killed in an aeroplane, Marsden,' she told me. 'Join the navy.' I could not understand her attitude, and was embarrassed at having to explain to John and Guy that I would not be joining them. We shook hands, promising to go camping again after the war, and parted. Before long both of them were killed in the air over Europe. My mother's refusal to sign that paper was one of the most fortunate journeying mercies I have received.

At the beginning of 1940, as I was still under eighteen and the war in Europe posed no immediate threat to Australia, my parents decided that before studying Law I should gain a smattering of culture. And so, my combative fervour temporarily dampened, I enrolled in Arts at the University of Sydney.

The 'Varsity', as it was fashionably known at that time, was an elite institution. As there was no free education, its students, apart from a small number of scholarship winners, mostly came from well-to-do homes. The academic staff were similarly select, and their rarity earned them a distinction not accorded to many of their counterparts today. They were the gods of Sydney's academic Olympus and those I remember—Professors 'Sonny' Holme, Lovell, Cole, Waterhouse,

Stephen H. Roberts and Arthur Lindsay Sadler, and the lecturers, Howarth, Maxwell, Oliver and Ward—were highly revered.

Professor Sadler was my greatest mentor. An Oxford MA, who had come to Sydney via Tokyo where he had taught for twelve years, he had been appointed Professor of Oriental Studies at Sydney in 1922. We later became close friends, but in 1940, as a raw student, I was just one of the many to whom he imparted some insight into the refinement of higher education. About fifteen of us had gathered in his lecture room in the south-east corner of the quadrangle. As we were very new, we were there well before the appointed time, and were occupying ourselves awkwardly by examining his collection of rare artefacts which hung or leant against the walls. There were suits of Samurai armour, swords, leg-cutters, Buddhas, Japanese screens, masks, braziers, robes, items associated with the Tea Ceremony and other treasures from the time of the Hideyoshi and the Tokugawa shoguns.

The door opened precisely on time and in strode Sadler. A dapper man, dressed in a Harris tweed suit and woollen tie, and sporting pince-nez, he presented an alien figure to our insular gaze, although later we accepted that as his constant mode of dress. After shuffling some papers on his desk, he looked up and said, 'Good afternoon, ladies and gentlemen.' I glanced about for subjects deserving of these titles and, on realising that he was addressing us, felt a surge of pride.

This greeting exemplified the professor's attitude to his pupils; a man of simple dignity, he spoke to us as equals, with no posturing. He often entertained his students, individually or in small groups, at his home, 'Rivenhall', in Warrawee. In response to his formal invitation, simply printed 'At Home', we would arrive to be greeted by Sadler and his Anglo-Japanese wife, Eva, and entertained at a tea ceremony in the Japanese tea house which he had built in his garden. These occasions, primarily designed, no doubt, to familiarise us with the ceremony, were possibly also an attempt to refine our social experience. I was taken aback by the first invitation and accepted only at my mother's insistence, but in common with many fellow students I now recall the professor's tea parties as some of the highlights of my 'Varsity' days.

In his first lecture, Sadler announced that we were to study Japan and its people, outlining its history and the antiquity of its culture, particularly comparing it with the Anglo-Saxon race. Over two thousand years ago, he told us, when our ancestors had been painting themselves with woad and conducting cruel human sacrifices, the Japanese were producing elegant ceramics. For two thousand years they had considered themselves a special race and had sought supremacy by whatever means promised success—hard work, trade, isolation, diplomacy or war. When one procedure failed they would try other means. He ended with the statement that the Japanese were a fearsome people with scant respect for human life and suffering and 'God help any European who falls into their hands.' All too soon I was to see for myself the tragic truth of his words.

In 1940 Australia was gearing itself for a war in Europe and at sea. The Royal Australian Navy was already largely dispersed in the northern hemisphere, and the army and air force were being expanded in preparation for operations there. Recruiting posters were appearing everywhere, and men, some of whom had been unemployed since the Great Depression, were enlisting in large numbers.

Together with many other undergraduates I joined the Sydney University Regiment and, as a private in 'C' Company, No. N42339, began an army career during which I was never to hear an angry shot or see a drop of blood spilt in action. Suitably kitted, we spent weekends and vacations under canvas learning the rudiments of military arts, most of which seemed to be digging slit trenches and latrines, filling palliasses, and renewing our acquaintance with the World War I .303 Lee-Enfield rifle, bayonet and Lewis gun—all familiar to me from my days in the Knox Cadet Corps.

The latrines made a particular impression on me. In terms of sanitation, I could chart my life from childhood, progressing from the outdoor pit at Seven Hills to the inadequate water closets at Wahroonga and Cooks River, and the final luxury of a two-lavatory home at Redfern. As the war progressed, I frequently rated my situation in terms of the provision and quality of these facilities.

For a start, as a rabble of individualists, we did not take our activities seriously. The regiment differed from the regular army in that all ranks were drawn from friends and classmates. In fact, our officers sometimes ranked below us in age and academic performance, and some of the privates and corporals, freshly imbued with notions of social equality, resented this. Our indignation focused on the distinction between our latrines—which offered little in the way of dignity or privacy—and the officers' 'throne', which was enclosed by hessian and entered by a door with a metal handle. So incensed did we become at this apparent discrimination that a larrikin group, of which I was one, wired the door-handle to a truck battery designed to administer an electric shock to the officers and gentlemen. The prank received swift retribution and, as I was by now a corporal, I was reduced in rank to private for several weeks, with a consequent reduction in pay.

During that year we camped in various sites and in varying degrees of discomfort around Sydney. On night manoeuvres near Mona Vale, we waded across Narrabeen Lagoon up to our necks in water, holding our rifles in the air above our heads, and slept soaking wet in the bush. On another occasion we pitched our tents under the avenue of trees leading from the grand gates to John Burns's mansion near Pennant Hills. This had become an army headquarters, and we relished its bathrooms and plumbing.

At the end of 1940 we spent our first long camp at the vast military establishment at Ingleburn. There we were inoculated against typhoid and vaccinated for smallpox, and our training took on a more serious note although, alarmingly, it had more to do with retreating than attacking. Route-marching and physical toughening increased; wearing painfully ill-fitting boots, we trudged along dusty roads singing the marching songs of the British Army in World War I about Tipperary, packing up our troubles in old kit bags and lighting our pipes with lucifers. More to our liking were our appearances in recruiting parades through Sydney. Swinging along George Street with rifles at the slope, bayonets fixed, bands playing, flags flying and crowds cheering, we hoped to give the impression of returned battle heroes rather than rookies.

Mindful of my mother's urgings to keep in touch—an injunction hardly necessary for a compulsive correspondent such as I—I wrote home regularly, sparing them none of the less pleasant aspects of camp life, the flies, dysentery and tinea, but ending on a brave note, 'I'm not grumbling at this life. I like it.'

During this time, major changes were taking place in my family. In December 1938 my elder sister, Mary, had married Boyce Rowley Horsley, who had been my father's curate at St Peter's, and thirteen months later my sister Noel married Arthur Hugh Darling, a grazier from Gunnedah. Both weddings took place in St Paul's, and the receptions, thanks to my grandparents' continuing generosity, were held in marquees on the 'Chislehurst' croquet lawn. The elaborate bridal gowns, flowers and other wedding paraphernalia were, of course, the gift of our grandfather Edward Carr Hordern, from whom we still received treats beyond my father's means.

Six months later E. C. Hordern was gone. His funeral service, held at St Paul's Anglican Church, Chatswood, was crowded, and a cortege of eighty cars followed the hearse to Gore Hill Cemetery, where he was buried in the extensive grave he had established thirty years before for his brother, John Lebbeus Hordern, and other family members. Although now closed to burials it is still an impressive site. A circular plot large enough to accommodate more than sixty graves, it is surrounded by a stone wall surmounted by iron railings. A flight of marble steps leads through an iron gate to a tall granite monument which, engraved with many names, still serves as an important family memorial.

When Edward Carr died, I went with my mother to convey the sad news to Bompie, himself confined to bed. He took it sombrely. 'I'm next,' was all he said. And six months later he too was dead. His funeral was a very different affair from that of my grandfather Hordern.

The service, also at St Paul's Chatswood, was attended only by the family and close friends and a few members of Sydney's literary and artistic community. Like my Hordern grandfather, Bompie too was buried at Gore Hill, but his grave was no larger than necessary to accommodate him and his beloved first wife, Mary. With his death I began to grow up: over the past year I had lost two of the most powerful influences of my childhood.

Japan's bombing of Pearl Harbor on 7 December 1941 suddenly brought war close to Australian shores. Within a few weeks Hong Kong, Singapore, Borneo and the Dutch East Indies had fallen, Port Moresby was directly threatened, and Darwin had been devastated by the same Japanese carrier-borne aircraft which had smashed the American fleet at Pearl Harbor. Most of our seasoned soldiers were in the Middle East or prisoners in Singapore, while the navy and many of our airmen were fighting in the northern hemisphere and, with no front-line aircraft to match the Japanese fighters and bombers, we were defenceless.

With panic in high places, the country was put on a full war footing and like many others in the Sydney University Regiment I became a full-time soldier. By courtesy of the government, my worldly goods were now a rifle and bayonet, gas mask, knapsack, kit bag, a fairly well-fitting uniform, a pair of heavy tan boots, gaiters, a slouch hat, forage cap, pullover, waterproof cape, ground sheet, water bottle, towel, socks, underwear, toilet and eating equipment. And they went everywhere with me. My pay was about eight shillings a day and, having regained the dizzy rank of corporal, I indulged myself by buying a small swagger-stick with brass fittings to carry when on leave.

We were now permanently camped at Ingleburn but, as the risk of a Japanese invasion fleet appearing off the coast was so great, the Barrenjoey Peninsula and other likely landing places were fortified with barbed-wire entanglements, machine-gun posts and tank traps, and we were sent to defend the Port Kembla steelworks.

Loaded with military impedimenta, we were trucked by 'blitz buggy' to Kembla Grange, and from there marched to the foothills of Mount Kembla to establish defensive positions overlooking the port and town. Once there, we were warned of the gravity of our situation. We were 'as close to active service as we would ever be without being on it', our officers told us, and must be ready for action at any time. Such was my youthful confidence that I wrote to my parents, 'If the Japs come here, we will be straight into them.'

Armed with picks and shovels, we settled in. We dug latrines, slit trenches and weapon pits, laid out a camouflaged camp complete with kitchen and mess tables, and sited machine guns. That done, we sat for several weeks, looking down onto the splendid coastal panorama below, and praying that we would not wake one morning to see a Japanese armada coming over the horizon.

Apparently the perceived threat soon faded. Returned to Ingleburn we were told that our service in the Sydney University Regiment was over, and that we would be distributed among other units of the Australian army. I was to be a bombardier in the 110th Light Anti-Aircraft Regiment, stationed at Kensington Racecourse.

This was a welcome change. I exchanged the parched Ingleburn countryside for the racecourse's manicured lawns and gardens, and pitched my tent under its shaded avenues. The food was better, and whenever we got a few hours' leave we could catch a penny ride on the tram and be in the heart of Sydney twenty minutes later. But the greatest blessing was our access to ablution and latrine facilities designed for peace-time punters which, by our standards, were luxurious. There were even rumours that the sergeants and officers had hot showers.

Then followed halcyon days. In serene autumn weather we began learning about the newly acquired 40 mm quick-firing Bofors gun, with which the regiment was being equipped, while outside the tents the leaves drifted down to form a gold and saffron carpet which rustled under our feet as we patrolled the grounds on sentry duty. We began digging trenches again, but this time among the flower beds and lawns, so that the ground was already softened by gardeners' spades. We also erected obstacles on the racecourse to prevent Japanese aircraft or gliders landing there.

As our training progressed, we speculated about our destination and rumours proliferated. Some said we were off to New Guinea, the Northern Territory or Darwin, to defend some of the many airstrips being built there. Others had it that we would be kept in the south to guard docks and airfields until the Japanese threat lessened.

But none of this happened. One day, without warning, we were trucked to Circular Quay and transferred to two ships anchored in the harbour. The *Queen Mary* and *Queen Elizabeth*, two of the world's greatest liners, had just disembarked American troops destined for New Guinea and the Solomon Islands, and we were to man their guns while they were in harbour. I joined the *Queen Elizabeth*; as we came alongside, her grey bulk loomed like a cliff above us. We climbed through a hatch in her side and, after walking along seemingly interminable passageways cluttered with overhead pipes, reached an open space on deck where the guns were explained to us. While not as efficient as the Bofors against low-flying planes, we were told, there was the compensation that even if not scoring a hit, a big shell just missing a torpedo-carrying aircraft might throw it off balance and spoil the pilot's aim. Then, having been allocated our cabins, we were sent to familiarise ourselves with the ship.

Our quarters were impressive. Some of the more fortunate had bunks knocked up in cabins and staterooms designed for millionaires. My berth, deep in the bowels of the ship, was dark, airless and stinking of stale tobacco, but I had no complaints. We had every comfort, I told my mother: 'Hot and cold water, warm and cold air conditioning, electric fans, bed lights, lifts, inlaid and tapestried walls, grand pianos, etc.' Our mess room was one of the *Queen Elizabeth*'s former dining saloons, fitted with long benches and tables, and it went without saying that the lavatories were well beyond our normal expectations.

The ship had not been cleaned since the American soldiers had left, and I noticed a white envelope lying on the deck. Printed in large letters in the top left-hand corner were the words 'THE WHITE HOUSE WASHINGTON'. It was empty, but later, on climbing into my bunk to test the mattress, I found another. This had not been opened. I broke the seal and read:

THE WHITE HOUSE
WASHINGTON

TO MEMBERS OF THE UNITED STATES ARMY EXPEDITIONARY FORCES:

You are a soldier of the United States Army.

You have embarked for distant places where the war is being fought.

Upon the outcome depends the freedom of your lives: the freedom of the lives of those you love—your fellow-citizens—your people.

Never were the enemies of freedom more tyrannical, more arrogant, more brutal.

Yours is a God-fearing, proud, courageous people, which, throughout its history, has put its freedom under God before all other purposes.

We who stay at home have our duties to perform—duties owed in many parts to you. You will be supported by the whole force and power of this Nation. The victory you win will be a victory of all the people—common to them all.

You bear with you the hope, the confidence, the gratitude and the prayers of your family, your fellow-citizens, and your President—

Franklin D Roosevelt

President Roosevelt's letter to his troops

It moved me then, it moves me now, and makes me proud of my American blood.

I was assigned to one of the big guns. At first it was a novelty to open its well-greased breech block and peer up inside the rifled barrel. For a while, too, we enjoyed training it on to the lantern of the Macquarie Lighthouse, Fort Denison or Government House. But soon all this palled. There was no hint of enemy action; no alarm sounded, no gunfire boomed at sea, and, to our great relief, no enemy torpedo bombers swept in over South Head. With the sun dancing on the water, we leant over the rails languidly watching the traffic passing on the harbour, while the residents of Sydney in turn scrutinised us. Passing ferries heeled slightly as their gaping passengers crowded to one side, motor boats and yachts cruised slowly by, and boys and girls waved from their sailing dinghies skimming under our stern and across our bows. Only the discreet warships, slipping in and out to sea, appeared to pay us no attention.

Days passed, while the bored soldiers of the 110th Light Anti-Aircraft Regiment played cards on deck or lay about smoking, reading and sleeping. Then, late one evening, we were transferred back to Kensington. And in the morning the two great ships were gone.

But my time on *Queen Elizabeth*, watching those sleek grey warships slide past, had made me think. My brief taste of life aboard ship, even at anchor in the harbour, had opened up a new world to me, and in my mind's eye I followed the naval ships out to sea, wondering what their life was like, what would be their ports of call, and what adventures awaited them. My mother's words, 'Marsden, join the navy', sounded constantly in my ears and I heeded them.

It was quickly done. I offered my services at the naval recruiting depot in Martin Place and, two weeks later, at HMAS *Rushcutter*, was interviewed by a panel of naval officers. When asked why I wanted to join the navy, my reply that it was to get out of the army, seemed well received. Had I done any sailing? they asked. This lucky question allowed me to take them aboard the *Temptress*, have an early morning swim at Refuge Bay, and, if the wind was westerly, an easy run out to sea. After a few more questions about my general interests and knowledge, the interview ended, and I returned to sentry duty at Kensington.

Shortly afterwards came a letter telling me that I had been selected to be a 'Sub Lieutenant RANVR (on Probation)' and, bidding a buoyant farewell to my army mates, I reported to HMAS *Rushcutter* for what the letter called 'further orders'.

At *Rushcutter* I entered a new world. The preliminary medical examination, with which I was now all too familiar, offered no surprises, but the slops department was an eye-opener. As a corporal in the army, I had been dished out with a uniform, slouch hat, socks, gaiters and boots and food from a camp kitchen. Now, after grave consideration of my size, I was given several sets of underwear, black shoes, half-Wellington boots, a Burberry, a naval officer's cap and badge, leather gloves, a white silk scarf, handkerchiefs, shirts, ties and toilet gear. Most gratifying of all was an order on Anthony Hordern and Sons Ltd, Universal Providers of Brickfield Hill, Sydney, for 'made to measure' blue and tropical white uniforms and a greatcoat.

This was another new experience. At Hordern's the head of the gentlemen's tailoring department, Mr Rook, greeted me as 'Sir', explaining the quality and weights of the cloth from which my uniforms were to be made. I would have several fittings, he told me, and if the cut of any garment was not entirely to my satisfaction it would be altered. Unaccustomed to such respect, I found it embarrassing, but accepted it awkwardly as part of a world at war about which as yet I knew virtually nothing.

After the drab khakis which I had been wearing my new uniform caused me great satisfaction and, as I left Anthony Hordern's gleaming with gold buttons, cap badge, and thin wavy sub lieutenant's stripes, I could not help taking complacent sideways glances in shop windows. Never before had I worn such finery and, to give it the exposure it warranted, I invited a girl to the pictures that night. But here pride betrayed me. As befitted my new status, I had bought tickets in the Dress Circle, where we rubbed shoulders with several American and

British naval officers. During the interval a heavily decorated Royal Navy captain in our row edged his way out past me and, heady with glory, I greeted him, 'Good evening, Sir'. He ran a cold eye over my pristine splendour, and said loudly, 'Good evening, Sub. You look awfully new.' That was my first painful lesson in naval etiquette: one does not address a senior officer unless spoken to.

In June 1942 I was sent to Flinders Naval Depot. This, my second rail journey to Melbourne, was a far cry from the ride to the Jamboree in a 'dog box' seven years earlier. Having tipped the guard a shilling, I had a sleeping berth to myself and, after changing trains at Albury, dined in style on the luxurious *Spirit of Progress*.

About noon the following day I reached the depot and was enchanted by its opulence. I was now developing a taste for the good life and my former grouches about officers' privileges were forgotten. The day after my arrival was a freezing Sunday and, seated at a table snugged up close to a big log fire, I began one of the many letters I would write home during my next five years in the navy. Reading them over sixty years later, I see that while my location and circumstances changed continually, the extravagance of their prose remained unaltered.

> You would simply be carried away by the Naval Base here. Everywhere there are glorious green lawns, immaculately kept flowerbeds, shrubs, emerald green and perfectly trimmed hedges—dream paths, beautiful palms and everywhere one looks one is in an atmosphere of ships and the sea. Spanish guns, British guns, guns captured in the Boxer Rebellion, German guns. Figureheads of sailing ships, masts, binnacles, wheels, compasses from the old *Sydney* etc. are on every side. The beauty & symmetry, cleanliness and neatness of the place is without parallel ... Beautiful red brick buildings everywhere. Hot showers. We sleep in beautiful beds—10 in a room. Our beds are made for us by stewards.
>
> Then there is the Ward Room. That is the equivalent of the Officers' Club ... There are rooms and rooms of it. Huge spacious

fireplaces with roaring log fires. Luxurious lounge chairs and sofas—wirelesses, billiard tables, library, periodical shelves. Then there is the dining room. Long tables of the most beautifully polished wood. Huge paintings of sea battles and the landing of Captain Cook, stretch right across the walls.

Then the food!!! You sit down and a steward … says 'Asparagus soup, sir'. Then follow roasts, potato chips, sweets, pineapple, fruit, finger bowls, toast etc.—then you walk out into the club rooms and drink coffee and stand by huge fires etc. There is a piano here too.

In the grounds of this establishment there is a zoo with wallabies, kangaroos, emus, possums, and all kinds of parrots. There is a sort of a river winding through with green lawns & willows & little bamboo bridges over it. We are on a bay here and there are sailing boats you can take out when you like …

My time in this paradise passed quickly. After being instructed in naval tradition, its customs and etiquette (if only I had known this before going to the pictures!) and absorbing the basic principles of seamanship during a short stint at sea in the 922-ton training vessel HMAS *Bingera*, we were considered fledged, and sent on our various ways. Some, destined for 'General Service', went to widely dispersed ships or shore establishments. I was returned to Sydney to serve in a new class of ship in the RAN—the Fairmile.

I now began a series of preparation courses for future Fairmile officers. Having suffered so much in World War I from U-boats cutting off her food supplies, and being haunted by the spectre of starvation in any future war, Britain had for years encouraged some of her most able scientists to work on means of hunting U-boats, and by 1942 their technology was the best in the world. Classified as 'top secret' and referred to as 'Asdic',[1] it introduced us to quartz crystals, high-frequency motor alternators and the Doppler effect, which concerned the nature of echoes bounced back to a searching ship from underwater transmissions. These might be coming from a whale, a school of fish, a wreck, a submarine or some other object, and we learned how to assess them, what an exploding depth charge could do to a submarine's hull, and what happened inside a submarine when sea water got to its batteries. The business of killing so horribly other young men also fighting for their country did not concern most of us. Knowing something of the sufferings of civilians in countries recently occupied by the Germans and Japanese, we were intent only on winning the war.

At the Woolloomooloo gunnery school we learned about fighting off attacking aircraft, and at HMAS *Penguin* were introduced to the mysteries of navigation, the relationship between time and longitude, the Celestial Sphere, sextants, azimuths, compass correction, dead reckoning, tidal prediction, meteorology, the barometer, temperature, wind, and Buys Ballot Law which, as most of us were destined for tropical service, we were told might help us survive a cyclone or typhoon.[2]

All this took several months. Then, crammed full of theory, we were packed off to sea to put our knowledge into practice. In late 1942 I was appointed to HMAS *Abraham Crijnssen* on east coast convoy duty and began to learn at first hand some of the facts of life in the war at sea.

4 | CONVOYS

Until the end of 1941 there had been little enemy activity in Australian waters, although in 1940 two German raiders had laid mines off the New South Wales coast, in Bass Strait, Spencer Gulf and the approaches to Hobart and Albany. Their first victim, the SS *Cambridge*, was sunk off Wilsons Promontory on 7 November of that year.[1]

With Japan in the war, however, shipping in Australian waters faced greater dangers. The Japanese I-class submarines were formidable. About twice the size of German U-boats, they were faster on the surface and more powerfully gunned than many of the small RAN ships opposing them. They carried fourteen torpedoes, and some were equipped with midget submarines and reconnaissance aircraft. And their crews were carrying out fearful atrocities; in seven instances of sinkings in the Indian Ocean they had machine-gunned survivors in the water or on rafts.[2]

In May 1942 their attack on shipping in Australian waters began in earnest. In the first week of that month they sank two ships off New Caledonia, and the following week attacked the Russian ship *Wellen* 30 miles off Newcastle. They now had five submarines on the east coast and from these were launched the midget submarines which attacked Sydney on 31 May 1942. Eight days later they bombarded Sydney and Newcastle.

To counter this threat, Australia had begun building Bathurst-class minesweepers, known as corvettes. These 650-ton ships were fitted with Asdic, armed with 4-inch, and smaller guns, and had a top speed of about 16 knots. On 8 June the Navy began a system of convoys, using some of the corvettes as escorts. But these convoys could not guarantee safety: the next day the *Orestes* was shelled south of Jervis Bay while travelling in convoy, and on 12 June the *Guatemala*, straggling astern of a convoy, was torpedoed and sunk 40 miles from Sydney Heads.

From that time the Japanese attacks intensified. Between June and August 1942, enemy submarines attacked fifteen ships off the east coast, sinking seven of them. Altogether, between 1942 and 1944, twenty-eight ships were sunk or damaged in these waters, and along the coast from Port Macquarie to Eden the flotsam of dying ships—sodden clothing, furniture, books and bodies—became a familiar sight.

This was the situation when I joined HMAS *Abraham Crijnssen*. One of four Dutch minelayers stationed in the Dutch East Indies at the outbreak of the war with Japan, she had been the only one to escape. Camouflaged with trees and foliage, and crammed with Dutch civilians, she had made a night dash for Australia, successfully eluding Japanese search aircraft. About a hundred miles off the West Australian coast she had run out of fuel, but was spotted by an RAAF recon-naissance plane and towed into Geraldton. Taken to Sydney, she was leased to the RAN and refitted as a corvette for anti-submarine and convoy duty.

But even after the *Crijnssen*'s refit there was much about her that was foreign to Australian seamen. Whereas we understood imperial measurements—5-inch guns, pounds, feet, fathoms and miles—hers were metric, and all notices around the ship were written in Dutch. For this reason the RAN decided to retain twenty-four of her seamen, her chief quartermaster, de Jong, and one of her officers, Lieutenant Bertis Van der Weyder, to help the ship's operation.

Her only captain in the RAN was 'Chappy', the 26-year-old Lieutenant Arthur Irwin Chapman RANR(S), who had already been at sea for ten years.[3] Apart from the permanent service RAN men who made a career of the navy, there were three classes of reserves: the RANR(S), merchant seamen who could be called to the colours, the RAN Reserve (RANR) and RAN Volunteer Reserve (RANVR), civilians who undertook training in peace-time and could be mobilised in a state of emergency. The younger officers of the RANR(S) who had spent much of their lives in ships were generally fine seamen and compared to them, we were, as we were sometimes called, 'Saturday afternoon sailors'.

Chapman's command was to be unique in the history of the RAN. In addition to the Dutch, his crew would be made up of twenty-five Australians: himself, three officers and twenty-one seamen and, to make up her war complement, a similar number of British sailors, survivors of the recently sunk HMS *Jupiter*.

This amalgamation of seamen of various nationalities in a ship of Dutch origin under Australian command made the *Crijnssen* one of the first examples of multi-culturalism in the RAN. It also posed particular problems for her captain. The morale of the Dutch was understandably low. Their country had been overrun, in many cases the fate of their families was unknown and, with their navy virtually destroyed, they now had to serve in their own vessel under foreign command. The British sailors, having lost their ship and being out of touch with home and family, were similarly dispirited.

Chapman brought tolerance and diplomacy to this delicate situation. Having been reared in the merchant service, he had a more liberal attitude to the navy's *King's Rules and Admiralty Instructions* than officers of the RAN might have shown, and bent them to suit *Crijnssen*'s unique situation. His superiors had given him some leeway in this regard. In correspondence with me many years later, referring to my confessions of deplorable lawlessness, he wrote,

> Obviously you broke all the wartime rules without any trouble ... we broke quite a few rules too in other directions ... I remember the Chief of Staff telling me that 'C' [*Crijnssen*] was an

unusual arrangement and would have its problems with a three-navy complement. It gave me a great feeling of power when he said, 'Whatever those problems are, we don't want to hear about them.' It was simply another way of saying, 'If you don't make "C" work, you're not the man for the job!' To make it work we made rules and did things which were not in the book, with the object of keeping our three navies happy in one small space and at the same time producing a fighting ship.

His first problem was not long in coming. On the morning the ship was to be commissioned at Garden Island, Chapman went on board carrying a commissioning pennant, the White Ensign and a picture of King George VI, which he expected to hang in the wardroom, as was the custom in the RAN. Following him was his first lieutenant, Bob Hart, bearing the Union Jack and a picture of the American film star Rita Hayworth. This photograph of the seductively posed actress, across which some wag had written, 'To the boys of the *Abraham Crijnssen* from Rita Hayworth', was also intended for the wardroom. At 8 a.m. the pennant, with its long white tail and red cross of St George, rose to the truck of the ship's mast, the colours and the Jack were hoisted, and the RAN had a new ship, HMAS *Abraham Crijnssen*. But as the transfer was only a temporary arrangement, the Dutch officers on board saw the *Crijnssen* as still their ship, and when Chapman and Hart joined them at breakfast in the wardroom they found hanging there a portrait of Queen Wilhelmina of the Netherlands and an engraving of Admiral Crijnssen, after whom the ship had been named, whipping a British squadron in the Dutch wars. Rather than giving offence by replacing Wilhelmina's portrait with that of George VI, Chapman took the British king below and hung him in his cabin. Rita Hayworth, however, offered no slight to national pride, and was welcomed. She took her place in the wardroom alongside the queen where she brightened the bleary eye of many a tired breakfaster coming off watch after a gale-swept night.

The RAN's purpose in leaving a Dutch officer on board was to help Chapman understand and handle cultural differences among the crew, and from this time he and Van der Weyder, consulting together, made some unusual decisions. One was to appoint two coxswains, one being de Jong and the other, Rhys-Jones, a Welshman, who had previously served in the Royal Navy. He had seniority, but Chapman assigned them a cabin together, hoping that through this proximity they would achieve harmonious cooperation.

The issue of 'grog' was another problem solved in an unconventional way. By tradition, the Royal Navy provided a daily tot of rum to their seamen, while the sailors of the Royal Netherlands Navy were accustomed to an issue of beer. But Australian sailors enjoyed no such privilege. At the time of the foundation of the RAN in 1911 it had been established that, in lieu of grog, they would be allotted an extra threepence a day, and this rule still held. The Dutch and British sailors, as members of the RAN, now had no legitimate entitlement to a grog issue, but Chapman and Van der Weyder, to avoid the resentment such a deprivation would cause, made a deal: the Dutchman would rig the books to bring on twice the beer required for his men, and this would serve all the seamen on board.

The wearing of beards was another tricky matter. An RAN sailor must obtain permission before growing a beard, and is then obliged to remain unshaven for a stated period of time. There is no tolerance of half beards or moustaches, it is a matter of all or nothing. But to the Dutch coxswain's neat Vandyke, Chapman turned a blind eye.

When I joined *Crijnssen* I was assigned a cabin just under the bridge. This was a small compartment and in it, apart from a bunk, was a safe containing the code, signalling, and other secret books. They had weighted lead covers and, in the event of possible defeat, it was my duty to throw them overboard.

Besides myself, there were four other officers in addition to Chapman and Van der Weyder. They were the first lieutenant, Bob Hart, the anti-submarine officer, Lieutenant Cole, the engineer,

Lieutenant Woods, and Lieutenant John Moyes RANVR. Moyes was an entertaining shipmate. He had recently served in a destroyer in the Mediterranean and was writing a book, *Scrap Iron Flotilla*—the first of his three successful war stories. Published in 1943 by the Sydney Bookstall Company, *Scrap Iron Flotilla* was followed by *Sea Digest* and *Mighty Midgets*. Two other notable members of the ship's company were a little brown dog, part corgi, called Kos, and a black cat. Members of the original crew, they were completely at home on board. The animals appear in some of my very rough photographs taken on the *Crijnssen*, but I was proud of one shot in Sydney Harbour during a convoy turn around. Puss had been relaxing on a coil of rope which was whisked from under her. She stalked off, leaped on to the gun and made her way along the slippery barrel to its mouth and, perched high above the deck, began washing herself. I clicked the shutter and caught a black cat on a black gun against the Harbour Bridge.

Two days after I had joined the *Crijnssen*, we left on convoy duty. During this time I had puzzled over how to meet my mother's requirements about writing home while at sea, and had decided to keep a journal which would form the basis of letters to be posted as our circumstances allowed. This was my second attempt at a diary and it proved more satisfactory than that written at the Jamboree seven years previously. We were not supposed to keep journals and this was lawless, which perhaps reflected my attitude to authority. Its pages are full of juvenile appraisals of often dramatic and dangerous situations, but they are on-the-spot pictures of my war at sea.

I felt a sense of exhilaration as we slipped the bridle of the buoy and, in company with a corvette, steamed out through Sydney Heads to meet the convoy. For a novice this was an engrossing sight. The ships, forming up in two columns, were a motley collection—smoky freighters, ore carriers and sea-worn tramps—and, as they communicated only by flags or signal lamps flashing Morse code, I was confronted by a seeming confusion of blinking lights and flag-hoists fluttering from yardarms as we shepherded them into their proper stations. Some belonged to Broken Hill Proprietary Limited and bore the prefix *Iron*. They carried ore from Whyalla to Newcastle, and over the next few months we would steam thousands of miles with them. Before I left the *Crijnssen* in February 1943 the *Mobilube*, *Kalingo*, *Star King* and *Iron Knight* had all been torpedoed. They were old friends and we mourned their loss.[4]

The convoy formed, we set off at 10 knots with the *Crijnssen* and the corvette on its port and starboard bows. Our Asdic set pinged incessantly, searching for submarines. So far my military service had been free from menace but this was now serious business. The enemy —no longer a distant force posing hypothetical threats—was at hand, with the advantages of invisibility and superior power, and we lived in a permanent state of apprehension.

As a probationary sub lieutenant with no sea experience I learnt the ropes by standing my watches with more experienced officers, and I had much to learn. Apart from maintaining our own station by keeping at a constant distance and bearing from the convoy, we had to ensure that the ships did not creep up or fall back on one another. It was like continually shepherding a group of unruly children along a highway, except that in this case the dangers were invisible. Any straying from position earned the offending ship a peremptory signal: 'Resume your proper station.'

With coal burners there was also the problem of smoke. When changing watches, the firemen sometimes overfed the furnaces, sending clouds of black smoke billowing into the sky. This could betray our presence to an oriental eye peering through a periscope, and prompted a speedy order: 'Make less smoke.' Quite soon, the routine of coaxing ships into place, admonishing stragglers and berating smoke-makers became familiar to me. By day we took some comfort from the land-based Hudson or Beaufort bombers which circled, flying just above the mast and talking to us in Morse code with their signal lamps. But at dusk they went home, leaving us alone in the dark and anxious hours.

Although I had travelled on ships before, I still had much to learn about the sights and sensations of being at sea, and my journal fed on these observations. To watch the sun rise over the ocean's rim was a constant source of wonder. From the small stock of university textbooks brought with me, I had been reading Arnold and Fitzgerald, and sometimes, when fighting sleep on watch, I would recite passages from them. Just before dawn one morning an oceanic version of the *Rubaiyat*'s opening stanza appeared before my bleary eyes. The stars began to pale, the sky lightened and the colour of the ocean faded from purple to grey. Then the sun burst from the sea, its first rays catching the top of our mast in a gleam of gold. As it rose, its glow crept down the mast to touch the ensign in a glittering play of red, white and blue, then down to the guns and depth charges, and to gild the merchant ships ploughing along through a calm blue sea with white foam sparkling beneath their bows. Now fully awake, I recited to myself:

> *Awake! for Morning in the Bowl of Night*
> *Has flung the stone that put the Stars to flight:*
> *And Lo! the Hunter of the East has caught*
> *The Sultan's Turret in a Noose of Light.*

For me, Fitzgerald's imagery became fact, not in an Arabian desert setting, but off Jervis Bay in the Pacific Ocean.

Another novel experience was to smell the land from far offshore —a phenomenon which must have preceded many discoveries in the age of sail, it rated a journal entry:

> This morning I was on the bridge at 4 and though the old quartering moon wasn't capable of much illumination I could just make out the dim shapes of the ships in convoy about a mile and a half on the stb'd beam. We were over 50 miles from land and I was leaning over the wing of the bridge when suddenly a westerly wind started blowing. It had evidently blown over hundreds of miles of land before it crossed the coast. It was filled with the rich scents of the forest … the aroma of flowering gums and eucalypts and all the bush.

Gales, although by now not novel, also set me scribbling and one we encountered in January 1943 was worth recording. We had left the Heads and turned south, ploughing into a big sea. The howling wind was tearing the tops off the waves as we climbed up their forward slopes and dropped with a shuddering plunge into the green valleys below. 'Pile-driving', we called it. Everywhere was violence and noise, except for the albatrosses cutting across our bow in silent flight, wing-tips feathering the waves in steep turns. They revelled in wild weather.

All day, lashed with wind and spray, we fought on, while below decks doors banged and everything loose slid about. One vicious wave burst a bulkhead, hurling sleeping sailors from their hammocks onto the deck. One broke his collarbone, and as the *Abraham Crijnssen* carried no doctor, the sick-berth attendant strapped his arm with bandages and adhesive tape, which held until we reached port and transferred him to hospital.

This gale held on stubbornly. The convoy's speed was down to 4 knots and when two days out from Sydney we were already one day behind schedule. The ships, all out of station, were straggling over the ocean, presenting easy targets for any prowling submarines. Then the corvette's captain reported a critically ill man on board; he must land him. We watched apprehensively as it disappeared over the northern horizon, leaving the convoy totally in our care. It later rejoined us with the news that the sailor had died. Like all gales, this one finally passed, and in gradually abating weather we reassembled our flock and ran on.

The menace of lurking submarines was constantly with us, and there were many false alarms. On one convoy, a patrolling RAAF Hudson swooped low overhead to tell us that a submarine had been sighted nearby. We saw nothing, but that night I took to my bunk wearing a half-inflated Mae West, and paid for my prudence by rolling about there like a bailer in the bottom of a boat. Next day there were more reports of a conning tower seen in the vicinity. One moonlit night, picking up an SOS from a torpedoed ship, we left the convoy to investigate. I was asleep when Action Stations sounded and, pulling my Mae West over my pyjamas, snatched my helmet from its peg and ran to my station beside the main gun. We sighted a lifeboat but found it empty, and returned to the convoy, leaving it drifting on the glittering sea. 'It seemed almost unbelievable to me standing there in my pyjamas', I later wrote, 'that not far from all this beauty were men struggling for their lives in oily water, perhaps bleeding and bruised, while their ship plunged down below the waves.'

My most memorable experience in the *Abraham Crijnssen* began in Bass Strait about 4 p.m. on Australia Day 1943. In bright sunshine, with a calm sea slightly ruffled by the breeze, we were escorting an 8-knot Sydney-bound convoy. *Crijnssen* was stationed out on its port bow, zig-zagging at 10 knots, and HMAS *Bundaberg* was on the starboard bow. The ships, all in station and free of black smoke, made a pretty picture, and I was counting the hours until I could get ashore in Sydney.

It had been an uneventful watch. The Asdic transmissions came through the amplifier with monotonous regularity, making no contact. But, just as the afternoon watch was changing, sharp clear echoes began bouncing back from something below us 700 yards on our port beam. They were not from a whale or school of fish and, as the target was moving, it could not be a wreck. Cole identified it as a submarine. Signalling 'I am investigating a contact', Chapman rang for full speed on the engines and men ran to their action stations. So did our dog, Kos. Whenever the alarm sounded, he scrambled up the iron companionway on his stubby little legs and sat himself on the signal-pad desk where he could get a dog's-eye view of things.

In a show of force which might have sunk us, we immediately dropped two depth charges. This prescribed action, called a 'counter attack', was designed to deter the submarine's captain from firing torpedoes by causing violent explosions close to her, and, for this purpose, the first two charges on the stern rollers were given the shallowest setting of 50 feet so that they would detonate quickly. But here we struck trouble. The minimum speed for a 50-foot setting was 13 knots, but we had not yet reached that speed and the depth charges went off close under our stern. As Chapman later commented, 'They lifted us a bit.'

This was one of Chapman's typical understatements. The explosions were like near-misses from 500-pound bombs, causing the ship to shudder violently. I was standing beside Chapman on the bridge when a large section of the steel base of the 20-inch searchlight on the top of the mast fell between us, missing his head by a few inches. The compass jumped out of the binnacle and my telephone line to the guns went dead. Now gathering speed the *Crijnssen* heeled over as she altered course towards the submarine and dropped a full pattern of depth charges set to explode at 100 feet. Again the ship jumped and shuddered:

> columns of water shot about 50 ft. into the air with plumes of white spray, which looked like some fairy fountain in the brilliant afternoon sunshine. We circled the spot. Oil and a scummy substance appeared on the water. Our guns were trained on it preparing to blast hell out of anything that appeared. The other escort signalled that she could hear the sound of engines under the water and a sort of tapping noise so she went in and attacked with depth charges ...

While *Bundaberg* and *Abraham Crijnssen* were hunting this contact, the convoy scattered and made off eastward at top speed. Two RAAF bombers appeared overhead and circled the patches of water discoloured by the depth charges. Dead fish floated to the surface all around us and when a wounded seal, with blood running from its ears and mouth, floundered alongside, Van der Weyder—displaying, I felt, more zeal than necessary—possibly to put the poor animal out of its misery, leant over the wing of the bridge and shot it five times with his Luger.

Soon after our first attack the captain began receiving reports of damage. Glass gauges in the engine room were smashed, rivets sprung, and water was entering the steering motor compartment. Sent below

to report on the condition of the wardroom and galley flat, I was
shocked at the mess. The pantry looked like a china shop after the bull
had left, the floor littered with broken plates and glass. Our fifteen cups
had hung close together on a row of hooks, like sailors' hammocks on
a crowded deck, so that, when the *Crijnssen* rolled, all would swing
together without touching, but the explosions had smashed them
together, leaving only the handles hanging. The wardroom was a
shambles too. Its heavy inkstand, hurled from the table, lay upside
down on the deck, and the carpet was covered with ink, papers and
upturned furniture. The queen lay face up on the deck, glass smashed,
frame wrecked, and the admiral's victorious squadron had developed a
90-degree list. But Rita Hayworth sat there unmoved, smiling down
on the wreckage below.

The *Bundaberg* and *Abraham Crijnssen* had dropped many charges
on the submarine but no wreckage or bodies had appeared on the
surface, and the *Bundaberg's* captain, the convoy's senior officer, now
decided to abandon the search. Night was coming on, the convoy was
already a smudge on the horizon and other submarines might be
lurking near Gabo Island. Leaving the submarine to cope with whatever damage our attacks might have caused, we reformed the convoy
and saw it safely to Sydney.

The submarine presumably made her way back to Japan. Examination of enemy records after the war suggested that she might have
been either I-178 or I-180, one of which torpedoed the hospital
ship *Centaur*, or the I-21 which sank or damaged five ships off our
coast.

In this attack the *Abraham Crijnssen* had suffered more serious
damage than we first thought, and on return to Sydney we spent a
week in dry dock replacing all the sprung centreline rivets in her stern
frame. Chapman was called before a naval board of inquiry which questioned his decision to attack instantly with charges set to 50 feet, and
he left on the next convoy fearing he might be relieved of his command.
But in the fullness of time he received a copy of the board's finding,
with the terse comment by Rear Admiral G. C. Muirhead-Gould,

'Counter-attack justified'—'navy-speak' for 'Well done, thou good and faithful servant.'

On 16 February 1943, at the end of another convoy, I stood with Chapman on the bridge of the *Crijnssen* as we entered Sydney Heads and steamed past the Sow and Pigs Reef, through the boom gate near Watsons Bay, and picked up our mooring at No. 10 buoy with Garden Island's signal tower busily blinking at us. We would be at sea again in a day or two and these were the usual messages about defects, fuelling, victualling and arming. A boat came alongside with mail and less urgent signals, and one related to me. I had been appointed sub lieutenant of His Majesty's Australian Motor Launch *814* and I was to 'repair to my duty on board forthwith'.

I never set foot on the *Abraham Crijnssen* again. She survived the war and in 1945, again under Dutch colours, witnessed the Japanese surrender at Koepang in Timor. She is now preserved for posterity in Holland, and although little is noted there about her time under the White Ensign, her service in the Royal Netherlands Navy is well documented. Chapman's monthly Reports of Proceedings to the Naval Board, however, and less formal accounts such as this, are some memorial to HMAS *Abraham Crijnssen*'s contribution to the defeat of Japan.

I was sad to leave her. She was a happy ship on a dangerous beat and her duties were never dull. My sea training had begun in her under a first-rate mentor, and I was confident and proud to serve under him. However exhausted he might be, Chapman was never off duty, constantly having to make vital decisions. I still have two special memories of him.

We were approaching Cape Everard on the Victorian coast, out on the starboard bow of the convoy and bucking into a head sea. It was after midnight. Chapman had been on the bridge far longer than any of us and was dead tired. He checked his watch, said, 'Hordern, I am going to my cabin, call me when you see the light', and went down the iron companionway. All I then knew of Cape Everard was that a stone obelisk there commemorated the first sighting of the

Australian coast by Captain Cook in 1770. But close examination of the chart told me that Cape Everard's lighthouse sent out two white flashes every 30 seconds and they were visible for 20 miles. At the time I expected to see them, I glued my eyes to the binoculars and before long there they were, two friendly flashes every 30 seconds. I slid down the ladder and knocked on the captain's door. No answer. I entered and found him stretched out on his bunk, snoring. 'Sir, we have raised Cape Everard light.' No reply. I spoke more loudly. 'SIR, WE HAVE RAISED CAPE EVERARD LIGHT.' Chapman remained deep in sleep and, to rouse him, I touched him on the shoulder. Instantly alert, he said in a tone I can never forget 'Don't touch me!' Chastened, I repeated my message and left the cabin wondering what I had done wrong. A couple of minutes later he was on the bridge, peering at the light and checking our position. In 1945 I would come to understand how offensive it was for a tired and anxious captain to be manhandled from his sleep.

Chapman never lost a chance to teach us, and my other special memory recalls an incident when he was being the schoolmaster. At the end of a hard convoy, we were lined up on the leads to take us through the middle of the boom gate, a heavy steel net opened and closed by a winch on the boom vessel. As the top of the net was level with the water and hard to see from a distance, signals informed approaching ships if the gate was open or closed. The 'open' signal was a hoist of two large black cylindrical shapes on the vessel's yardarm. The captain had been on the bridge for many hours and now, weary, red-eyed and stubble-faced, was still there conning the *Crijnssen* safely home. A brief order to the quartermaster, a slight movement of the wheel, and we were lined up directly on the leads to take us through the centre of the gate. He swept the harbour with his binoculars, trained them momentarily on the boom vessel's yardarm and said, 'Hordern, how do I know that the boom gate is open'? I replied earnestly, 'Well sir, you have two black balls ...' Picking up his binoculars, he swept the harbour again, and, with the suspicion of a smile said, 'Hordern, I'll have you know that my balls are not black.'

Even the quartermaster laughed.

5 | A FAIRMILER

The moment I saw ML *814* lying in Elizabeth Bay, I fell in love. Her raked bow and sleek lines, her 2-pounder Rolls Royce Mark IV gun on the fo'c's'le, and, behind it, her armour-plated wheelhouse, bridge, mast and well-proportioned funnel, gave her the appearance of a miniature destroyer. She was about to sail and I boarded her immediately.

Fairmiles were the brainchild of Albert Noel Campbell Macklin, an English naval reserve lieutenant, engineer industrialist, visionary and adventurer, who had served with the Dover Patrol during World War I. In the 1930s, recognising that, in another war, England would need fast small ships to counter the German E-boats, he had begun building them on his industrial estate at Fairmile in Surrey for the Royal Navy. By 1941, one 'Fairmile' was being turned out every thirty-six hours, and in all 703 were built in England alone. Some were produced in kit form for assembly overseas, and twelve of these found their way to Australia, where altogether thirty-six B-type Fairmiles were built for the RAN. They were the smallest class of warship in the Australian Navy, having an overall length of 112 feet, a beam of 17 feet 10 inches, a draught of just over 5 feet and displacing about 90 tons. Each carried two 'CQR' or plough-share type anchors of 80 and 120 pounds respectively, and their heavy 3/16 inch chain cable was worked by a back-breaking hand-operated winch on the fo'c's'le. They were powered by twin 650-horsepower Hall-Scott high-octane petrol engines, and could carry just over 2300 gallons of fuel. The Fairmiles' top speed differed depending on who had built them, but at close to 18 knots they used approximately 90 gallons of petrol per hour and had a range of 600 nautical miles. If slowed to 12 knots their range increased to 1500 miles.

The RAN used these versatile little craft for many purposes—escorting convoys, hunting submarines, ferrying troops, freighting stores and ammunition, bombarding enemy positions, rescuing airmen from the sea, landing commandos, and evacuating civilians far behind enemy lines from under the noses of the Japanese.

They carried a crew of just under twenty. The three officers occupied the wardroom aft and the coxswain and motor mechanic shared a small cabin on the port side for'ard, with the communal head alongside. The remaining crew were quartered in bunks in the mess deck. The galley was equipped with a kerosene-operated stove and refrigerator, but there were no showers on board. The captain had no servant, as was common in larger ships, and there was no sick-berth attendant or trained cook. A crew member would be appointed cook, and sailors took turns to serve meals in the wardroom. Apart from that, the officers fended for themselves. Sometimes they paid sailors to do their 'dhobying'; otherwise, like everyone else, they washed their own clothes in a bucket on deck. There was little place for formal relationships between officers and men in such conditions, particularly on remote service.

I was welcomed on board by a tall, rangy lieutenant, who at first sight reminded me of the American film star Gary Cooper. 'My name's Chips,' he told me, 'I'm the first lieutenant here—just joined from a minesweeper—what do we call you?' That was my introduction to Bernard Page Western Wood. Born in Toowoomba in 1908, Chips had been jackaroo, sportsman, banker and member of the 11th Light Horse Regiment before the war. We were to share hard times together and have remained close for over sixty years.

When I told Chips my name, he rightly judged it 'a bit of a mouthful' and, as he associated it with Anthony Hordern and Sons—at that time a household word in Australia—he decreed, 'We'll call you Tony.'

Chips led me down a companionway into the wardroom where the captain, Lieutenant Reg Kennedy RANVR, was sitting at a table littered with official papers. Like Chips, Kennedy was a big amiable man in his thirties; in civilian life he had been a West Australian farmer, and was veteran of many actions with German E-boats in the English Channel. He knew his job, and under him ML *814* was in good hands. He welcomed me aboard and told me that we were off to the war. Traditionally, he called me 'Sub'. I called him 'Sir'.

I looked around the wardroom which was to be my new quarters. It was nothing like the steel box I had had to myself under the bridge in the *Crijnssen*. It had a table, three chairs and, against the for'ard bulkhead, a chest of drawers beneath a fixed mirror which, by reflecting the light from the companionway hatch, made the living space look slightly larger. There was a bookshelf on one side of the mirror and on the other a glass-fronted case containing the officers' .45 Colt revolvers. Two settees, one on either side of the wardroom, completed its furnishing. At night their backs folded up and hooked to ring bolts in the deck above to make four bunks. Four small scuttles let in a little light. Chips allocated me the top starboard bunk and the bottom drawer in the chest for my gear. Then, after issuing me a pillow, two pillowcases, a blanket, steel helmet and Mae West, he took me on a tour of the ship.

ML *814* had recently been launched by the Sydney boat builders Halvorsen Brothers. She had taken nine months to build and cost £30,000. Everywhere was gleaming paint and varnish, and the powerful smells of marline, Manila cordage, linseed oil, paint, sisal, spun yarn and Stockholm tar, from forepeak to tiller flat, gave further proof of her newness.

Except for depth charges, the Fairmiles' armament varied, depending on what was available from the Navy or could be acquired—often unofficially—from other sources, and I was impressed by what I found on *814*. As well as the 2-pounder gun on the fo'c's'le, she had two Vickers .303 water-cooled machine guns on the bridge and another just behind it, an Oerlikon 20 mm cannon, two Thompson sub-machine guns, six Lee-Enfield rifles with bayonets, hand grenades and demolition charges. On her port wing was a Schmurley rocket apparatus—a contraption designed to bring down low-flying enemy aircraft. It was fired by a lanyard which, when pulled, released a rocket into the air with a fierce 'woosh', raining sparks down on the open bridge and enveloping us with smoke. Several hundred feet up it would explode, releasing a parachute from which trailed a steel wire. It was supposed to wrap itself around the approaching aircraft and bring it down. I never heard what enemy airmen thought of it but it terrified me.

To complete her equipment, ML *814* was fitted with a Type 134 Asdic set, partly housed in a streamlined metal dome which projected about 2 feet below the keel. There was also a Y gun for throwing two depth charges simultaneously out on either side, and fourteen more housed in racks on deck, from which they could instantly be rolled overboard. The Carley rafts, lashed on either side of the wheelhouse, were stowed with emergency rations, water and a few medical supplies, and a 10-foot dinghy hoisted in davits completed her lifesaving equipment. In all ML *814* was a trim little fighting ship.

She had one unusual feature, however. In contrast to most of our warships, which were then grey, she was tricked out in zig-zag lines of white, light blue and green—reportedly the inspiration of camouflage experts at the University of Sydney. But this decoration, like many academic schemes, was impractical. Ships in the tropics needed frequent repainting, and where we were heading only battleship grey or jungle green paint was readily available. Before long, ML *814*'s distinctive colouring began to fade and she had to be repainted. Then, like most other naval ships of the time, she became a sombre grey.

On 17 February 1943 we lay in Elizabeth Bay alongside another new Fairmile, ML *817*, commanded by Lieutenant Athol Townley RANVR, a Tasmanian who later became a minister in the federal government between 1954 and 1963. The *817* was also about to go north, and we were to meet up with her again.

At dawn next day we ran out through the Heads and turned north for Darwin, over 3000 miles away. The south-easterly swell lifted our stern and shoved us forward in a plunging corkscrew motion and in the stuffy mess deck and engine-room below, some men became queasy. On the bridge Signalman D'Arcy Kelly began to vomit, and went on vomiting throughout his watch. The following morning, when I told Kennedy that he was still very ill, he picked up a tumbler and bottle of whisky, promising, 'I'll show you the cure for seasickness.' We found the wretched Kelly, head in hands, slumped on the potato locker and, when Kennedy poured a large tot of neat spirit and told him to swallow it, he obeyed dumbly. A few minutes later the whisky returned, but Kelly showed new signs of life. Later on, when we ran into rough weather again, several other crew members applied unsuccessfully for 'the treatment'.

During the short run to Brisbane we acquainted ourselves with our new home, practising exercises for man overboard, fire drills in various parts of the ship, firing the dreaded Schmurley rocket and exercising the guns by shooting at boxes thrown into the sea. By night we anchored in small secluded coves. The coast of northern New South Wales was still largely untouched by tourism and development, and we would row ashore in the evening to swim and walk along its virginal sands. It was hard to believe that we were at war.

But on 20 February, when we ran up Brisbane River proudly displaying our zig-zag camouflage and flying our largest White Ensign, we felt closer to the action: American bombers and fighters circled above, a United States submarine with part of its bow blown off lay in Pinkenba Reach and further on we passed the stern half of a Liberty ship moored in the river. Anxious to be on our way, we berthed at

Nixon-Smith Wharf and began watering and refuelling in preparation for an early start next day.

But Kennedy's advice to me that we were 'off to the war' had been premature: as we were about to leave for Townsville, bureaucracy intervened. A signal from the Navy, concerned about the engine performance of this new type of ship, ordered us to delay our departure for testing. On the first leg of the voyage the twin Hall-Scotts had run splendidly but, as an exasperated Chips said, 'They only start tinkering with the bloody things when they're working well.'

Remaining in Brisbane was no hardship, however. The Nixon-Smith Wharf was only a short walk from the centre of the city, which was full of friendly and hospitable people. It was also full of American servicemen, who, as well as being loaded with seemingly limitless Yankee dollars, had the additional benefit that they were exotic, and spoke like people in 'the movies'. This put us at a great social disadvantage: our means of getting about the city on foot or by public transport looked less than dashing beside that of the Americans, who would hail a taxi to cross the street, and local girls, having been dined by them at leading hotels, lavished with orchids and chocolates, and seated in a cinema's most expensive seats, found Australians rather niggardly escorts. But perhaps our greatest handicap was that all Fairmilers travelling north had been ordered to send their white uniforms, or 'Number Tens', home, and with the Americans sparkling in their whites and gold braid, our crumpled khaki shorts and shirts cut little dash.

Soon we were able to compare our lot with that of US servicemen at closer quarters. One morning two small ships flying the Stars and Stripes steamed up the river and moored just ahead of us. They were Yard minesweepers, direct from the United States, and this was their first sight of Australia. Shortly after they moored, one of their captains came aboard and, in a slow southern drawl, introduced himself as Lieutenant Partee Crouch. On meeting Chips I had been struck by his resemblance to Gary Cooper; when Partee spoke, I could shut my eyes and hear Gary speaking. As the minesweepers were dry, we invited their officers for a drink and compared notes on our respective vessels and naval customs. Apart from our having liquor on board, we had to accept that the results were heavily loaded in favour of the United States. Shocked to hear we had no showers, they offered us the use of theirs and, on boarding the minesweepers, we were agape at the high standard of their equipment, accommodation, washrooms and galley. And they treated us to a dinner of steak and fresh vegetables, fruit salad, ice cream and coffee—all beyond a Fairmiler's wildest dreams. But the greatest gulf between us and these charming Americans was economic: my pay as a sub lieutenant was about £3 a week; my equivalent in the US Navy drew about £19.

As days passed with the engines still under examination, the Navy began to find odd jobs for us, and one of these required a visit to Moreton Island, with a night return to Brisbane. When we were nearly home, running down the middle of the dredged channel from the Pile Light, the lookout reported a ship's navigation lights ahead. She was the SS *Buranda*, outward bound. The night was clear and, as we were on a collision course, Chips, who held the watch, gave the helm order 'starboard easy'. This was a merchant service term sometimes used by naval reserve officers, and equivalent to the navy's 'starboard five' or 'starboard ten', which indicated an alteration of five or ten degrees. The coxswain, Ordinary Seaman Partridge, altered course to pass down the *Buranda's* port side within a line of wooden piles marking the edge of the dredged channel where, according to the chart, there would be plenty of water beneath our Asdic dome. But as we came abreast of the *Buranda* we felt a slight bump and Chips, switching on the anti-submarine set, found it dead. In a split second we had lost a highly secret item of equipment weighing nearly half a ton and worth £3000.

At the subsequent Court of Enquiry, Partridge's explanation that he had acted in response to the order 'starboard easy' horrified the regular officers on the Board. 'Never heard of it' was their dismissive judgement. 'The Brass', as Chips called them, were professionals: they had entered the Naval College as boys, learned how things should be done, and expected them to be done accordingly. Some reservists, on the other hand, although fine seamen, were unaccustomed to the rigid naval discipline and were unaware of, or unmoved by, the finer points of naval law. As the Navy was not to be their life-time career, the possibility of blemishing their service record was no great threat, and this insouciance must have tried the patience of some permanent service officers. Possibly the use of this unfamiliar term led the Court to suspect irregularities aboard ML *814*, and their suspicions would have increased on learning that Chips had been overheard to pronounce that the dome's loss was '… the best bloody thing to happen. That blob under the ship always worried me.' ML *814* was hauled up on Peters' Slip at Kangaroo Point to have another fitted, and we foolishly thought that was the end of our troubles.

More than a month after leaving Sydney we were still in Brisbane, bored and chafing to be off. One day a Harbour Defence Motor Launch, HDML *1074*, arrived from Port Moresby under the command of Lieutenant Norman Greaves RNVR; she had seen hard service in New Guinea, had crossed the Coral Sea in bad weather, and was salt-stained, leaking badly, and everything below deck—dirty clothes, wet oilskins and bedding—smelt of sweat and mildew. Her crew—half-naked, with flowing unkempt hair and beards—looked like a bunch of pirates. To my impressionable eye they had an enviable buccaneering aura, and from that time I cherished a vision of achieving just such a swashbuckling image.

On 26 March 1943 I came of age. Most of the day was spent at sea testing our new Asdic dome, but in the afternoon we returned to Moreton Bay and anchored off a white beach in water so clear that we could see the anchor embedded in the sand. We swam from the ship and walked along the beach, and that night fished from the deck under a bright moon and a sky full of stars. There would have been many worse ways of spending one's twenty-first birthday.

On our return to Brisbane I received eight letters, and one from home with details of some of the presents they were holding for me. These were mostly gifts of money, but included a water-colour by Fred Elliott, a former friend of my grandfather White, of the birth of the

The children of the Hordern family with our parents in 1923 (from left to right, Noel, Mary, Marsden, Hugh). We spent an idyllic early childhood in various rectories, all of which had their quirks. St Andrews, Seven Hills (below) lacked electricity, running hot water and a water closet.

A move to Wahroonga in 1929 brought us closer to the extended Hordern family whose life centred around our grandparents' ornate Chatswood mansion (above), 'Chislehurst', set in gardens, bushland and paddocks with an orchard, stables, cows, horses, glasshouse, aviary, tennis court and croquet lawn. Here we met for occasions such as our grandparents' fiftieth wedding anniversary (below). I am third from the left in the front row.

In 1937 our father became rector of St Paul's, Cleveland Street, Sydney. We were growing up and going our own ways, and the last photographs of the family all together show Ian, John and me as members of the church choir (right) and the eight of us just before Mary (left) and Noel (centre) were married (below).

Having shed the school uniforms of Knox and Malvern, I was soon in other uniforms of varying qualities and colours. 1941 saw me in sloppy army fatigues, firing Lewis Guns (above) and on leave sporting a new swagger stick as I escorted my godmother Phyllis Perdriau down Martin Place (below left). By 1942 I had become a sparkling sub-lieutenant—still with everything to learn (below right).

In 1942, I trained to be a Fairmiler at HMAS Rushcutter. I am second from the top right with classmates and instructors; Lieutenant N. B. Wallis, my future captain in ML 823, is second from the right in the bottom row.

My first ship, HMAS Abraham Crijnssen, leaving Sydney on convoy escort duty in 1942.

ML 814 sets off to war (above). Below are most of the ship's men, top row:
R. C. Ling, R, Hayes, D. Partridge, Brewer, J. Nelson, J. Livingstone, D. Ashford,
G. Constable; middle row: 'Chips' Wood, Reg Kennedy, M. Hordern, D. Davey;
bottom row: T. Trewick, J. Old, in Brisbane where ML 814 was delayed. This was
no hardship for us, although, in our crumpled khaki shorts and shirts, we could
not compete ashore with the Americans, resplendent in their gleaming whites and
gold braid.

In the Gulf of Carpentaria, playing pirates (above). Top row, left to right:
D. Kelly, R. Lewis, D. Kay, J. Nelson, J. Old, R. Hayes; middle row: R. Ling,
T. Trewick, J. Livingstone; bottom row: M. C. Hordern, Brewer, 'Chips' Wood,
D. Partridge, G. Constable. It was a wrench to leave ML 814's close-knit family.
We had been bonded by hard service and I was never to find better companions.

On discharge from hospital in Sydney I applied for a ship working with the army
in the islands, but tropical service was out for six months and I became First
Lieutenant of ML 823 (below) operating off the Australian east coast.

In December 1944 when I was appointed to command Harbour Defence Motor Launch Q 1347 (above), being totally responsible for any ship was not on my agenda. I tried to decline the appointment on the grounds that I was irresponsible but eventually I toed the line. Jack Page, Ken Akers and Len Clarkson pose on the fo'c's'le (left, top); Clif and I familiarise ourselves with Q 1347's Oerlikon gun (left, bottom).

Royal Australian Navy. The money soon disappeared but the picture remains a treasure. Another major present was a matured endowment policy for £100 with the Mutual Life and Citizens Company of Sydney, which my parents had taken out at my birth. It represented the best part of a year's pay, but I had nothing to spend it on and did not claim it until 1946.

A less welcome letter also greeted us in Brisbane. The Naval Board conveyed its 'displeasure' at the loss of ML *814*'s dome and disapproval of 'the casual manner in which Lieutenant Wood had run His Majesty's Ship ashore'. Kennedy brushed this off as a formality: the loss of a dome had been a regular occurrence in the English Channel. But a follow-up signal plunged us into gloom: Kennedy had been relieved of his command and appointed First Lieutenant of the corvette *Inverell*, and his replacement was on his way to take over.

Soon afterwards, our new captain, Lieutenant Charles Carlton Skarratt RANVR, arrived on board, and posed an immediate problem by announcing himself as 'Charles, call me Chips, Skarratt'. It would have been impossible for two-thirds of our officers to be called 'Chips', and only his speedy departure saved us from having to handle that dilemma. The tall, languid Skarratt had served in the English Channel in Motor Anti-Submarine Boats (MASBs), before returning to Australia to join a corvette which had recently been attacked in the Gulf of Carpentaria by Japanese aircraft. The Japs, he told us, were very active on the North Australian coast, and it was clear that he was reluctant to return there in ML *814*.

I had some reservations about Skarratt, writing to my parents, '... as opposed to the other skipper, he has a very "la-de-da" English voice and not the type of man you imagine suited for steamy tropical fighting', but ended philosophically, '... nevertheless he is a good man & we will get on well together I know.'

So much for my worldly wisdom. Skarratt was gone within a week. We never met again, although I later became a friend of his first wife—a red-headed English beauty who settled in Sydney. On returning to civilian life, Skarratt embraced the diverse occupations of pig farmer and bookmaker and, as a 'stylish 72-year-old veteran bookie', made headlines in the *Sydney Morning Herald* of 23 December 1989 when found murdered at his waterfront Woolwich home, his feet bound with his trouser belt and with black electric tape 'wound around his mouth'.

Eight days after I had reported on Skarratt's arrival, Lieutenant R. R. Lewis RANVR—who, like Skarratt and Kennedy, had seen service in the English Channel—came aboard. But, unlike Skarratt, he accepted his new posting in good spirits. 'He's nothing like the one we lost ... he's not a bad chap', I told my parents. 'I call him Reg, and of course he calls me Tony.'

Our engine tests were finally completed early in May 1943 and we received a signal to sail for Townsville. We were to join a convoy, but would not be making the voyage under our own steam. While we had been detained in Brisbane, MLs *815* and *817* had left for their operational areas in the north, and assessment of their engine performance had confirmed the ruling that the Hall-Scotts needed a substantial service every 500 hours. And so it had been decided that to reduce wear on ML *814*'s engines we should be towed to Townsville by a ship in a New Guinea-bound convoy. This was welcome news. We congratulated ourselves that on the passage to Townsville we would be able to sleep without the roar of engines in our ears, would be free of navigating worries, and our watch-keeping duties would be much lighter. But our vision of a dream ride soon became a nightmare.

We found the convoy assembling near Cape Moreton. As well as freighters carrying war supplies, it included a troopship, and that called for a destroyer among its escorts. We passed our towline to an American Liberty ship, and settled back to enjoy the trip. But it soon became apparent that the convoy's speed was too fast for a comfortable tow, and once we left the shelter of Moreton Bay a heavy quartering sea made us yaw and scend in an unpleasant corkscrew motion. The large swell, sweeping up under our stern, would lift us, then roll away ahead and, as we fell back on its reverse slope, it would lift the Liberty ship, which would surge forward, causing the towline to tauten and jerk our bow sharply. This was harsh treatment for ship and crew, many of whom had lost their sea legs during our long spell in port, and some of them, including the cook, lay immobile about the deck. Until they recovered I prepared bully beef and cheese sandwiches, with tea, lime juice or water, for any left with an appetite.

As we moved into the tropics north of Cape Capricorn we began to learn more about the Fairmiles' shortcomings. Although excellent sea boats, they had weaknesses. Being long and narrow, they needed careful handling in a steep head sea to prevent pile-driving, and when running before a large following sea there was the risk of the square stern being caught and driven sideways down a wave, which could broach the ship. Furthermore, having been intended primarily for use in the cold English Channel, they had been designed on the assumption that they would spend only short spells at sea, and that when in port the crew would be billeted ashore. Little consideration had been given to their accommodation, and quarters were cramped, hot and stuffy. There were no awnings on deck to shade us from the burning sun, and despite our best efforts with salt-water soap and a bucket of sea water we all smelt overpoweringly of sweat.

At 2 a.m. on our second morning out I was wakened by a heavy jerk, telling me the tow had parted. The swish of water past the hull ceased, and we lay rolling beam on to the wind and sea as the convoy disappeared into the darkness. It took about three-quarters of an hour to haul in our end of the tow and splice another length to it while we hurried on to find the blacked-out Liberty ship. She slowed down for us to pass the tow, and this was dangerous work for both of us. As a stationary straggler from the convoy she was a sitting duck for any lurking submarine and when we went close to her tall steel side as she lay plunging and rolling, it looked like a moving cliff about to fall on us. After several attempts we caught her heaving line, her men secured the hawser, and off she went at top speed to catch up with the convoy.

She was just in time. At about 4 a.m. Verey lights—the signal for a submarine alarm—soared into the sky, the destroyer raced off and we heard the ominous boom of depth charges.

Before dawn, the tow parted again, and this time we passed the ship our heavy anchor cable made of 9/16 inch forged steel links. But even that did not hold, and dawn found us exasperated and exhausted, rolling in a nasty sea and struggling to haul in what was left of it. Reg called a council of war which agreed that this towing business was madness: it had given us 300 miles of tension, discomfort and danger, and we would not try it again. The Hall-Scotts started with a satisfying growl, we sped north, and soon the convoy was nothing more than a bad memory and a smudge of smoke on the southern horizon.

Our course lay north-westerly through the Capricorn Channel and, being out of sight of land, we now had to rely on celestial navigation, fixing our positions by the Marcq St Hilaire or 'Intercept' method.[1] In the English Channel Reg had had little occasion to navigate by the sun, moon and stars, and he was happy to leave most of it to Chips and me. The day after leaving the convoy we both took our sextant altitudes of the sun, calculated our intercepts, and plotted the positions we had obtained on the chart. They differed by 7 miles, and such uncertainty was perilous in coral waters strewn with out-crops. As night was coming on, it was important to know exactly where we were, and Reg decided to settle the matter by taking an altitude himself. After shooting the sun and poring laboriously over the cosine and haversine tables and azimuth diagram, he marked a little dot on the chart. Exactly halfway between Chips's position and mine, it was beyond all dispute and a great joke, but we passed an anxious night.

We now discovered the delights of cruising in the tropics. Entering the Whitsunday Passage, with its calm waters, white beaches and enticing bays, I wrote to my mother, 'We have been threading our way through a maze of woody islets set in the bluest of blue seas.' The sun was becoming fiercer by the day and, to provide shade for those on watch, we made an awning from a small piece of canvas found in the tiller flat. The bridge soon became the most popular place on board, with off-watch sailors sitting around under our feet, trailing fishing lines, or singing to the accompaniment of Stoker Doug Ashford's concertina.

On leaving the sparkling waters of the Whitsunday Passage and rounding Cape Cleveland, the view became less serene. Cleveland Bay, an assembly point for arriving and departing convoys, was full of ships, and Townsville, which lay spread before us around the waterfront, had a military air. Having been a base for American aircraft engaged in the Battle of the Coral Sea, it had been bombed by the Japanese and we could see American, Australian and occasionally Dutch aircraft taking off or circling to land. And, as I later told my family, the town throbbed with service men and women:

> Practically all men & women one sees here are in khaki, hardly
> any civilians here at all. If you go to a picture show or to a cafe
> in town you can only see uniforms ... Navy, Army, Air Force,
> Yanks, AWAS, Wrans, WAAAFs, Nurses, VADs etc. ... The other
> night I had tea in one of these cafes and there must have been a
> hundred service men and women there and only 2 civilians ...

Our engines were now due for their 500-hour overhaul, and while our motor mechanic, Jock Livingstone, and stokers Jack Old and Doug Ashford, worked on their gruelling task in the engine room's stifling heat, I took the opportunity to explore the town, often in company with David Price, midshipman from ML *817*, which we had last seen the morning we left Sydney. Being en route for New Guinea, she had overtaken us in Brisbane, and was now herself held up for a few days.

David and I spent pleasant off-duty hours swimming, sailing the Fairmiles' dinghies in Cleveland Bay and going to the pictures and dances. Wandering along streets lined with banyan trees and coconut palms, we admired the fragrant frangipani and brilliant bougainvilleas in the gardens, but avoided places like the Queen's Hotel, which, overlooking Cleveland Bay on the Strand, was patronised by the Americans, and therefore rather beyond our means.

Meeting two WAAAFs at a dance, we invited them to have a meal with us on board Athol Townley's ML *817* next evening. David had obtained Townley's approval for this and had been told that since he and the first lieutenant would be dining ashore, we could have the wardroom to ourselves.

Next night we collected the girls from the air force barracks and escorted them down Flinders Street to our berth at Hyne's Timber Wharf. Helping them down to the deck, we were surprised to hear soft music floating up the companionway and, on entering the wardroom, found Townley, resplendent in the forbidden Number Tens and gleaming in white and gold braid. Years later, in Tasmania, I got to know Townley better and to appreciate his social skills, but never saw them used more effectively than on that night. Playing the genial host, he welcomed the girls, offered them drinks and quickly had them captivated by his debonair charm and stories of wartime exploits in Europe. It soon became evident to David and me that this had become the captain's dinner party and, after a muttered consultation, we announced a change in the evening's plans: we were off to dine at the Queen's. And that cost us a pretty penny.

On 15 May, we left for Cairns on an all-night passage. For much of the night we were blinded by torrential rain, but it cleared in time to give us a distant sight of the town nestling beneath wooded hills capped with fleecy clouds. Still relatively untouched by war, life moved at an unhurried pace in Cairns; another colourful garden town, its sleepy boulevards and verandahed bungalows were a far cry from the sophisticated tourists' mecca it is today.

We were ordered to berth alongside the SS *Cardross*, a smoky old coal-burner capable of about 8 knots, and to our disappointment learned that she would be towing us to Thursday Island. We had been looking forward to that stage of our reef cruise, hoping to visit Lizard Island, and hanging onto the stern of the *Cardross* was a grim prospect. And the picture painted by her gloomy mate was even more sombre. The *Cardross*, he told us, was slow and difficult to manoeuvre even on her own, she was carrying 400 tons of high-explosives, and the waters around Torres Strait were patrolled by Japanese aircraft.

Fortunately, our passage to Thursday Island did not live up to the mate's fears and was far more comfortable than our tow behind the Liberty ship had been. The *Cardross* was slower, the water, sheltered by the Great Barrier Reef, was calmer and—apart from missing our visit to Lizard Island—all went well.

At first glance, Thursday Island—its luggers with furled sails lying in the light blue water off the palm-fringed shore, and the jetty steaming in the sun—could have been the setting for a scene from Somerset Maugham. But a second look dispelled that notion. The harbour was busy with naval escorts and merchant ships full of war supplies coming and going, and an occasional United States torpedo boat, stationed there to defend the island from surface attack, sped across the water. And ashore the island was full of soldiers carrying rifles and tommy guns wherever they went; the Japanese had effectively used paratroops when they had taken Koepang from the Dutch and Australian troops in Timor, and the army was taking no chances. Although in May 1943 the Japanese had more on their minds than Thursday Island, they were still keeping an eye on it: while we were there, a Japanese reconnaissance plane flew overhead.

Our visit to the island had an unpleasant sequel. Soon after arrival, Chips and I went aboard the *Cardross* to use the seamen's washrooms. The shower was welcome, and we left feeling clean and refreshed, but paid for the luxury later. The heads on the *Cardross* were filthy, and next day we were both attacked by crabs—an extremely aggravating affliction which stayed with us until we found medical help in Darwin.

After a brief stay at Thursday Island we continued on our way to Darwin. We were now travelling alone; the south-east winds which had been with us since we passed Cape Capricorn were still blowing strongly, and from Torres Strait we rolled westward past Booby Island and a red light-ship with 'Carpentaria' painted in large white letters across its sides.[2] Approaching the Wessel Islands, we entered what was known as 'Bomb Alley'. This area was less than an hour's flight from the Japanese base in the Aru Islands, and the corvette *Latrobe* had recently been attacked there by twelve of their aircraft. Apprehensively, we sharpened our lookouts and exercised the guns.

By now, the heightened presence of danger had welded us into one cohesive group, and to capture the spirit of the moment we posed for a mock-piratical photo. Brandishing bayonets and knives, we were already on the way to achieving the swashbuckling image I had so envied in Brisbane.

The passage to Darwin remained uneventful. Giving the low-lying Arnhem Land coast a wide berth, we rounded Cape Croker, turned south into the Gulf of Van Diemen, and on Sunday 23 May 1943, passed through the gate of Darwin's massive boom to become part of Darwin's navy.[3]

6 | DARWIN'S NAVY

Although we had heard of the raids carried out by the Japanese on Darwin over the past fifteen months, I was shocked by the damage they had caused. Everywhere I looked were wrecked and gutted buildings surrounded by piles of smashed timber, rubble and broken glass. And we were horrified to hear stories of the human destruction too: the mutilated body of a young girl hanging in a forked tree near the Post Office, and the corpses of drowned sailors floating in the harbour being devoured by crocodiles. Little of this had filtered south.

The harbour presented a desolate sight, with the superstructures of sunken ships projecting at odd angles from the water. Alongside the main jetty, which had been heavily bombed, the capsized hull of the *Neptuna* lay like a huge stranded whale, and the rusting remains of the *Zeelandia* brought back memories of the family voyage to Tasmania in her ten years before. Then, she had been all gleaming paint and varnish; now, sharks and turtles swam above her spacious promenade deck and dining saloon, and fish darted past the cabins where we had slept.

We were now truly in a war zone. Most of Darwin's civilian population had been evacuated, and the town thronged with servicemen. About seventy RAAF Spitfires, various formations of Beaufighters,

Hudsons, Mitchells, Vultee Vengeance dive-bombers, Catalina flying boats and a squadron of USAF Liberators—which, since the beginning of 1943, had made nearly seventy raids on Japanese targets north of Australia—were based in the area.

But despite the town's vulnerability, there was far less blackout discipline than I had seen down south. Vehicles were still driving at night with glaring headlights, while in Sydney the headlights of cars were shaded or reduced by black paint to small slits of light.

A bulky mailbag awaited us. Some letters, having made the long dusty trek through the desert from Adelaide, had been weeks on the road; others had come by air in four days. Answering them raised the unpleasant business of censorship. As it was forbidden to mention military movements, ships' officers had to censor the men's mail. This was an embarrassing job at any time, but particularly odious for officers on Fairmiles, because of the close friendship often existing between them and the men. To ease our problem, Charles Inman, senior Fairmile captain in Darwin, came up with the solution that the officers of each Fairmile censor the letters of the other. Officers' mail was censored ashore at the Darwin depot, HMAS *Melville* and, looking today at the yellowing pages of some of my letters which passed through *Melville*'s hands, I wonder, as my mother must have done, what indiscretions could have prompted such heavily inked obliterations or, in some cases, the removal of entire sections by razor-blade.

A few days after we arrived, Cyril Alcorn, the Naval Chaplain, came aboard to invite us to church the following Sunday. The chapel was packed with soldiers carrying steel helmets and, as we walked in, one of them started playing the organ softly. A big man with gentle expressive eyes, Alcorn had a warm and affectionate relationship with his flock. He did not stand on undue ceremony, introducing the hymns with whimsical asides, but nevertheless preached one of the best sermons I had heard. Faced, as all Christian clergy of that time were, with the complex problem of extolling patriotic valour without condoning violence, he gave us a statement of encouragement and faith:

we must wage war relentlessly until we were victorious, returning peace and security to our country. But, he cautioned us, that victory must be one which would do credit to God's kingdom on earth, and in the hour of that victory we must 'keep alive in our hearts the spirit of mercy and compassion'. In the meantime we must wait upon the Lord for strength to bear the sacrifices we would have to make. As sermons were part of my father's life, I sent him a résumé of it.

The closing hymn, which opened, 'Dear Lord and Father of mankind', emphasised for me the contrast between the Christian message and our present situation. As we sang of 'Sabbath rest' and the 'dews of quietness' calming inward strife, a formation of Liberators roared overhead, and we knew that up there other young men, who might die before the day was out, were on their way to blast some Japanese base north of Australia.

On first joining *814*, I had been disappointed to find no wireless in the wardroom but now, thanks to the Australian Comforts Fund, we had radio contact with the outside world. One dubious benefit of this was that, together with the rest of the allied forces in the southwest Pacific, we were subjected to regular haranguings by 'Tokyo Rose'. Iva Toguri, a US citizen born in Los Angeles in 1916 of Japanese parents and educated in America, had gone to Japan in 1941 and remained there to disseminate propaganda. Her broadcasts, directed against the US forces, were particularly insidious because her American accent and friendly 'girl-next-door' style of speaking recalled the girls they had left behind, making more fruitful the seeds of doubt and suspicion which she sowed in their minds by playing hit songs such as 'Don't sit under the apple tree with anyone else but me'. She also touched raw nerves among Australian troops with honeyed innuendos about Americans in Australia receiving the 'warmest of welcomes' from the wives and sweethearts of the Australian soldiers 'so fruitlessly sacrificing their lives in New Guinea's swamps and jungles'.

Picture shows at Darwin's Myilly Point were popular, and on 29 May I reported home on my first attendance there:

Last night I went ashore to the pictures which are held if the moon and the enemy permit. There must have been several hundred steel-helmeted, khaki-clad troops there, & we sat down on chairs and boxes and some even sat on their steel helmets. It was there that we heard music—the first for some time—you never realise how you miss music until you haven't got it. The pictures were thrown on a piece of canvas & the loud speaker etc. worked from a truck like those police trucks with loudspeakers.

Before the show began several senior officers arrived; everyone stood, and the amplifier blared out the first verse of the national anthem. Then, as the Americans were our allies, we remained standing for the 'Star-Spangled Banner'. The brass sat down, but the troops raised a protest: Joseph Stalin was also our ally, so why not the Russian national anthem too? A roar 'What about Joe?' rose from the picture show's patrons.

In Darwin we were quickly put to work. ML *815*, commanded by Lieutenant Charles Inman, with Harold Sturt as his first lieutenant and my *Rushcutter* classmate Jim Morrison her junior officer, had preceded us by some weeks and had already been in the thick of what became known as the Battle of Blaze Point. After forty-one Japanese planes had attacked the aerodrome and floating dock, they had been chased and intercepted by Spitfires about 40 miles out to sea. In the ensuing battle, fourteen Spitfires were lost or damaged, and ML *815* had rescued three of their pilots from the sea. One of them, Flying Officer Ken Fox, had spent eight hours drifting in a dinghy before being picked up.

At dawn on 1 June we sailed for Millingimbi, a voyage of about 350 miles eastwards along the Arnhem Land coast. A Methodist mission station had been established there in the 1920s and in 1941, anticipating the Japanese threat, an RAAF base, too, which now had six resident Spitfires from 457 Squadron and over 300 RAAF ground crew. The air-strip was also being used by Beaufighters from

31 Squadron to strike at the Japanese float-plane base at Taberfane, in the Tanimbar Islands. Millingimbi was within easy range of the Japanese aircraft at Selaru Island, about 340 miles to the north-west, and on 9 May the Japanese had bombed the air-strip, killing ten airmen, a soldier, and an Aborigine. Next day, in another attack, they had destroyed one Beaufighter and sunk HMAS *Maroubra*, loaded with 30 tons of stores for the base; the Spitfires had shot down two enemy fighters and lost one of their own. In the latest action, four days before we arrived, when thirteen Japanese planes had attacked Millingimbi, two Spitfires and three of the raiders were lost. Our job was to provide submarine protection for the American ship *Admiral Halstead*, which was shortly to arrive with stores and aviation fuel.

On the first night out we ran into the worst weather I had experienced in a Fairmile. We were heading into steep seas, and for twelve hours the ship, swept by wind and spray, was burying her bow in their crests, dropping off the top of one wave and pile-driving with a crash into the hollow behind it, only to be picked up by the next wave and shot skywards again. The fo'c's'le deck opened up and water poured through, soaking the men trying to get some sleep below. Fortunately not prone to sea-sickness, I took over the wheel during the middle watch while the quartermaster vomited continually.

We reached Millingimbi next afternoon, feeling our way carefully in through its poorly charted waters, and anchored near the mouth of the inlet. Here we refuelled from the small supply vessel HMAS *Chinampa*, with turtles swimming around us and crocodiles basking on the muddy banks. When the *Admiral Halstead* arrived we began our patrol around her and I was sent off with two men in the dinghy to deliver an RAAF liaison officer to the air base. The tide was low, the dinghy grounded well out, and we struggled ashore up to our knees in sticky mud with lurking crocodiles much in mind. Several well-built Aboriginal men met us and led us along a path to the RAAF headquarters. Almost as we arrived, the air-raid alarm blared, and the roar of Rolls-Royce engines filled the air as the Spitfires took off right beside us and soared into the sky.

All thoughts now were to get back to our ship. We ran to the shore, ploughed through the mud to the dinghy and rowed feverishly back to her. The Spitfires disappeared over the horizon and our first little flurry in Darwin's navy ended with us patrolling monotonously around the *Admiral Halstead*.

Homeward bound to Darwin we savoured some of Northern Australia's dry season delights as we slipped smoothly through a mirrored sea flecked with gold and, as the sun sank to touch the sharp, scimitar-like edge of the horizon, its rays covered the western sky like a vast crimson fan. In the short tropical twilight this spectacle faded quickly, supplanted by the southern stars burning brilliantly above our heads.

That night I held the first watch, from 8 p.m. to midnight. We cruised comfortably along at 14 knots with our cutwater slicing through the glassy sea like a sharp knife, spreading bow waves endlessly out on either side, while under our stern the big three-bladed propellers churned the sea into a foaming wake brilliant with phosphorescent light. After a while we passed close to an island and, notwithstanding its extravagant prose, my journal entry still recalls for me the magic of that night:

> The evening breeze soft and warm, brought to us from an island nearby the distinct savour of frangipani and tropical flowers. The stars flamed across the deep velvety blue of the tropical sky. Venus smiled brightly down with a steady warm glow and, exactly as the picture books tell, the new moon slept with the old moon in her arms. The White Ensign streamed stiffly from the Jack and the engines' pulsing roar hurried us homeward through the night to our base with our mission accomplished.

On 5 June, when we returned to our No. 5 buoy in Darwin harbour, HMAS *Tonga*, a former motor yacht requisitioned by the Navy, came alongside to replenish our tanks. As *Tonga's* living quarters were even more restricted than ours, we invited the crew to secure their lines to us so that they could at least walk a few paces on our decks. Like so many men I met during the war, her captain, Sub Lieutenant Max Mattingly, remained a friend for life.

Some of the small craft like *Tonga* serving under the White Ensign in Darwin were not equipped with adequate heads, and their crews had little privacy. One of them, moored close to us, had a wooden platform with a hole in it, rigged out over her taffrail where men could sit at ease. One morning I noticed a figure enthroned there wearing a straw hat and reading a book with his bottom a couple of feet above the water. About half a mile away a boat, moving at high speed, was leaving a wake of steep waves which were moving swiftly and silently towards the lugger's stern. The first wave lifted it sharply and dropped it into the following trough. The next struck the reader's nether regions so violently that he lost his hat and book, and barely managed to save himself from being pitched off his perch.

The nature of our operations in Darwin varied, and their outcome depended on factors ranging from weather to enemy action. Not all went as planned, and our next mission had to be aborted. A convoy sailing from Thursday Island to Darwin was due to pass through Clarence Strait at night, altering course near some sunken rocks and low-lying islands about 50 miles from Darwin. Because of the strong tidal streams in the area, the position was normally marked by a light buoy which was visible by day or night, but to prevent its use by Japanese submarines or disguised luggers it was now lit only when needed by allied ships. Our job was to find it, with the help of a local pilot, and light it.

The night was very dark and the sea shrouded in mist, and while we were groping for the buoy we saw a strange blinking light in the distance. After poring over the chart with the pilot, Reg and Chips decided it was probably a Japanese lugger trying to lure the convoy onto the rocks. We approached it cautiously, guns manned, but the light vanished suddenly and, as the area was poorly charted and full of dangers, Reg signalled a warning to Darwin and we withdrew. The convoy anchored until daylight, and we returned to No. 5 buoy with the strange flashing light remaining one of the many mysteries of war.

The Territory's fecund wildlife amazed us. After seeing a soldier, fishing with a handline from the Commonwealth Airways Jetty, catch four fish which together weighed about one hundred pounds, and watching two Aborigines drifting in a dinghy over nearby shallows spear a dozen superb fish in a few minutes, we decided to use our technology to supplement our dreary rations. Working with ML *815*, we tied several demolition charges together and detonated them halfway between the two ships. The explosion was alarming, but the catch fed forty men.

Our thoughts were never far from food; we continually grouched about its scarcity, and in a letter home on 12 June, I did my share of complaining:

> Our main moan here is diet—nothing much fresh. De-hydrated (tinned) potatoes, no eggs at all, ever, no fresh milk at all, never seen any fresh fruit, and that's what we all crave. We are all fit and well but everyone in the ship was weighed and we've all lost between half and one stone ... There is one chap here who lives in Sydney & once in a while his wife buys him some greenish apples which take about three weeks to come by ordinary mail & are ripe on arrival. I don't like to keep asking for things, but if you'd send say half a dozen apples (green) now and then, it would be wonderful. We've forgotten what a piece of fruit looks like. There are banana palms ashore—but you can guess how many bananas are on them.

My parents responded generously, and for the rest of my time in ML *814* they sent tins and packages of cakes, apples, oranges, barley sugar, Ovaltine, malted-milk tablets, cordial crystals to mix with water, and other treats. These were shared around in small portions and eaten sparingly.

Gradually, the food improved: '... fresh spuds have been reaching us more lately, & things could be a lot worse', I wrote in July. But there was still plenty to complain about:

> There are some completely tasteless, hard biscuits, which the Navy issues us—they are 99% inedible—so one of the stokers had an idea—he soaked a lot for a long time in water, mashed them into a pulp & we got that half cold for 'porridge' for breakfast this morning—it was terrible, and I, and the others, threw it overboard, so we had a piece of toast and a cup of tea for breakfast ...

Our first air-raid was, from our point of view, uneventful. Reg and Chips were about to go ashore when the Air Raid Yellow flag rose at the signal station overlooking the harbour, warning that enemy aircraft were approaching. Our Action Stations alarm blared and within seconds we had slipped the bridle of the buoy and were racing for the boom gate with every man, steel-helmeted and wearing his Mae West, at his post. Our duty was to get to sea at top speed and wait in our air-sea-rescue position about 20 miles from Darwin. As we passed Emery Point, the yellow flag came down and up went the Air Raid Red, signalling that the Japanese were overhead. We could not see them, although before our engines started we had heard the Spitfires revving up and watched them climbing into the sky on the other side of the town. Now the anti-aircraft batteries on the esplanade near the Darwin Hotel opened fire, and the brown smudges of their exploding shells appeared high up. We reached our position, but the bombers had passed over the town and gone on, perhaps to attack the Beaufighter strip at Coomalie Creek or the Liberator base at Fenton Field, and we were recalled. Later we heard that the Spitfires had engaged about forty-two bombers and fighters and had shot down fourteen with a loss of two of their own.

The aerial warfare between Australians and Japanese was intensifying in retaliation for the attacks made on Darwin and our airfields by the Japanese. Beaufighters from 31 Squadron had attacked Taberfane, destroying six float-planes on the water and one in the air. Our reconnaissance planes had also discovered that the Japanese were building an airstrip on Selaru Island, and the RAAF planned to attack it with twelve Vultee Vengeances and six Beaufighters. Our part in the action was to rescue any airmen who were shot down. We left for the area on the eve of the attack and sailed after dark, having spent the afternoon checking charts, guns, ammunition, water and rations in the life rafts. By daylight we had reached our position and were drifting alone, deep in Japanese waters. Nervously conscious of our vulnerability, we ranged our binoculars continually across the sky and when, at about 10 a.m., black dots appeared to the south, the tension on board rose. But after minutes of anxious scrutiny we identified them as the strike force and, breathing more easily, watched them disappear over the horizon towards Selaru. After what seemed hours of watching and waiting, the wireless set buzzed, the telegraphist decoded the message 'Return to base' and, needing no urging, we set off for home at about 15 knots.

Early that afternoon, while I was scanning the ocean with my binoculars, idly watching the broad white ribbon of our wake on the blue sea, I suddenly spotted a black periscope about four miles astern moving quickly through the water and trailing a plume of spray. I went cold and, with my stomach churning, pushed the alarm button. Within seconds everyone was at Action Stations, peering at the periscope which was now clearly following us.

The situation was terrifying: we were virtually defenceless. The Japanese I-class submarines were much faster on the surface than we, and our guns useless against them; all they had to do was overhaul and ram us, or shoot us out of the water. Reg rang down for maximum engine revolutions to give us our top speed of 18 knots, and sent an emergency Enemy Report to Darwin.

The Hall-Scotts responded at once. Smoke poured from the funnel and we gained speed, drawing slowly away. Our hopes rose but, just as my stomach was beginning to settle, a conning tower emerged, water cascading from its sides, and on the submarine's deck was a large black gun pointed straight at ML *814*. Now the sub also put on speed, throwing up a large bow wave, and began overhauling us rapidly. Frenziedly, Reg rang down for still more revolutions, but Jock Livingstone could do nothing. Not only could he not give us any more revolutions, he told Reg, but if we maintained our present ones the 'bloody engines would blow their tops'.

With all hope gone, I had a bright idea: as we had nothing to lose, why not try to take them with us by waiting until they were almost upon us, and then, with all our depth-charges set to explode at 50 feet, make a sudden 180-degree turn, rush alongside the submarine, shooting at the conning tower, and release all our charges at once? The subsequent huge explosion might sink her too … This suggestion was received on the bridge with dead silence.

When the submarine was only about a mile astern, Reg desperately decided to challenge her, and when D'Arcy Kelly began flashing the Morse code international challenge, 'What ship? What ship?', a bright light blinked back the welcome message, 'dit dit dah, dit dit dit': 'US'. Sick with relief, Reg told D'Arcy to signal, 'Welcome to Darwin, gateway to the north'. 'Thanks', they replied, 'but we have already been welcomed with bullets.' Earlier, while running on the surface, they had been shot at by our returning Beaufighters. We reduced to a relaxed 14 knots, they came up almost alongside, and we chatted through megaphones. They were returning from a patrol in the Sea of Japan, having 'sunk some Nip ships' and were also going to Darwin. They had not forgotten Pearl Harbor and, after fuelling and re-arming, were going back north to 'kill some more of the bastards'. We picked up our buoy in Darwin harbour about midnight, profoundly grateful to be home.

13 June was as fine a day as Darwin has to offer in the dry season—a bright clear morning with a gentle breeze ruffling the harbour and brown kites circling on thermals above the town. But our peace was soon shattered by the roar of engines as Spitfires took off on the other side of town and began climbing steeply into the sky. Then the Air Raid Yellow signal went up on Fort Hill. There was confusion in the

harbour as ships began manoeuvring to avoid attack and, as we headed for the open sea, the big red flag signalling 'Enemy aircraft overhead', went up. And there they were right above us.

The first wave of Mitsubishis, coming in fairly low, met a hail of steel from the ships and shore batteries. At the start the shells burst astern, above, and below the tightly packed formation; then the gunners got the range and brown blotches appeared among the aeroplanes. One aircraft began to smoke and dropped out of the formation. The gunfire stopped and from high above the Spitfires swooped onto the bombers, and we heard the staccato rattle of machine-guns and cannon. By now the Japanese were over the airfield, and we could see their bombs bursting in red balls of fire with clouds of smoke and dust. Then they dropped lower and began machine-gunning the buildings, setting fire to installations and motor transport. We heard later that some men were killed in this attack.

We were still moving fast towards the boom when the Japanese Zeros, the bombers' fighter escorts, became locked in dogfights with the Spitfires. I had never seen an aerial battle before, and watched fascinated as they zoomed, banked and dived to get on to each others' tails, while from the middle of it all came the constant sounds of wildly revving engines and hammering guns.

But my attention was soon diverted to the low-flying bombers; thirteen of them were returning and heading straight towards us. As controller of the 20 mm Oerlikon which had an effective range of 1000 yards, I had to estimate their distance and calculate when to open fire. For the moment they were too far away, but their approach was menacing. Then we had a journeying mercy: their leader dipped his starboard wing, turning out to sea, and they all followed him back towards Timor. The fighter fracas continued above us for a while as the Zeros fought to buy time for their bombers, but when we reached our rescue position out at sea all was peaceful there.

On our way home one of those silly incidents occurred which often happen in war and often end in tragedy. The morning's events had left us on edge and distinctly 'trigger happy', and when the bridge lookout reported an approaching aircraft we went immediately to Action Stations and trained our guns onto it. Flying fast at about 1000 feet, it began a shallow dive straight towards us but, just as we were about to open fire, it rolled away in a steep turn, revealing the blue and white roundels and elliptical wings of a Spitfire. One of our young countrymen was indulging in a display of exuberance which nearly cost him his life.

Next morning our peace was again shattered by gunfire as the battery in front of the Darwin Hotel began firing at a Japanese Dinah taking photographs from about 28,000 feet. Some of the shells exploded close to it, and as it sped away they hung there, forming perfect smoke rings in the clear morning air. Picturesque, but dangerous too, as any of those jagged steel fragments, in returning to earth, could kill as surely as a bullet or a bomb.

The next Japanese raid forced Chips to make a difficult decision. At about 9.30 a.m. Reg and Jim Nelson, the coxswain, took the harbour duty-boat ashore on ship's business. They had just landed on the wharf when we heard the familiar roar of Spitfires' engines and saw the yellow flag go up. Our duty was to get to sea at once, and Chips sounded Action Stations. We left the buoy, picked up speed, and were about 300 yards from the jetty when Reg and Jim appeared on it, beckoning frantically. Chips ignored the waving arms: 'Too close to those bloody oil tanks, Tony,' he told me, and rang down for full speed ahead. Our captain and coxswain, seeing themselves abandoned, also put on full speed and headed for the nearest air-raid shelter. We reached our air–sea–rescue position and remained there for several uneventful hours before returning to face Reg's outrage.

Darwin's powerful tides punished the ignorant and unwary. An American sailor who had left his dinghy secured to a jetty by a short painter at the top of the tide returned to find it hanging almost vertically by the bow, and everything in it that had not been lashed, floating out to sea. And although I had studied the local tides and was aware of their power, they still caught me out.

We often berthed at the Commonwealth Airways Jetty close to Darwin's main wharf. This was a tricky berth for a 112-foot ship, being angled out towards its end like a badly drawn figure seven, so that it was difficult for us to approach and leave it moving in the same direction.

Reg, Chips, and most of the crew had gone to the pictures, leaving me on duty. We were lying at the long face of the jetty, moored by bow and stern lines with fore and aft springs. The heavy timbers of the jetty's angled section slanted out across and a few feet in front of our bows. As I knew there was to be a big tide of around 24 feet that night and that at mid-tide the water would be rising nearly an inch a minute, I told the watch-keeper to check the lines frequently and keep tightening them as they slackened in the rising tide, which was flooding in from astern and pushing us forward. Having seen to that, I went to the wardroom to write up my journal.

To begin with, I could feel the ship moving slightly as she lifted in the tide now boiling past her stern, but after perhaps thirty minutes it suddenly dawned on me that she felt dead in the water and that the table seemed to be slightly tilting towards the bow. Racing up the companionway, I found the deck deserted, the bow line completely slack, hanging in a loose bight, the stern line bar taut, and the ship's stern, pointing out from the wharf, held fast by the tide. As the mooring lines had not been shortened, she had moved forward as she rose, and a couple of feet of the fo'c's'le were already jammed under a big beam of the jetty. The bow was being dragged down at about an inch a minute, the propellers lifting out of the harbour at the same rate. I was horrified: unless we could free her in a matter of minutes and move her astern against that fierce tide, we would be in deep trouble.

I pressed the red alarm button on the bridge, the crew appeared promptly, and we all stood on the bow, hoping to weigh it down sufficiently to free it by manually pushing the ship backwards. But we could have been flies trying to shove an elephant. Someone suggested flooding the forepeak with the fire hose, hoping that the weight of the extra water there might drag the bow down but, as this would have damaged the stores and equipment in the forepeak, I decided instead to try going astern on the main engines. After positioning the crew as far forward as they could get to weigh down the bow, I told Jock Livingstone to start the engines and, feeling very scared, rang down on for 'Slow astern together'—500 revolutions. But the propellers, now almost at the surface, had lost much of their grip; as they spun they threw a lot of spray into the air and the ship did not budge. I tried 'Half astern together' and the growl of the Hall-Scotts became a muted roar. Froth from the fury astern, shining in the down-lights on the cross-trees, came rushing past the bridge, and the pressure on the bow seemed to lessen. I rang 'Full astern together', and all hell broke loose. The roar rose to a scream of engine revolutions and thrashing water combined. At 1800 revolutions per minute the propellers hurled a curtain of spray high into the air, the harbour boiled under our stern and, with a sound of rending timbers, ML *814* tore herself free from the wharf, shot backwards against the tide and regained an even trim. I stopped the engines, put them gently ahead and picked up the buoy, feeling relieved and rather proud to have brought my first experience of acting command of a King's ship to a satisfactory conclusion with no worse damage than a bent guardrail and a few split planks.

On 28 June the Japanese called again, this time drawing blood from ML *814*. As we were passing Emery Point on our way out to sea, they appeared above us, flying towards Vestey's Meatworks, with anti-aircraft shells bursting around them. Reg, Chips, Jim Nelson and D'Arcy Kelly were on the bridge, and from my position beside the Oerlikon gun I watched through my binoculars as their bomb-bays opened and bombs began tumbling out. Some exploded in red balls of fire with flames, clouds of smoke and debris leaping into the air. Others fell between us and the shore, throwing up columns of water. They were moving in our direction and, as they came closer, the ship shuddered from the blasts, and fragments of metal and bullets from the battle above made smaller splashes in the water around us. Now under heavy ground fire, the Japanese dropped lower and began machine-gunning buildings and vehicles before turning and heading out to sea, with two planes trailing smoke and one losing altitude. I returned to the bridge to find Chips, who had not been wearing his helmet, holding a blood-soaked handkerchief to his forehead and blood running down his face. This 'nick', as he termed it dismissively, was our first and only air-raid casualty.

On 30 June, when the Japanese struck again with twenty-one Zeros and twenty-seven Mitsubishi bombers, there was a furious air battle in which eleven Spitfires and twelve Japanese planes were said to have been lost. We were sent to search for a Spitfire pilot reported floating in the sea about 35 miles offshore, but when we reached his supposed position at 5 p.m. we saw nothing except wheeling seabirds and a low swell gently rising and falling on the sea. A search plane appeared, circling us warily, and a light blinked from its cockpit, 'Nil Sight'. Night fell, and we continued searching for a tell-tale light until about midnight, when the wireless buzzed, and we were ordered home.

Our next task took us to the Drysdale Mission at Napier Broome Bay in Western Australia, whose air-strip was used by the RAAF to strike at the Japanese in Timor. These raids drew reprisals, and the base needed supplies and aviation fuel which were to be shipped there in the slow old freighter SS *Alagna*. We were to escort her there and back and help unload her cargo.

As the crow flies, Drysdale is only about 200 miles south-west of Darwin, but our route across the Joseph Bonaparte Gulf and round Cape Londonderry was much longer than that, and it took us two days to get there. We left Darwin on 9 July 1943 in glorious dry-season weather: by day, blue sky above, blue sea below, and by night the sky ablaze with great lights. At about 3 a.m. on the second morning out we passed through a spectacular submarine battle between small fish and large predators which rushed in among them with slashing jaws filling the waters with phosphorescent fire.

We crawled on westward, constantly scanning the sky for Japanese planes and when, at about noon, I picked up a silver gleam in the sky, I hurriedly pressed the Action Stations alarm. We warned the *Alagna* and stood to our guns, all eyes fixed on the suspicious speck, but to our embarrassment the *Alagna*'s captain, who knew his stars better than we, dismissed it as only a planet shining in the sun.

On the afternoon of 11 July we shepherded the ship into Drysdale's pretty little Mission Bay and anchored a couple of hundred yards inshore of her off a beach fringed with coconut palms. As the unloading would not start until the morning we fished, and I began a six-page letter home which, with the censor in mind, I headed 'Somewhere in the North about 12 July'.

Soon after we anchored, several black figures appeared on the beach and three of us rowed in to meet them. Like those at Millingimbi, these men were big and strongly built and, when we pointed to a bunch of coconuts, one climbed the tree and threw them down to us. We took them back on board to supplement our rations. As we had just thrown overboard eighteen loaves of mildewed and rotten bread, and that night our meal was a slab of dry meat, a piece of stale mouldy bread smeared with yellowed margarine and a cup of tea, the nuts were very welcome.

The tasks allotted to Fairmiles often called for initiative. In Mission Bay there was no jetty, and unloading the *Alagna*, as I informed the family, demanded ingenuity:

> The problem here was how to unload the cargo of stores and motor vehicles where there were no wharves or port facilities whatsoever—and such a gradually shelving sea bed that the ship had to stand out 400 yards from the beach. Jack Old and I found an old lugger and managed to get the engine running inter-mittently, and with another sailor, Mackenzie, we managed to improvise a ship-to-shore ferry for the unloaded cargo. Rafts were made out of 44 gallon drums lashed together with timber laid across. Each would hold about 9 tons. Two of the ship's lifeboats were lashed together and also used and the cargo unloaded on to these improvised rafts. When loaded in the lugger, we would tow them as near to the beach as we could get,

and then let them go, and the natives would wade out and pull
them in and unload them in about 3 feet of water. The first day
we unloaded 60 tons up to midnight …

After landing all the stores, vehicles and aviation fuel, we returned to
Darwin satisfied that we had done something to strengthen Drysdale's
striking power. But that did not guarantee its safety. On 27 September,
twenty-two Mitsubishi bombers, escorted by Zeros, attacked the
station, damaging the base and killing one of the missionaries and five
of his flock.

26 July 1943 broke fine and clear, promising a brilliant day. But, as I
was enjoying the morning air on the bridge with D'Arcy Kelly, a light
blinked from the signal station '*814—814—814*'. Reg was ordered to
report to the Operations Office 'forthwith'. Something was afoot. A
special boat collected Reg and a Jeep was waiting for him on the
wharf. A couple of hours later it returned with dust flying from its
wheels, and a worried-looking Reg climbed aboard. Chips and I met
him at the gangway, he motioned us down to the wardroom, flopped
into his chair, flung his cap onto his bunk, and swore loudly. 'What a
job they've got for us. We're off to bloody Timor and I'll miss the
nurses' dance.' That was pretty rough justice: when invitations came
for social functions ashore, Reg generally drew the lucky straw.

His story was this. Together with *815*, we were ordered to prepare
for an operation—code-named 'Mosquito'—to succour our commandos still holding out against the vastly superior Japanese in Timor.
When the Japanese had landed there in February 1942, they had
captured and executed some of our soldiers; others had taken to the
mountains, where they were carrying on guerilla warfare. Some Portuguese civilians, hiding out with our men in the mountains, were
encumbering them, and our task, arranged by a brave and flamboyant
Portuguese guerilla leader, Lieutenant M. de J. Pires, was to go and get
these people out.

The Japanese had strong forces in the area, and supporting our soldiers there had already cost the RAN dearly, with the loss of the destroyer *Voyager*, the corvette *Armidale*, and many men. About 6 miles west of our rendezvous there was reported to be an airfield; Dili was a Japanese air base, and there were possibly float-plane bases at Maobesi Bay and Besikama, close to our proposed landing point.

Our orders were precise. As the Japanese would be listening for radio traffic, we were to maintain strict radio silence. On the way over, a Beaufighter from 31 Squadron would give us air cover for some of the daylight hours until we were close to Timor; then we would be on our own. We were to cross the Timor Sea slowly at 10 knots to save petrol for a high-speed dash home. We were to anchor off an open beach near the mouth of the Dilor River, and would have to row in through the surf to embark the civilians. As well as getting the Portuguese out, we would be taking in food, medical supplies, weapons and wireless equipment, and also landing one or two brave souls who had volunteered to join our commandos there.

While Reg was briefing us I thought of the fates of the *Voyager* and *Armidale*, and I half wished myself back with my friends in the 110th Light Anti-Aircraft Regiment, now comfortably camped on Queensland's Atherton Tableland.

Next day, Flying Officers Ray Whyte and Bob Ogden from 31 Squadron came aboard for a beer and a chat. Ogden, known as 'Oggie', sporting a large handle-bar moustache, might have stepped straight out of *Biggles*. They would be covering us for about 200 miles and thought it a horrible assignment: their Beaufighters, armed with four 20 mm cannon and eight machine guns, were not designed for this sort of caper. Their game was to sweep in fast and low, rake their target and get home at top speed, and circling around two Fairmiles crawling across the Timor Sea did not appeal to them.

But talking to them gave me confidence until I asked Oggie what he would do if we were attacked by a Zero. He took a thoughtful pull at his glass, smiled, and said that all he could do would be to make one pass at it, wish us luck, and go hell-for-leather home 10 feet above the sea. After considerably more refreshment, the pilots went ashore leaving us in a thoughtful frame of mind.

I watched the preparations with butterflies fluttering in my stomach. A big wooden skid was built over the quarterdeck for a 28-foot canvas boat. Outside Timor's surf we would have to push it into the water but, as we would not be able to lift it back and it was too costly to abandon, we must tow it back to Australia, and that would slow us down. Our depth charges, which weighed 4 tons, were removed to lighten our load. Most of our secret code books were sent ashore; they must not fall into enemy hands.

Shortly before we left, an intelligence officer came aboard. I met him at the gangway and he gave me a fake Japanese ensign to fly on the way over as a *ruse de guerre*. I was suspicious, even though sailing under false colours sounded better in French. He did not ask me to sign for the flag and I passed it on to Chips, who was talking signals with D'Arcy on the bridge. They didn't like the sound of it either, and we decided that if we were to be caught, it would be under the White Ensign and not the Rising Sun, reasoning that the Japs had not signed the Geneva Convention and that if they caught us like that they might use blunt swords. As there was no need to worry Reg with such trivia, Chips told D'Arcy not to put it with the 'decent' flags but to 'shove it in the potato locker'.

Cyril Alcorn came on board just before sailing time. Regardless of whether we were Catholic, Protestant or atheist, he gathered us around the 2-pounder gun, and in a moving prayer, committed us into God's hands as we were about to 'pass through the waters'. One wag made the crack that the waters were passing through him right then. That raised a nervous laugh, but it helped to know that God was now officially on our side. Shaking our hands, Cyril gave us each a piece of rather soft Comforts Fund chocolate and, remembering the terrible fate of the *Armidale*'s men who had drifted for days on a raft and died slowly, I put mine away for raft rations. Taking our few last letters to parents, wives and sweethearts, Alcorn promised to post them 'if necessary', but assured us that he would be giving them back to us in a week or two. I kept mine for forty years before destroying it, but kept the envelope.

Finally, a Portuguese pilot, Baltazar, and Lieutenant G. Greaves and Sergeant Jim Ellwood arrived on board. The two soldiers were members of the SRD, the army's cloak-and-dagger men. During the next few days Jim and I exchanged the stories of our lives and discussed our hopes for the future. I admired Ellwood's nobility: he had already been in Timor and was returning voluntarily to join our men there in the mountains. Soon after we landed him, he was captured and tortured, but he survived the war, and over half a century later we met again and relived old memories.

At about midnight on 27 July 1943, the two Fairmiles slipped out of Darwin and next day anchored in Kings Cove on Melville Island, close to the ruins of Fort Dundas. We found there a former coaster, HMAS *Terka*, under the command of Lieutenant Ken Shatwell, who later became Dean of the Faculty of Law at the University of Sydney. He hailed us cheerily as we berthed alongside him to replenish our petrol tanks from drums on his deck, and full of bonhomie and chat, superintended the business with a glowing pipe in his mouth. This shocked us, for we had rigid safety rules about fuelling: rubber-soled shoes had to be worn, lest a spark from a nail on the armour-plated deck should start an inferno, all electrical switches had to be broken and smoking was absolutely taboo. Noticing our concern, Shatwell airily waved his pipe at the *Terka*'s funnel, and we took his point. By comparison with the smoke and sparks belching from it above the fuel drums, his pipe seemed innocuous.

Kings Cove was a haven of peace, its air full of bird songs, and the next twenty-four hours there were balm for our taut nerves. Three Aborigines arrived in a dugout canoe, inviting us to go crocodile shooting, and Jim and I took a couple of rifles and joined them. Once ashore, they treated us to a memorable display of the hunting skills which had fed their people for millennia. They brought down birds with stones, and showed us how to make little cakes by knocking the tops off an ants' nest, removing a handful of eggs and rolling them in wild bees' honey. We were suitably impressed:

> ...there is here too a fat grub that lives in the mangrove root— and in truth—with sharks, snakes, crocodiles, fish, birds, mussels & roots, this apparently inhospitable country to white men's eyes, can be a veritable larder...

Although these Tiwi islanders—some naked, with tribal cicatrices on their bodies and front teeth knocked out—looked alarming, they were friendly, and anxious to show us the sights. They took us to see a crashed Japanese Zero and the ruins of Fort Dundas, built in 1824 by the order of Earl Bathurst in the hope that Melville and Bathurst Islands would become another Singapore:

> ...the remains of the fort were a deep moat, square and wide, & an old well and a stone blockhouse now crumbling in decay amid the silences of the Melville Island bush. We found some old glassware and bottles over a hundred years old. At the Mission we met a bluff R.C. Father who teaches these natives a rough and ready form of Christianity. He had brewed some beer of wild honey, hops and yeast—a very potent and unpalatable concoction & quite black. We savoured it without too much enthusiasm, but he knocked off a large tankard and slapped his belly in appreciation.

That night the islanders staged a corroboree. Met by furiously barking dogs, we—about twenty men from the three ships in the cove—were led into a clearing and sat down to wait:

> ... before long the dancers with balls of eagle feathers about their necks began to arrive. The women and children sat in an outer ring & the show started. The ... spectacle was accom- panied by a rhythmic clapping & a low guttural sound for musical

background. The dancing, with wild screams, furious twirlings, and frantic stampings of bare feet on the ground, raised clouds of dust which dimmed the brilliance of the fire and made the trees appear to recede and assume the proportions of ghostly figures, and all the time the clapping and stamping continued. Most of the meanings behind the dances were fairly evident but a bright lad … translated some for me. There were buffalo, crocodile and shark hunts. Then the dance telling of the coming of a ship, and the women entered the firelit circle and joined the ecstatic dancing of which they never seemed to tire … towards midnight we made our way back to the boats and out to the ships swinging quietly to their cables in the stream.

One of the dances portrayed dog fights between Zeros and Spitfires. Arms outstretched to represent aircraft wings, the dancers made passes at one another, uttering staccato sounds like machine-gun fire. Occasionally one would be hit and would start spinning, still with arms extended, until he lay a crumpled heap on the ground, the firelight flickering on his body. That remains one of the most memorable theatrical productions I have seen—its stage a dusty fire-lit circle, its sound effects the actors' voices, clapping hands, stamping feet and barking dogs.

About noon next day we left Kings Cove on our 300-mile crawl across the Timor Sea, the cloudless sky offering perfect visibility for any Japanese reconnaissance pilots. At night, the constellation of Scorpio with its great red star, Antares, arched above our mast. It also shone on the nurses and soldiers dancing and drinking beer in Darwin, and Reg cursed his luck.

Shortly after 1 a.m. on 29 July our wireless began buzzing: it must be something important, for we were on radio silence. Tensely, we waited some minutes while the telegraphist consulted his code books and deciphered the message. It finally came as an anti-climax: we were to return to Melville Island to await further orders. We learned later that the Japanese had been closing in on our men on Timor, and Pires, fearing an ambush on the beach, had broken radio silence and deferred the operation. He also asked for desperately needed food.

For two days we lay in Kings Cove, biting our fingernails, while the Japanese maintained their pressure on Pires's men. On 1 August, with an easing of the situation on Timor, we sailed again, this time refuelling at Snake Bay on the north coast of Melville Island, and once more launched out across the Timor Sea in perfect visibility. At length Timor's towering mountains loomed on the western horizon, and when an aircraft appeared, we trained our guns on it, challenging it with the Aldis lamp. It was our friend Ray Whyte in his Beaufighter come to hold our hand, and as we trudged slowly on he circled above us.

As the long afternoon wore on and the two Fairmiles crept closer to Timor, we draped sacks over the wheelhouse windows to prevent the westering sun flashing warnings to the Japanese. Thinking of the men on *Armidale*'s raft, we also stowed extra cans of water and tins of bully beef in the Carley rafts. The escorting Beaufighter, now over 250 miles from home and getting low in fuel, came round for his final sweep. As he flew about 50 feet above the bridge, the roar of his Hercules engines drowned all conversation, and the roundels on his wings and his cannon muzzles seemed larger than I had ever seen them before. He banked steeply, and a light blinked from his cockpit window. Eight letters only, but all that he could say: 'Good luck'. Then he levelled out, opened his throttles and sped off over the south-eastern horizon to Darwin, leaving the two Fairmiles alone on the Timor Sea.

As it was now late in the afternoon, we began to breathe more easily, reckoning that the Japanese air patrols would have gone home too, and I went below to get some sleep in preparation for whatever the night might hold. I had just dozed off when the strident clatter of the alarm bell jerked me awake and the ship shuddered as she increased to fighting speed. Grabbing my Mae West and helmet, I scrambled on deck to find all eyes focused on a Japanese aircraft circling over the northern horizon. Making a leisurely turn, it flew straight towards us. Then, as we watched breathlessly, it turned and flew off towards the island. The pilot had not sighted us in the gathering dusk and was going home.

When we were close enough to pick out individual trees on the island, and were, according to Baltazar, heading directly for a Japanese position five miles south-west of the rendezvous, we turned and ran along the shore. Soon we saw a faint blue light flashing the secret letter; then three fires, 50 yards apart, erupted on the beach. This was the final signal our men were to make, but could we trust it? What if someone had been caught and tortured, revealing the secret? What if this was an ambush? The first boat ashore would find out.

We anchored just outside the surge, using a Manila line rather than our chain cable, and leaving an axe beside the winch. At the first sign of trouble ashore we would have to cut and run—and bad luck for anyone left on the beach. The engines stopped, and we could hear surf breaking on the sand and smell the spice wafting out from the shore.

Chips was the first to go in. We pushed the heavy boat over the stern and he went off with four sailors to land Jim Ellwood and assess the situation. For about fifteen minutes we waited, peering anxiously through the dark. Then he was back, with word that the commandos were ready and waiting for us.

Now it was my turn. We loaded the canvas boat with tommy guns, ammunition, food, medicines and tins of two shilling pieces— Australian silver to pay the Timor natives who had lost confidence in Japanese printed currency. I climbed down the scrambling net into the boat and grasped the long steering oar. We wore heavy army boots in case we were stranded ashore and had to take to the mountains; despite my nervousness, it flashed across my mind that we looked like the pirates of Penzance. But no one was singing.

Standing in the stern of this heavily laden 28-foot wood-and-canvas contraption, my anxiety was increased by the prospect of having to steer it safely through the surf. Since my boyhood days on Pittwater I had never beached a boat of any kind in such conditions, and I dreaded capsizing. The first surge lifted the boat, hurried us forward and slipped away under the bow, breaking ahead. Several more followed before we were into broken water and, although the surf was low, it was still a job to keep her running straight. Then wild-looking naked figures rushed into the water and hauled us on to the sand. We shook hands and, as the Japanese were thought to be near, exchanged guarded greetings, keeping our voices down.

It took some time to clear the boat of its cargo, but while they were working I saw an astonishing sight: two of the men grabbed tins of bully beef, hacked them open with knives and wolfed the contents down like half-starved dogs. Then, ponies appeared on the sand and, while the commandos were loading the supplies onto them, a number of men, women and children walked out from the trees behind the beach and began climbing into the boat. They kept coming until there were too many for safety; with the boat already dangerously low in the water, I told the soldiers 'no more', and standing waist-deep in the water, they pushed the crowd back. Just as we were about to leave, I glanced along the beach, and there, in the shallows, stood a tall old man in a white suit and Panama hat. In my mind's eye he stands there still, dignified and authoritative. He did not call to me, or make any effort to save himself—he just stood staring at the boat, and watching his people go. I could not leave him: I waded quickly back and grabbed him. He was thin and frail, I could feel the bones through his shirt. We did not speak: there was nothing to say. Hampered by my weapons and our soaking clothes, I dragged him through the surf, shoved him over the side into the boat beside my oar, and jumped in. The commandos pushed us forward, the sailors bent their backs to the oars and pulled us through the surf, and soon we were into calmer water. Once there, the old man turned and looked back at the island in the starlight. Then he took something from his hand and, giving it to me, spoke for the first time in precise English: 'If you ever go to Portugal, show this.' It was a handsome silver ring inlaid with a rampant gold lion on a field of jade green—perhaps the armorial bearings of some family with centuries of service in the East. Now nothing remained for him but memories. He had lost everything except that ring, and that he gave away. I did not ask his name and I have never been to Portugal, but I still treasure that memory and his ring.

After several more boat trips, having embarked all the people we could take, we headed for home, engines at full throttle, using 90 gallons an hour of the precious fuel we had saved by our slow crawl across the Timor Sea. With the heavy canvas boat bouncing astern, we flew along at 17 knots, hoping by dawn to be a hundred miles from the Japanese airfields.

Daylight revealed a pathetic sight on the crowded deck: our human cargo were huddled around the guns, lying in their own filth, vomiting and soaked with spray. We cleaned them up as best we could and gave them tea from our chipped china mugs. Soon after dawn a black dot appeared in the sky, and once more we went wearily to our guns. But as the dot grew larger we recognised the stubby hunched-up look of a Beaufighter, and then the blessed blue and white roundels on its wings: our friends from 31 Squadron had come to shepherd us home. At last the low brown blur of Australia appeared on the horizon. We shot through the boom gate, landed our wretched cargo, and returned gratefully to No. 5 buoy.

For this operation MLs *814* and *815* were mentioned in despatches and received a salute from the acting Portuguese governor in Timor:

> Profoundly grateful to Sea Land and Air Forces Darwin for Gallant and Splendidly successful rescue my Nationals under extremely trying circumstances all concerned Stop We are yours to command for the duration to help against common enemy Stop Viva Australia Viva os Aliados

The Japanese float-planes in 'Bomb Alley' gave us our next job. On 6 August, two of them attacked the 8000-ton SS *Macumba* off the Arnhem Land coast. The escorting corvette, HMAS *Cootamundra*, scored a hit on one of the attacking planes, shooting off a float, but a well-aimed bomb struck *Macumba*'s engine-room, sinking the ship and killing or wounding many of the crew. The *Cootamundra* rescued some survivors, and we were sent off with a doctor at top speed. Up to this point I had seen few war casualties, and as we came alongside the corvette I was horrified to see a row of corpses lying on her deck. The shocked survivors, still wearing their yellow Board of Trade life-jackets, stared blankly at us. At the wharf in Darwin, a line of ambulances was waiting to take the wounded off in stretchers, but for a while the dead were left on the quarterdeck with sheets over their faces. This made for a sad journal entry:

> I don't suppose their families know they are dead yet. As the survivors came off they gave 3 cheers for the corvette which has saved their lives & half an hour later the bodies were lowered into a boat and taken away. It was a lovely sunset with little red clouds flecking the blue sky & reflecting in the calmness of the sea, it seemed too beautiful to die.

When ML *814* entered Darwin's floating dock at the end of August, I was given three days' leave and, with Jim Morrison from ML *815*, travelled to Captain Campbell's farm at Adelaide River about 80 miles to the south. This was a blissful interlude. We slept in airy huts on a tree-lined river bank, relishing the smell of earth and the sound of birds. We swam in the river's clear waterholes, and feasted on fresh eggs, tomatoes, beans, potatoes, pineapples and pawpaws. Best of all, we were invited to a meal at the hospital, where there were girls from the Voluntary Aid Detachment; listening to their feminine chatter and laughter was, we decided, even more invigorating than fresh tropical fruit. Some of the girls came swimming with us, and in the evening took us to a concert staged by the local troops.

Then it was back to life afloat. In the increasingly humid weather, and without a shower on board, it was almost impossible to keep clean, and we began getting skin disorders. When I developed an itchy rash with large areas of skin peeling off my hands and feet, the Port Medical Officer, Lieutenant Commander Pat Reilly, diagnosed tropical tinea, and put me into Darwin's Military Hospital.

This collection of low buildings, painted with large red crosses, had many patched-up holes in its roofs, but it was heavenly to lie in an airy ward between crisp white sheets, with the scent of frangipani wafting through the open windows. I spent about a week here before being released for duty.

While swinging round the buoy waiting for a job, we passed the time as best we could in maintaining the ship, fishing and washing our clothes. Some of the sailors made pearl-shell trinkets for their women-folk and brass ashtrays and serviette rings from shell cases. I also lightened my hours recording daily trivia, writing letters, and reading whatever came to hand—mostly material sent from home. I devoured weeks-old copies of the *Bulletin*, *Women's Weekly*, *Woman*, and the *Sydney Morning Herald*, before passing them to others hungry for news of the world we had left behind. Fashionable titles of the time, such as *The Keys of the Kingdom* and *The Importance of Living*, also found their way to us, as well as the Army Education journal *Salt*, published for troops in forward areas to keep them informed on the progress of the war and events at home. It had articles by renowned writers such as the historian C. E. W. Bean, but also provided a literary forum for servicemen. Many of their contributions were poetry; as Denis Healey, British Cabinet Minister and a former beachmaster at Anzio in World War II, later explained, 'Thousands who found the pressure almost too much to bear turned to writing poetry as the only way of releasing it—for the first and often last time in lives.' As World War I had produced its rich harvest of war poets, so the muse flourished among the death and destruction of the Second World War.

One of these poems, which I copied into my journal, opened with the question:

Soldier sleeping in the train
What's awhirl within your brain?
Do you dream of wafted wattle?
Are you in the midst of battle?
Pleasure yours or pain?

To this, another soldier responded a few weeks later:

What's awhirl within my brain
While I'm sleeping in the train?
Who can tell what vagrant fancies
Who translate the mixed refrain?
Fleeting dreams that twist and double
Break and burst like pin-pricked bubble,
Nights on leave and girls at dances
Days in swamp and rain ...

That's what whirls within my brain
While I'm sleeping in the train.

I longed to be able to write like that, for I, too, found solace in poetry at that time. The works of Matthew Arnold, Swinburne and Francis Thompson had come with me from the *Abraham Crijnssen* and were now old friends. Swinburne's jingling *Dolores* soothed, and parts of *The Hound of Heaven*, with Thompson fleeing from the truth that would set him free, influenced and stimulated my own efforts and, although I never aspired to publication in *Salt*, I took some pride in them.

As the sun swung south, the heat and humidity increased in our airless accommodation and we envied the Fairmiles based at Eden, Jervis Bay or Coffs Harbour on the cool New South Wales coast. My letters home dwelt on the delights of feeling cool, and I dreamt about holidays at 'Green Gables' with blazing log fires and hard frosts.

One hot sticky night, when Reg and Chips had gone to the pictures, I was writing in the wardroom; sweat dripped from my chin on to the paper and when I lifted my wrist the page stuck to my arm, and

I had to dry my face and arms with a sweat rag. That week I had been reading a lot of poetry; it was running in my head and I began a piece to send with my letter. It was a mishmash of images: Keats's 'Season of mists and mellow fruitfulness', Shakespeare's 'cool south', Thompson's 'arches of the years', 'Soldier Sleeping in the Train' and Vera Lynn's song about bluebirds over the white cliffs of Dover, and promise of peace ever after '...when the world is free'. I called my effort 'Dreaming'.

Long after my mother's death I found the poem, which she had kept with my letters in her attic. Presumably I liked it when I wrote it but now I see it as a very poor companion to 'Soldier Sleeping in the Train':

I cannot see
The hills and valleys that I used to love,
Or watch the free
Unbounded mountain breezes lightly move
The evening clouds across the sky.
These things may still
Be there, & living yet for other eyes—
But here they fill
My dreams as though a door of Paradise
Were opened quickly by some passer by.

I do no know
The joy of loving hearts I knew one day.
The breezes blow
Across three thousand miles, but on their way
Fierce sunlight scorches them & they grow faint
And here they seem
Soft echoes of their former selves, like leaves
That lose their green
And summer lustre, soon as Autumn breathes
Over the vines and boughs her golden paint.

Sometimes I sleep
And in the starry night time see again
The cool showers sweep
Through trees and fields. But here it does not rain
Save in a wall of stickyness and heat.
Sometimes I dream,
And in my dreams the ugliness of war
Its wounds and pain
Are but a memory, and pale before
The misty door that leads to my retreat.

The night is long
And there are times when fires of hope burn low.
And times the song
That tells us of a world we long to know
Falls like an empty promise on our ears.
One day will dawn
A day when this unloveliness shall cease,
And we return
Back home again—to live and die with peace
And Mem'ries, down the valley of the years.

Shortly after I returned from hospital, a signal arrived appointing Chips to HMAS *Rushcutter* and promoting me to first lieutenant of ML *814*. A nineteen-year-old midshipman, John Dowey, was on his way from Sydney to take over my duties as the ship's third officer.

This brought home to me how much I had depended on Chips's wisdom and experience. Reg, although affable and hearty, had a different view of life, and things had not always been easy with him. It was Chips's tolerance and maturity which had kept the ship happy and, shaking his hand as he boarded the boat to go ashore, I wondered how I could ever fill his shoes. But life went on. John Dowey, who hailed from Russell Lea in Sydney, had arrived, looking very dapper.

He settled in quickly and we got along well, beginning a close friend-ship which is even closer now.

My action station was now on the bridge beside Reg. For the extra work and responsibility of my new position, I received an additional one shilling and sixpence a day, and—even more welcome —an extra drawer and locker and two more hooks on which to hang my clothes.

My devoted parents maintained the flow of luxuries and, as they now had three sons on active service, they must have been continually preparing, packing and posting parcels. Among my pre-Christmas treats in 1943 were tinned tongues, oranges, apples, Milo, Ovaltine, Pyrex tooth powder, tinea powder, cakes, shortbread, biscuits, chewing gum, newspapers, magazines and books. Not all of these travelled well across the desert:

> ...the ovaltine ... had all melted and gone into a thick sort of toffee & hardened ... I had to cut the tin away ... and break it with a tomahawk ... many thanks for the fruit—some were rotten but only about 5%.

And as Christmas approached most of us sent presents to our families, usually in the form of banknotes, to buy gifts. Some of the sailors made artefacts or sent souvenirs we had found on our travels. I stitched a canvas bag for my father and sent my mother a small platter fash-ioned from mother of pearl found on the beach at Thursday Island. Jack Old, always clever with his hands, made a brooch for her from another piece of shell; its centrepiece was one of the gold buttons from my uniform embossed with the admiralty crown and anchor. I found it among my letters after her death.

Towards the end of the year we were ordered to prepare for an imme-diate operation to rescue survivors of an American Liberator which had been shot down near the island of Moa, just off the Timor coast.

The pilot and six of the crew had been killed; the remaining four were floating in a rubber dinghy.

Great secrecy surrounded our preparations. We were all confined to the ship, our depth charges removed, and extra drums of petrol lashed on deck. Moa, over 300 miles from Darwin, was close to three Japanese airstrips on Timor. The round trip was expected to take about three days, and for most of the time we would be alone and deep in enemy waters. But fortunately for us, just as we were about to leave, an RAAF Catalina flying boat from Darwin, escorted by our Beaufighter friends, lumbered across the Timor Sea, found the dinghy, landed beside it and plucked the men to safety. This superb display of airmanship and navigation saved the lives not only of the Liberator's men, but probably ours too.

By late October the wet season had set in. At noon the sun glared almost vertically down on us. Every day it rained heavily and when it cleared steam rose from the deck. Below decks was like a Turkish bath. On 24 October our first 'Cock Eye'—a violent electrical storm—struck at 2 a.m. It was a hot, humid night, and we had been lying alongside a large steel ship; the warning from the signal station enabled us to get away before its full violence struck and so save our soft Huon pine sides from a pounding against her hull. On deck was pandemonium. Illuminated by the lights from our crosstrees, shouting men, crouched against the wind, fought to control lines and fenders, while around us jagged lightning streaked, thunder boomed, and the torrential rain drove almost horizontally into our eyes, stinging them like little darts.

Casting off from the ship, we headed out into short steep waves and flying crests and with little idea of exactly where we were in relation to the nearby wrecks; Reg was resolved to anchor at the first opportunity. Struggling along the deck, John Dowey and I joined the fo'c's'le party trying to clear away the anchor and take soundings, and as soon as we reported 7 fathoms, Reg waved his arms and shouted over the storm 'Let go!'. Away went the anchor with its cable links making a fearful clatter. Normally we would pay out three times as much chain cable as the depth of water, as the links, embedding themselves in the sand or mud, contribute greatly to holding the ship. But even after we had paid out 21 fathoms, the ship continued driving fast down wind. Out went another 10 fathoms, but still she drove, and it was not until we had paid out 60 fathoms of heavy chain cable—her total scope—that ML *814* took up with a heavy jolt.

That salvation was a legacy from the departed Chips. During our Fairmiles course at HMAS *Rushcutter*, it had been impressed upon us that the last link of the anchor cable should not be shackled, but lashed to a ringbolt on the stem post in the chain locker by six turns of codline, so that, in an emergency, the ship could be released quickly by cutting the lashing and abandoning the ground tackle. But before ML *814* had left Sydney, Chips, foreseeing such a situation as this, had provided for it. Reckoning that if the cable was still running out fast when it came to its end, the codline lashing would snap like a thread and we would lose our anchor and cable unnecessarily, he had fastened the last link to the ring bolt with a heavy iron shackle. That night, his foresight preserved our anchor and saved us from drifting helplessly in a harbour strewn with wrecks. The heavy jolt felt throughout the ship as the cable at last took up was her salute to him.

The next day was John Dowey's birthday; we caught a shark which gave us all a fresh meal and a welcome change from the glutinous 'M&V'—the Navy's standard meal of tinned meat and vegetables. Our food was still poor, and on 25 November I acknowledged another parcel from the Rectory:

'V. many thanks for exceptionally welcome parcel received 2 days ago containing Drink crystals, nuts, foot powder, apples, sandals & a tin of biscuits. The crystals were marvellous I made them up right away & it has been just wonderful as there is only water and beer to drink ... Please do not send my anymore nuts as I have ample, also have plenty of anti-tinea powder now as the Comforts Fund has given us an issue of it. The apples did not carry too well this time and I think it is unwise to send any more. Please don't send me any more Hordern Brothers cakes as I don't think they taste too good by [the time] they reach here. I would appreciate a HOME made one—but only very occasionally (once every 2 or 3 months or so) as I do NOT want to put you to any bother … You must remember that the climate through which goods travel is very hot & they may lie out in the sun for long periods … Today the temperature in our wardroom is just on 100° and I took the thermometer on deck where it quickly went to 140° and I put it in the shade again.

On 4 November Ray Whyte invited me to fly with him in a Beaufighter which he had to test, and I jumped at the chance to get off the ship and take to the air. This was my first visit to Darwin aerodrome and I was struck by its bullet-marked buildings and bomb craters. Spitfires, Beaufighters and Hudsons were parked everywhere. A flight sergeant handed me a set of headphones and parachute, instructed me on their use, and asked me to sign a certificate absolving the Air Force from any responsibility for my life. Then, with the parachute hooked uncomfortably between my legs, I waddled out to Ray's Beaufighter. It had seen hard service and obviously been frequently repaired. Attacked by a Zero over the Tanimbar Islands, it had received over 300 bullet holes, and Ray mentioned casually that on a recent strike two bullets had hit the windshield in front of his face.

We climbed up through a hatch in the fuselage and, settling into the pilot's seat, he told me to stand behind him and hang onto his shoulders. Then, plugging my headphones into his throat microphone, he pressed the starter button and the engines growled into life. A couple of miles away a powerful tropical squall was brewing up and the sky was full of menacing black clouds. I pointed to them nervously, but Ray assured me he would keep well away from them. He taxied onto the strip, turned in to the wind and opened the throttles.

Although fascinated by flight since a child, my experience had been only as an observer, and I now abandoned myself somewhat apprehensively to its new and thrilling sensations. As the heavy machine accelerated, roaring across the ground faster than I had ever moved before, a powerful force dragged me backwards and I had to cling tightly to Ray's seat to stay upright, while the instrument panel, with its air-speed indicator, altimeter and a host of other dials, sprang to life in front of me. At about 100 knots, very close to the trees at the end of the runway, Ray lifted her off, and for the first time I saw the feathery tops of trees flashing under my feet and buildings, roads, trucks and fences passing below us like a miniature landscape, diminishing in size as we climbed. At 1500 feet Ray moved the control column to the right and down went the stubby starboard wing as we made a steep turn over the town and headed for the harbour. Wisps of cloud —flimsy curtains of grey lace—tore past the cockpit, and the harbour's headlands, arms, bays and beaches appeared as they were laid out on the chart, but all in vivid colour and three dimensional. I could see the wind rippling the water, wavelets breaking on the sand and a toy ML *814* lying at No. 5 buoy. Another steep turn, another tightening of my grip on Ray's seat, and we went into a fast dive. The ship grew larger and larger until I could put names to the upturned faces on deck, and at about 50 feet above the mast, as the Beaufighter zoomed upwards into the sky, I was gripped by gravity. Still clinging to the pilot's seat, my jaw opened, viscera sagged and knees buckled. Next minute we were out at sea, skimming over the swells, then back to the coast, coming low over beaches, salt-water creeks and mangrove swamps. As we came into land, Ray lowered the wing flaps and the plane nosed forward alarmingly and skimmed over the trees before sinking onto the strip and rolling to a halt. He cut the engines, unplugged the microphone, and I climbed down, glad to feel mother earth firmly under my feet. But Ray had given me a peep of an eagle's world, and I was hooked on flight.

At dawn on 10 November our morning peace was shattered by Hercules engines overhead as Ray Whyte, 'Oggie' and his friends flew out to attack the Japanese in the Tanimbar Islands. Now it was our turn to wish them good luck. And they needed it. On his return, 'Oggie' told me that as he swooped in low, raking the Japanese with his cannon, their anti-aircraft shells had been bursting just below his wings.

As the sun moved further south, conditions on board became even worse. A bucket of sea water left standing in direct sunlight for half an hour became scalding, and mildew, cockroaches and bugs were our constant companions. When in harbour, some off-duty sailors went naked. Our wardroom meals, prepared in the for'ard galley, were carried by the acting steward along the deck and down to the wardroom table, so that from the table our first view of him would be his feet on the companionway steps as he descended, holding our dinners on a tray before him. On one memorable occasion the steward, a tall, well-built youth, came down the steps completely naked, with a sweaty section of his anatomy swaying above our plates. Reg, generally mild-mannered, exploded in rage, and our last view of the steward was his bare bottom and legs flying up the steps faster than they had ever moved before.

On 5 December a group of army officers and nursing sisters from the hospital planned a picnic in the launch *Valmarie* to Talc Head, several miles across the harbour from the town. Reg had been invited and, as our ship was at immediate notice for sea and he could not leave it for any length of time, he obtained permission to take ML *814* across to Talc Head so that the crew could have a 'recreational swim off the beach'. As we would be out of sight of the signal station, we were to keep a constant wireless watch.

The outing had been planned like a military operation but, like many military operations, it did not work out quite as expected. The *Valmarie* left early with a mixed dozen of soldiers and sisters and several mixed dozen bottles of beer and other refreshments to complement the more solid delights provided by the hospital kitchen. We followed later with more of the sisters, anchoring close to the launch just off the beach.

After Reg and the girls had gone ashore, the rest of us settled down for a quiet day on board. Some fished or washed their clothes—

a constant chore—while others began diving or jumping from the wing of the bridge about 15 feet above the water, taking care to keep well clear of the steel guardrails on the deck below. After several successful dives, John Dowey, in throwing himself out from the bridge, slipped, twisted in the air, struck the guardrail and crashed onto the armour-plated deck. Rushing down, I found him unconscious with blood running from a deep gash over his right eye. We carried him to the quarterdeck, laid him out and tried to assess the damage. He had bruises and abrasions on his arms and legs and had gone an alarming bluish-white colour, but I was relieved to find his pulse still throbbing. I pressed my thumb into the hole in his head to stop the bleeding while Jack Old went for the medical chest and D'Arcy Kelly hoisted the Church Pennant—the General Recall signal—to attract attention from the beach. I also sent a man in the dinghy to get Reg and ask if one of the sisters could come on board to stitch the wound. In the meantime we cleaned his forehead and applied a field dressing from the medicine chest, while one of the sailors fanned John's face. After a few minutes, to our relief, he opened his eyes.

Reg was unmoved by our call for help. The party on the beach was in full swing and was not to be disturbed; he instructed me to take John to Darwin and signal for an ambulance to meet us there. Then we were to return to Talc Head and pick him up. This round voyage of 9 miles was a challenge for me: it was the first time I had been officially in command of the ship, and I was relieved when we had landed John and returned to Talc Head by mid-afternoon without mishap.

My experience with the ship caught under the jetty should have taught me to respect Darwin's tides, but I was still careless, and that afternoon they nearly got me. Towards sunset, with no sign of the picnic breaking up and most of the men on board resting below, I dived overboard for a short swim, confident that a few strokes would bring me back to the Jacob's-ladder rigged over the side. Since we had anchored, I had not noticed the tide strengthening, and on surfacing I was shocked to see the ship sliding away from me, and realised with a chill that I was being swept swiftly out to sea. I could see no one on deck, and knew that unless I could reach that ladder quickly this would probably be my last dip. I am not a strong swimmer but, with fear and pumping adrenalin spurring me on, I struck out furiously and reached the ladder so exhausted that I had to cling to it for several minutes until I had sufficient strength to climb aboard.

At sunset Reg started waving his arms on the beach, sending a semaphore message ordering me to take the ship back to No. 5 buoy, adding that he would return later in *Valmarie*. This would not be easy. It was now dark, the tide was setting strongly, and there was no other officer on board to help with the navigation. Before leaving, I carefully calculated the distances and compass courses to steer, and after some anxious moments arrived safely back at No. 5 buoy. It had been an eventful day: I had gained a lasting respect for Darwin's tides and some useful ship-handling experience. And I had been very lucky. Reg also had been lucky, as he might well have lost both his officers.

Shortly before Christmas, hampers and parcels began to arrive. On 17 December I received a cake with almond icing made by Lizzie Sherwood, who had come to the rectory at Seven Hills in the 1920s. It had travelled well through the desert and I was miserly with it, only doling out little pieces to John and Reg. Letters from friends and relations told of other gifts on the way—mostly dried fruits and nuts, books and cigarettes. Everyone on board received a hamper from the Australian Comforts Fund: mine contained a face washer, handkerchief, shaving cream, toothpaste, plum pudding, Christmas cake, writing paper, envelopes, tobacco, cigarette papers, chocolate, chewing gum, tinned fruit and cream.

On Christmas Day *Tonga* moored alongside us and we shared our dinners. Max Mattingly, Reg, John and I ate ours on a card table on deck under a makeshift awning. The Salvation Army had sent some tinned turkey and ham, the cook had valiantly baked potatoes in the furnace-like galley, and as well as our canned vegetables and fruit, there was a Christmas pudding, made by the telegraphist's mother, and big enough for everyone to have a thin slice. We had not seen food like this for months, and as the wicks of our two kerosene-operated refrigerators had been carefully trimmed, we also had at least one glass of something cool to drink. John and I drank water, leaving Reg and Max to drink a bottle of beer. It was vastly different from the Christmases I had known, with carols, organ, choir and the high feast at 'Chislehurst'.

On this, the Empire's fifth Christmas at war, there was little peace for Darwin's naval signallers, who were kept busy sending messages of encouragement and good cheer. One was from the Prime Minister of Australia, John Curtin:

> At this period of Xmas I offer you all the deep gratitude of the Australian Govt. & people. For many of you this is the 5th. Xmas in the Australian fighting forces. Wherever you may be, and whatever dangers you may have survived, and whatever hazards lie ahead, be certain of one thing, the nation has been behind you as the final victory draws near. The year closing has been the brightest of the whole war, and one on which you can look back with pride. On every front the United Nations are on the attack. The enemy, whether in the Pacific or Europe or the Atlantic, is feeling the growing strength of Allied striking power. It has been for you a year of privation & hardship, and often agony. In New Guinea especially you have done things under conditions which fighting men nowhere in any war have ever suffered. To Australian fighting forces everywhere, throughout the Pacific, in the Mediterranean, Canada and Britain, in the Navy, with the Merchant Marine, the Army & Air Force & with the Women's Services I send the warmest thoughts & thanksgiving. Let us pray that next Xmas will see you all back victorious in your home and for whose security you have offered all there is to give.

Curtin's patriotism breathes through this signal. It seemed to come from his heart and chimes with the simple epitaph on his grave:

> *His country was his pride,*
> *His brother man his cause.*

On 2 January 1944 I sent my New Year's greetings to the family in a twelve-page letter. I was less optimistic than the Prime Minister about our victorious return home that year and if, on New Year's Day, our 2000 gallons of high-octane petrol had been a bit closer to a lightning strike, none of us would have got home at all.

> Dear Mum and Dad
> Well, all the best for 1944 & let's hope it brings the end of the war a lot nearer.
> We had a 'close go' yesterday morning just before dawn, a tropical storm ... there was a terrific pillar of fire which was bluish white, it came straight down ... with a great hissing rushing sound and burst about 20 feet above the water about 50 yards away sending sparks and forks of flame of blinding brightness ... all over the place. It was instantaneously accompanied by a most terrific explosion, louder than I have ever heard ... John was lying flat on the deck and a man standing with his hand on a steel shroud was knocked flat by an electric shock ...

Having already told my parents that I did not expect to see them again for many months, my next letter from ML *814*, written on 14 January 1944, told them I expected to be home in a week. And that was a pretty good guess. Nine days later I wrote to them again from a bed in a Sydney naval hospital.

For some weeks I had been having difficulty with my vision, and was losing my balance. The Port Medical Officer sent me to the army hospital at Katherine to see Colonel Lorimer Dods[1]—a 200-mile journey by steam train and truck. The hospital was a brown canvas town; I slept in a tent near the river and lived like a king. Once more I was in a land of ease and plenty and every day was sheer delight. I read, showered several times a day and ate well. I swam in the Katherine River, and at night dined in the officers' mess with girls from the Australian Army Medical Women's Service. And I was paid for it! After several days I was examined by a panel of doctors, headed by Colonel

Dods. Concluding that I was deficient in vitamin B, which was associated with beriberi, he ordered that I be sent at once to a hospital in a southern state for treatment.

Euphoric, I set off back to Darwin by rail. The carriages on the rocky little train from Adelaide River were fitted with tiered wooden bunks and as we puffed and rattled along through the night the haunting words of the soldier's poem kept running through my mind:

> What's awhirl within my brain
> While I'm sleeping in the train? …
> Fleeting dreams that twist and double
> Break and burst like pin-pricked bubble,
> Nights on leave and girls at dances
> Days in swamp and rain.

As yet I knew little of days in swamp and rain, but I did know that this was no fleeting dream about to burst, and that I was off to the cool south, leave, and perhaps even the chance of meeting girls at dances.

Despite the joys awaiting me, it was hard to leave *814*. We had been a close-knit family, bonded by hard service, and I knew I would never find better companions. However, John Dowey's star was rising fast. A few weeks before he had been a nineteen-year-old midshipman. Now, fully recovered from his head wound, he was an acting sub lieutenant and second-in-command of a warship in waters still dominated by the Japanese.

I packed my sea-bag and, just before my last farewells, walked around the ship to say my goodbye to her too and, thinking about our adventures together, remembered the Japanese ensign now in the locker under the chart table. When it had been thrust into my hands I had not been asked to sign for it, and when we got back from Timor no one had wanted to know about it. Thinking it might one day be of historical interest, I jammed it into the top of my sea-bag, looked for the last time on familiar faces, and set off for Sydney and some easy living.[2]

7 | EASY LIVING

The journey south was something of an adventure in itself; I was to fly to Brisbane, then take a troop train to Sydney, and in company with Charles Inman, who had just completed a long period of service as captain of ML *815*, I drove by Jeep to Darwin Airport. Our plane—a civilian De Havilland 86 Commonwealth-class biplane—stood waiting for us in front of a battered hangar and I approached it with some misgivings. Apart from the fact that this was only my second flight it was a sister to the VH-USF in which John Dowey had flown north to join us several months before and which, in taking off from Roma, had ground-looped, rolled on to its side and ended in a crumpled heap with a smashed wing. There had been no casualties, but it added to my apprehension.

It promised to be an interesting flight, however. Formerly used by Qantas on the Brisbane–Singapore leg of its London service, our plane had a range of 760 miles, and on the 2028-mile run from Darwin to Brisbane we would have to set down frequently to refuel. Qantas had established twelve landing fields about 168 miles apart along the route, and we would be calling in at some of the most remote air-strips in outback Australia.

The initial stop on our aerial odyssey was Katharine, where we stayed the night. Its hostel was the first establishment of its kind encountered by troops returning from the war zone, and its domestic staff the first women many of them had seen for months. The habits of many men reflected the all-male conditions under which they had been living, and Guinea Airways, which ran a weekly service between Adelaide and Darwin, had posted a notice above the reception desk:

Gentlemen, please modify your language and adjust your dress as there are women working in this establishment for your convenience.

On Charles blandly enquiring about the nature of this work, the burly proprietor, whose own conduct took little cognisance of this injunction, treated us to an outburst which also needed much modification.

Next morning, after a hurried breakfast at 5 a.m., we climbed back into the plane to find the pilot and local Qantas engineers discussing aerodynamics, with particular reference to the peculiarities of our aircraft. Frozen in our seats, we heard the pilot describe how, on the way from Darwin, it had been flying with its port wings low, and how he had to continually apply starboard aileron to keep it level. What would he do, he asked the engineer, if, on the next leg across the desert, the port wings continued to sink? In response, the engineer strolled languidly back to the hangar, returned with a shifting spanner and, putting his ear against the wires bracing the upper and lower wings, began twanging them and tightening nuts, his expression concentrated like that of a doctor using a stethoscope. After doing this for several minutes he had apparently achieved satisfactory pitch, and we took off, climbed to 200 feet and headed south in the pre-dawn darkness. An hour later the sun rose over the flat desert horizon like a ball of red fire.

The rest of the day passed in something of a blur, as we put down at a series of air-strips, most of them little more than paddocks with tin sheds. At Daly Waters, which I dismissed in my diary as 'merely a stunted group of trees around a dusty strip set in the midst of miles and miles of Nothingness', we were directed to an oven-hot iron shed shimmering in the sun, where we swallowed a tired meat sandwich and flushed it down with a cup of tepid tea.

On we went southwards, flying sometimes at barely 500 feet, the endless miles of desert country with its red-brown earth, stunted bushes and bleached animal bones rolling under our wings like a strip of scenery on a huge revolving drum turning round and round beneath us. Occasionally we would pick up a track leading to a small house in a clump of trees, with a litter of petrol drums and farm machinery nearby. At one place, as we flashed past at about 200 feet, a woman with a baby in her arms came out and waved; it shocked me to think that this might be her only other human contact that day.

At Camooweal, after crossing the border into Queensland, an Aboriginal girl served us a hot roast dinner in yet another stifling tin-roofed shed; then, taking off once more, we flew towards Mount Isa. The country was now grand and rugged and the air more turbulent and, as we approached the town at 3000 feet, a violent bump hurled us from our seats and sent luggage flying from the open racks above our heads. The pilot, momentarily unseated, received a bad crack on the head and, when he turned around to grin reassuringly at us, I noticed a small trickle of blood running from a cut on his scalp.

Mount Isa's aerodrome—a dustbowl—lay in an amphitheatre surrounded by bold hills, and the temperature in the building where we waited for our next flight registered 115° Fahrenheit. Then it was on to Winton and, finally, after flying over Queensland's mid-west cattle country, we landed late in the day at Longreach.

Now we were back in a civilian world we had not seen for many months, and our spirits rose at the sight of shops, houses with curtains in the windows, and women and children in colourful clothes. Our accommodation in the town's principal hotel was, by comparison with that of the previous night, near luxury: Charles and I each had a room opening onto a wide verandah and, in place of the grubby blankets to which we had long been accustomed, our beds were made up with crisp white sheets. This was so novel as to be disturbing: several times I woke wondering where I was, and noted in my diary next day that, unlike those nights in a scorpion-ridden tent at the Scout Jamboree, I had not 'slept well'.

> After taking off for Roma at dawn the next morning, we ran into heavy rain. The temperature dropped dramatically, and Charles and I, wearing only shorts and shirts, and shivering with cold, marvelled at the waterlogged land beneath us. When the pilot climbed to 2000 feet over the Darling Downs, the picture changed again: Farms are dotted about below us with a patchwork effect ... ploughed land and brilliant green of standing crops. Ahead of us are mountains over which we will be passing in a few minutes but may not see much of as we are just entering a layer of cloud—the dark wisps are tearing past, giving to an otherwise seemingly stationary aircraft, suspended in space, an effect of hurrying speed. This is glorious country. How strange it is to shiver and feel cold again.

In Brisbane, where I joined a troop train for Sydney, my easy living began. Conditions on these trains—especially if packed with servicemen heading north towards the war zone—were frequently nightmarish, but this was not crowded, and my status as an officer and invalid earned me the rare privilege of a sleeper.

Then it was only a short trip by car from Central Station to Darling Point and the haven of the naval hospital, Canonbury. This handsome house, built in the 1930s by the Tivoli Circuit entrepreneur Harry Rickards, was set in well-tended gardens running down to a stone wall at the harbour's edge. I was astonished and delighted to find myself in such elegant surroundings, but the contrast between this and my Darwin existence was so marked that it took me some time to relax and enjoy it. By day I lay mostly on my bed, gazing across a sunny terrace to the harbour's glittering prospect and reading, but at night my dreams transported me relentlessly back to *814*'s sticky wardroom, its cockroaches, mildew and bugs, and on waking I would feel disoriented and depressed. Even when that had passed and I had again abandoned myself to Canonbury's luxury, there remained a feeling of disbelief at my good fortune. Writing to my parents who were holidaying in the Blue Mountains, I reported that life was one continual feast:

> They are feeding me like a King—as much milk and orange juice as I can drink, & fresh vegs, eggs, meat, special pills, injections— if I don't get fat here I never will ... They are giving me a glass of Stout a day which altho' I told them I didn't like or want it, they said I had to have it, it is full of malt & hops and supposed to give you an appetite and make you fat.

In the next bed to me lay the emaciated figure of Lieutenant Commander George Tancred RAN, a renowned hydrographer, who had recently been charting the north coast of New Guinea under the very guns of the Japanese. Now, ravaged by malaria he looked to me like a dying man, his body a sickly saffron colour from his taking atebrin tablets, and his sunken bright eyes and his fits of shivering and sweating so upset me that when they gripped him I tried to look away.

While at Canonbury I received my first campaign ribbon—then known as the '1939–1943 Star'. Awarded to those who had been on active service between 1939 and 1943, it had three stripes: dark blue for the Navy; red for the blood of the Army; and light blue for the Air Force's battleground in the sky. In 1944 these ribbons were quite rare and I was proud of the little splash of colour on the left breast of my jacket. Subsequently, the qualifying period for this star was extended to the end of the war, and it became the '1939–1945 Star' or, as some irreverently described it, the 'EBM'—everybody's medal.

By mid-March 1944 my incipient beriberi was cured and, after taking fourteen days leave, I reported to the Fairmile Officers' Pool at HMAS *Rushcutter*. My immediate future lay in the hands of Lieutenant Commander Peter Anthill RANVR, a former racing-car driver and, having heard that the Fairmiles on the coast of New Guinea were having an exciting time bombarding shore positions, chasing Japanese barges and sometimes moving ahead of our troops fighting their way westward along the coast, I asked him to post me as first lieutenant to one of them. But, although sympathetic to my request, Antill replied that this was not possible, since my hospital discharge papers had put an embargo on tropical service for six months. Instead I was appointed first lieutenant of ML *823*, then operating off the New South Wales coast. Despite this setback, Peter and I became friends, and his invitation to me after the war to join him in founding a trucking business, which eventually became part of the transport company Antill Ranger, was one of the many post-war career opportunities with which I flirted and rejected. At *Rushcutter* I also renewed my friendship with Jim Morrison, my classmate from Flinders' days and my opposite number in ML *815* in Darwin. He had been recalled to become captain of an HDML—a smaller type of patrol boat than a Fairmile—and to celebrate his elevation we dined in style at Kings Cross before going on to the theatre and to see Edwin Styles playing in *Rope*.

I joined ML *823* in Sydney and found another life-long friend in her commander, Lieutenant Norman Bryan Wallis DSC, RANVR, whom we all called 'Captain'. The stocky 35-year-old Wallis, hero of the famous British commando raid on St Nazaire, who had been brought back to Australia to train Fairmilers, was to become a powerful influence on my life. An individualist and man of strong opinions, he was at times a law unto himself.

Educated at Sydney Church of England Grammar School and the University of Sydney, from which he had graduated in Economics in 1933, he received a commission in the Navy and was sent to England in 1940. There he became the captain of Fairmile ML *307*. In 1942 she had been one of three survivors of eighteen Fairmiles and motor torpedo boats which had attacked the German naval base at St Nazaire. For his part in this action, described by Churchill as a 'brilliant and heroic exploit … a deed of glory involved in high strategy', Wallis was awarded the Distinguished Service Cross. The black band around

823's funnel signified that she was the Fairmiles' flotilla leader, and I was proud to serve as his first lieutenant.

From Sydney we sailed immediately for Coffs Harbour, the 275-mile passage recalling for me the first leg of *814*'s voyage to Darwin. We kept about 10 miles offshore and had a lively run in a tumbling sea, but after three months on land I felt I was back in the real world.

The north coast of New South Wales was a dramatic contrast to the flat, hot dreariness of Arnhem Land. Here were thickly forested mountains, bold headlands, powerful rivers, and pretty little boat harbours. And none was more picturesque, or welcome to a sailor, than 'Coffs', as we called it. With its massive jetty built to freight the region's timber, fruit and dairy produce to their markets, Coffs was protected by two islands and two breakwaters. One ran out from the northern end of the harbour's beach to Mutton Bird Island half a mile offshore, and the other—later nearly my nemesis—extended north-east for about 500 yards from South Coffs Island, which almost joined the shore. These breakwaters protected the harbour; but in heavy easterly weather, a big swell rolling in through the entrance made it difficult to enter or leave it and raised a steep surf on the beach. In such conditions it was dangerous for a Fairmile to lie alongside the jetty, or even for men to disembark there from a dinghy.

Service on this temperate and spectacular coast was like a holiday on full pay. Although food still featured largely in my letters, I was now carolling its abundance: 'Fresh milk, butter, eggs, fish, fresh vegetables, etc.—do not send me anything.' And apart from this freedom from want, there was much else to be grateful for:

> Great to lie in my bunk at night lulled by the continual easy roll
> of the ship to the ground swell in the harbour, and look out of
> the porthole at the waves breaking on the beach about $\frac{1}{4}$ mile
> away—all steeped in silvery moonlight …

In the absence of extreme heat and humidity, even the discomfort of continuous driving rain could seem a blessing:

It is raining steadily outside and there is a mist and a fresh breeze from the south-east making us roll. I can hear the rain pattering on the deck above my head, &, when it gets hard hissing on the surface of the sea. We cannot poke our heads out of the hatch unless we are covered with oilskins, sea boots and Sou'westers; and even then the driving rain finds chinks in the armour & it trickles down the cracks around the necks. But I like it. Everything is fresh and damp, and clean and beautifully cool … I am enjoying today very much. The captain is not aboard, it is our day in, and the radio is playing soft music, all our work is just about done, I have my history book, a good novel and several letters to write—and plenty of good food, & everything is so dry and snug below decks, and cold and wet outside—so everything is happy.

This easy living was even more relaxed because, as we were the only naval ship in Coffs Harbour, there was no signal tower to summon us with flashing commands. We had regular duties and responsibilities but, apart from that, unless we received a submarine report or a ship was attacked in our vicinity, no one would trouble us. When not at sea, we kept a wireless watch at certain hours in case the Navy wanted to contact us; at other times, if something urgent cropped up, they would send us a telegram. This was delivered by the local postman; he would come down to the jetty, halloo across the water, and wait patiently until the duty watch-keeper rowed over in the dinghy to collect it. Most days at sea were spent on Asdic patrols and challenging merchant ships, calling on them to identify themselves and declare their destinations. When returning to harbour for the night we often stopped to throw a few fishing lines overboard, usually catching far more than we could eat. On off-duty days in the harbour, we swam, played sports on the beach and shot rabbits on Mutton Bird and South Coffs Islands.

Soon we were caught up in the town's social life. The people of Coffs took us to their hearts. They were pleased to have fresh blood in the town and we were overwhelmed by their hospitality.

The postmaster, Bert Yoole, became a special friend and his home our haven: after a spell at sea we could be sure of finding a hot bath and clean towels at Bert's. He often came aboard after work for a convivial drink, and when we were not taking his daughters to dances or the pictures, we would join the family around their dinner table. Like all country women of that time, 'Mother' Yoole was a marvel in the kitchen, and once, after we had returned from a long hard patrol in wild weather, she sacrificed her best 'chook' for us. The memory of that roast chicken, potatoes, pumpkin and home-grown beans remains with me still. Our hostess had other accomplishments: after dinner she would seat herself at the piano and bang out all the old favourites— 'Land of Hope and Glory', 'Old Lang Syne', 'It's a Long Way to Tipperary', 'Once a Jolly Swagman', and—for our friends still out there —'Eternal Father Strong to Save'—while we all sang along lustily.

At the beginning of 1944, although Japan had largely withdrawn her submarines from the Australian coast, the risk of an isolated attack by a roving submarine remained, and on our beat between Evans Head to the north and Smoky Cape, about 37 miles south of Coffs Harbour, we continually listened for echoes. As we could distinguish between different types—those from a whale, a reef on the ocean floor which might not have been marked on our Admiralty chart, and a school of fish—we soon discovered two excellent fishing areas, one about half a mile east of Split Solitary Island, where the bottom of the sea rises steeply from 12 to 3.5 fathoms, and the other 2.5 miles to the north-north-east.

Hudson and Anson aircraft from the Air Station at Coffs Harbour also patrolled the coast, sometimes carrying out bombing practice at sea, and together we planned a fishing operation which would combine our ability to locate fish with their capacity to stun them with bombs. The scheme worked well and produced some splendid catches. If, in the course of our patrols, we located a sizeable school of fish, and if a patrolling aircraft was nearby, we could signal him by Aldis lamp, drop a silver dye-marker over the spot, then turn away fast while the aircraft swooped in low to drop a bomb on the stain. Returning to the scene, we would scoop up the stunned fish with nets and, on reaching port, would find a RAAF ambulance on the jetty waiting to collect their share of the spoils.

But then we discovered a fishing ground against which all others paled into insignificance. We were on patrol and navigating by Admiralty Chart 1026: *The Solitary Islands and Adjacent Coast*, which was something of an elegant nineteenth-century traveller's guide and a lovely thing to use. Its copperplate, meticulously engraved in 1865 with charming little coastal vignettes showing the appearance of the land from offshore, must have been a godsend to many a long-dead mariner. But it showed few depths outside the 30-fathom line, and while patrolling there one day we discovered, through the medium of modern British science, a fisherman's paradise.

We had been slipping easily along over a calm sea at about 10 knots with our Asdic set pinging away monotonously, when suddenly the operator called out 'Echoes!', and everyone sprang to attention. On the bridge we could hear them through the voice-pipe to the wheel-house below; they were sharp—which might indicate a submarine, a wreck or perhaps a whale. The object was not moving and after cautious investigation we pronounced it an unmarked reef. The presence of a reef so far off the coast promised good fishing, and I carefully noted its position on the chart, making a pencil sketch relating the position to two islands and a prominent mark on a distant hill.

Some days later, returning from patrolling that patch of ocean, we stopped to test it. Rigging hand lines with three hooks on traces with a heavy lump of lead on the end, we dropped them until the lead hit the bottom. I have never seen such fishing. The response to our baits was so immediate that we tired of constantly hauling in a fish and learned to wait until we could bring in two or three at once. There must have been hundreds of snapper, morwong and other fish down there.

Working the reef now became standard practice when our patrol took us in that direction and its yield was prodigious; on one occasion eight of us caught 300 pounds of fish in two hours—the greatest haul being made by 'Captain'. I still have a faded photo of him, wearing nothing but a pair of shorts and holding a superb morwong, standing on a deck covered with fish.

Now we had a problem: the temptation to continue reaping this harvest was irresistible, but we were catching far more than we could eat and, looking around for an outlet for our surplus stock, we lit upon the Refreshment Room at Coffs Harbour Railway Station, constantly besieged by hungry men on troop trains. Its manager was only too glad to pay a shilling a pound for our catch. And so began a small co-operative business in which everyone on board became a working partner. Some caught the fish, some scaled and others gutted and cleaned; I kept the books and arranged for the fish to be collected on the jetty. The enterprise prospered, and by the time we went to Sydney for an engine overhaul we had enough money to buy amenities for the crew: two sets of cricket stumps, two bats, several balls, pads, sporting equipment for beach games, and a wireless for the sailors in the mess deck.

On 8 June while patrolling towards Smoky Cape, we sighted the masts of a ship on the horizon and clapped on speed to investigate. The silhouettes of many ships were familiar to us and, as we closed her, the two small funnels close together amidships and masts with cross-trees, identified her as the Navy's victualling stores issue ship *Merkur*. She had a special interest for me and, being on watch at the time, I brought the Fairmile close up under her bridge and called through a megaphone, 'Is Supply Assistant John Hordern there?' And in a minute my brother appeared. Running up to the signal platform, he stood beside the signalman—none other than D'Arcy Kelly, my friend and companion in ML *814*. We chatted for a few minutes before ML *823* turned away on her southward patrol, and soon the *Merkur* was hull down on the northern horizon. It had been one of those chance war-time meetings at sea between brothers and friends —in this case one carrying supplies for our soldiers fighting the Japanese up north, the other having the time of his life down south.

Four days later we had another sea encounter, this time with whales also on passage to the tropics. Sighting a pod, we altered course to have a closer look. About 60 feet long, they were cruising sedately, but every now and then one would throw its enormous body right out of the water and fall with a crash like a cannon shot, churning the sea into a flurry of foam. On our way back to Coffs we witnessed a much uglier display: a lone whale being attacked by killer whales was trying to escape them by leaping into the air and thrashing the water with its flukes. We had heard that killers harried other whales to exhaustion before tearing out their tongues and, as we were on the lone whale's side, we played with the idea of killing these killers with our Bofors gun. Finally, deciding to let nature take its course, we went on our way, reluctant to witness the bloody finale.

Whenever ML *823* returned to Sydney for an engine overhaul or some duty requiring the flotilla leader's attendance, we were given a temporary captain, and during my time on the ship, three men of widely differing background, appearance and character commanded it, illustrating the diversity of the Navy's family. Lieutenant Eric Sodersten, a small, dapper architect, took life seriously. Meticulous and conscientious on duty, he spent much of his spare time drawing sketches of clipper ships. George Stooke, large and rugged, tended to laugh a lot, except when handling the ship in dangerous conditions. No smiles then. Ray Penny was the most memorable of the three. The softly spoken son of a well-known Sydney solicitor, he was a fine seaman, good companion, and something of a twentieth-century buccaneer.

I can never forget our first meeting. ML *823* was lying at the Fairmile base at HMAS *Rushcutter* and I was sitting in the wardroom writing up the Armament Store Ledger and trying to account for the past month's expenditure of ammunition, some of which had been used for shooting rabbits, ducks and fish. Footsteps on the deck, and an Exodus-like figure with a Mosaic beard came down the companion-way. After announcing that he was my new captain, he got down to business. He was recovering from a bout of malaria, he told me, and as that was a thirsty business he wanted to know the state of the ship's liquor supplies. When I told him, he pronounced it meagre, but set to, reducing it further while treating me to a colourful account of his war.

He had recently starred as captain of the lugger *Fauro Chief* in a cloak-and-dagger affair, landing a party under Lieutenant Mader on Misima Island in the Louisiade Archipelago off the south-eastern tip of Papua New Guinea, to set up a coast-watching station. He had just put them ashore when a Japanese submarine surfaced nearby and sent a well-aimed shot through the lugger's wheelhouse, slightly wounding Ray. His only machine-gun returned fire, the submarine submerged, and he chased it dropping clusters of hand grenades hoping that the Japanese would think them distant depth charges. But although Ray came out of it well the incursion had been a disaster for the soldiers as Lieutenant Mader and his men were all killed by natives loyal to the Japanese.

On another occasion the *Fauro Chief* had been ordered to deliver sacramental wine to the mission station on Samarai Island, about 50 miles from Milne Bay, where they were expecting large Easter congregations. On the first day out, while nosing into a bay for a night's sleep, the lugger had run on a reef and, as it would be several days before the tide would be high enough to float her off, they had made the best of things, playing cards, fishing and swimming. They were still there on Maundy Thursday, and some of the crew, apparently wishing to observe the Holy Week feasts, called on their captain to perform the appropriate divine services. Somewhere between Maundy Thursday and Easter Monday they lost track of what services they had had, and when the lugger at last floated free there was only about a gallon of the wine left. By then, as it was too late to continue to Samarai, they held another 'service' and returned to Milne Bay naval depot, where the authorities, Ray said, had not been very understanding.

During Ray's temporary command of ML *823*, the ship was based in Sydney. He had lodgings nearby and when we had to put to sea at a certain time, I would have the ship ready with her engines turning over. Just before departure, he would speed down Beach Road,

Edgecliff, on a black Waratah two-stroke motorbike, zoom through the depot's gates, across the parade ground and out onto the jetty, parking the bike beside the bridge.

He had only been with us a short time when he was dispatched back to New Guinea and had to sell the Waratah. He offered it to me for £40 and when I countered by saying I had no experience in valuing motorbikes, he expatiated on its reliability and economy, insisted that £40 was a 'sacrifice price' and assured me that in business matters it was his unalterable principle 'never to take a friend down'. I capitulated and we shook hands on it. But, while signing the registration papers, Ray confided that he also had another unalterable business principle—'Never give a sucker an even break'. 'Was I a friend or a sucker?' I asked. To which he answered, 'Ask the Waratah.' I was sorry to see Ray Penny go, but we will cross his tracks again in these memoirs.

As well as receiving temporary commanding officers, from time to time we also had temporary sub lieutenants and midshipmen, and we returned to Coffs Harbour under George Stooke's command with a new midshipman. George was much less familiar with Fairmiles than Norman Wallis, and I, complacent in my piety and seafaring skills, took it upon myself to set the newcomers right, informing the family:

> ... the midshipman is coming along OK. I am training him hard
> and giving him a lot of work—but he and the other one know,
> oh so little about the sea and seamanship, that it is really a
> danger—for there are things like winches, anchor 'chains' etc.
> where, if you don't know what you're about men will get hurt. I
> am teaching him [the midshipman] navigation now—he is a
> good lad, teetotal, Presbyterian & reads the Bible.

This indirect reference to George was unkind, but he had just given us the fright of our lives. We had left harbour with a southerly gale brewing and it had worsened as we headed south with the wind tearing the tops off the steep swells and *823* taking green water over the bow. We were all wet, cold and miserable but, although it was too rough to operate our Asdic, and we were clearly wasting fuel and risking damage to no purpose, George held on doggedly. When the ship began pile-driving, George reduced speed, but continued heading into the teeth of the gale with the watch-keepers, cocooned in oilskins, sou-westers and sea boots, clinging to anything solid in an effort to remain upright. At last, to everyone's relief, George decided to turn and run for home. But by now that was easier said than done. After a few steep seas we had a lull. Down went the helm and round we came with the wind and sea dead astern of our Achilles' heel—the big flat counter—waiting for an overtaking wave to catch it and push us sideways down its slope. But although the sea seemed calmer the powerful swells charging up from Smoky Cape began overtaking us. George increased speed and the ship began yawing and rolling heavily. Then came a nasty moment which I shared with the family:

> On putting about to return to harbour we were caught by a huge wave and broached. I have never experienced such a sickening roll and thought we were gone. Clinging to the deck and looking almost vertically downwards at the angry ocean. We were caught by another which seemed like the end. George Stooke ... thereafter reduced speed and things became more stable.

War-time service often leads to chance meetings with old friends, and in Coffs Harbour I ran into Harry Stoyles, a former classmate at Knox Grammar School, now a warrant officer attached to 71 Squadron RAAF at Coffs Harbour. I invited him and a couple of friends to join us on our next patrol. It was breezing up when they arrived and once we cleared the breakwater ML *823* began leaping about in the lumpy sea with spray sweeping the decks. The airmen, except Harry, were very seasick but back on dry land claimed to have loved it, and in return Harry promised to arrange a flight for me in one of their aircraft.

The breezing up became another winter gale, and for the next two days it sent huge seas crashing over the breakwater, rolling us heavily at the buoy, and, as we were weather-bound, I went to the Air Station to claim my ride. Most of the planes were grounded, but Harry passed me over to his CO, Wing Commander Shorter, who was about to flight-test an Avro Anson. Climbing into a parachute harness recalled my Beaufighter flight, but this time instead of standing behind the pilot and hanging onto his shoulders, I sat in a proper seat and was given the job of manually raising the undercarriage by winding a handle about 120 turns. A force six gale was blowing, and from 2000 feet above the sea I enjoyed being able to watch the commotion below without becoming wet, cold and uncomfortable. The ocean was covered with long white streaks of spume and a sizeable surf was breaking on the harbour's beach; as we returned low over the harbour in very turbulent air, I could see *823* rolling heavily at her buoy. We landed in such a strong wind that the Anson came to a halt in a few seconds. It had been a stimulating jaunt, but returning to the ship, climbing down the slippery jetty ladder and jumping into the dinghy as it surged up on the top of a swell was the most hair-raising part of the day's outing.

For two more days we lay rolling in that gale, with cups, saucers and plates rattling about and sliding off tables. About 3 a.m. one morning the dinghy's painter parted and it was swept away to be smashed to pieces on the rocks. After daylight Stoker O'Neill and I, wearing heavy duffel coats and sea boots, borrowed a fisherman's skiff and went to salvage what we could from the wreck. We saved the oars and rowlocks, but while climbing back aboard the rolling ship I fell into the water. Floundering there in my heavy coat and boots, I was myself salvaged by O'Neill's strong arms.

The series of hard gales, which disrupted coastal shipping and caused widespread damage that winter, also caused some curtailment of my letters home, and my mother, reading press reports of the bad weather, became so worried that on 19 July she sent a telegram saying that they had not heard from me and were anxious. Embarrassed by this public display of maternal concern, I dashed off a sharp note which it pains me to recall and record. It must have hurt my mother but, unlike her, I only kept some war-time letters, and must have thrown out her gentle reply to this broadside:

> The idea of a mother with a son in the Navy, in war time, getting 'anxious' if she doesn't hear every two or three days is very silly. Weather or work may prevent us from writing or the mail being landed ashore, and therefore you have no right to start getting 'anxious' and following me up with telegrams ... it embarrasses me. It would perhaps be justified if you didn't hear from me for a month or so.
>
> I'm sorry to speak like this but I want you to understand the situation.

'Captain's' unpredictability was familiar to us all, but on one occasion it caused me a week of torment and sleepless nights. His wife, Peg, was expecting their first child and there had been a flurry of letters and phone calls to and from Sydney. Returning from the post office one day he looked unusually serious. Pouring himself a stiff whisky, he invited me to a game of chess and, after playing absentmindedly for a few minutes, volunteered that he was worried about his 'girl': the doctor thought the baby could arrive any day and he wanted to be with her. He was therefore giving himself a few days' compassionate leave, leaving on a troop train the next morning and had no idea when he would be back. Then, taking another pull at his glass, he leaned forward, shook my hand and said with a disarming smile, 'From tomorrow morning this ship is yours.'

It was like a punch in the face. I had seldom handled a Fairmile, let alone commanded one at sea. Japanese submarines might be on the coast; what would I do if a conning tower appeared, a submarine began chasing us and this time it was really Japanese? 'Captain,' I pleaded, 'you can't do this to me.' Desperately, I produced arguments: I was inexperienced and it was a bad season for gales. He listened quietly, but when the game was over he simply reiterated that he had complete confidence in me and that he was off in the morning.

Hissing steam and breathing smoke, the large black engine pulled into the station, 'Captain' climbed aboard the train and we shook hands. I wished him luck and said rather tremulously that if it was a boy he might at least call it after me. He gave me a cheery wave from the carriage window, and in a thoughtful mood I walked back along the jetty, climbed down its rusty ladder and rowed out to my unofficial command.

For a couple of days we lay peacefully at the buoy, cleaning guns, checking depth charges and servicing equipment in readiness for our next patrol to Smoky Cape. The night before we were to leave, the glass dropped and a cold southerly wind, gusting to force five in the Beaufort Scale, began scattering white horses across the sea. The midshipman and I listened anxiously to the weather reports, watched the barometer, and studied the *Beaufort Wind Scale* which told us that white horses first appear when the wind was force four, and a force five wind was between 16 and 20 knots. Officially it was a 'strong breeze' which built up waves about 9 feet high with white foam crests and flying spray. But submarines could operate comfortably in that sort of weather and at dawn we were to be out in it looking for them.

During the night wind gusts swept the harbour, sending the halyards slatting against the mast, but the weather got no worse, and at dawn I sent the usual signal that ML *823* was proceeding on patrol. As we went through the breakwater she plunged heavily into the large rollers running through the entrance, and once clear we turned south towards Smoky Cape and started pinging with the Asdic set. The weather worsened and we plunged on, wet and miserable in the cold wind. After a couple of hours it became too rough for the Asdic; I shut the set down and, forgetful of our experience with George Stooke, continued south keeping a visual watch for anything unusual.

About 9 a.m. the wind began gusting to force six, the seas had built up to about 13 feet, and now—more concerned about being at war with nature than the Japanese—I decided to run for home. I warned the men in the engine room to 'hang on', waited for what looked like a lull, and round we went.

Perhaps in retribution for my earlier judgement of George Stooke, I now faced a similar wild ride. The large following seas began picking us up and sending us surfing down their forward slopes, reducing the ability of our two small rudders to control the ship. From out at sea, as I lined up on the navigational leading marks ashore to take us through the breakwater, I could see the rollers heaping up in the entrance and felt frightened. With the leading marks in transit, the track in and out of Coffs Harbour passed only about 130 yards from the end of the eastern breakwater. I reduced speed to about 8 knots and glanced astern to see a succession of very big waves about to overtake us. The first caught the stern, lifted it and gave us a toboggan-like ride, slewing us towards the breakwater. We slipped back off it and I straightened the ship as well as I could by applying a lot of starboard wheel. Then the second wave caught us. This was bigger, and one of 'Captain's' stories flashed through my mind. He had been in a Fairmile entering Appledore on the south coast of England in a similar situation. The ship had broached on a big wave, rolled onto her beam ends, buried her deck rails and depth charges in the sea, and very nearly been lost. The wave flung us forward, again pushing the stern to starboard and shooting us almost out of control down across its face straight for the breakwater, by now very close and smothered with foam and swirling water. No one on the bridge spoke. With the almost useless wheel hard to starboard, the Fairmile was caught by the third wave and shot into the harbour, practically on her side. It was one of the closest calls I was ever to have at sea.

Several days later 'Captain' stepped from the train, smiling broadly. Shaking my hand, he said, 'Thanks, Tony', and told me that mother and son were doing well, and they had called the boy Anthony. It almost made up for that rollercoaster ride.

As the sun moved quickly south winter turned to early spring, and life on the north coast became even better. I described for my family the delights of Coffs Harbour in September:

…we have been having a great time. All we wear is shorts and perhaps a singlet. Just after dawn we slip over the side into the dinghy and row through the sparkling surf to the white sandy beach. Here we play quoit tennis and run around on the sand, dive into the clear water and spend a bit of time shooting the waves and having the time of our lives. Then into the skiff and … out to the ship rolling gently to the low swell a few hundred yards from the beach. After a breakfast of fried eggs, Crispies etc, we are all ready to go to sea … After a day at sea on patrol in the sun and the sea breeze we come back and in the evening we either play chess, cards or go to the local pictures or a dance … last Sunday I went to church and enjoyed the service, tho' the singing was a bit flat. The local Girls' Friendly Society are holding a dance on Thursday to which we are invited.

'Captain' was a great teacher. His most effective method of instruction was to delegate a duty and oversee its performance. Occasionally he would give me the task of drafting his monthly Report of Proceedings, sometimes developing a point or stringing out a comment. He mostly approved of my drafts and did not greatly alter them. He used unimportant incidents to teach his juniors or make them think, and when he said, 'Listen, son,' he generally had something worthwhile to say.

One bright morning he read us a lesson on the dangers of the sea. I held the forenoon watch and, as he stepped onto the bridge, I blithely assured him that everything was 'peaceful and safe'. He glanced at me with half a smile and said, 'Listen, son, there's always danger.' I looked around nervously as he eased his stocky frame into a corner of the bridge, inhaled deeply from the fag end of his cigarette, flicked it into the sea, and launched into one of his favourite pastimes—educating young officers.

We were running north along the coast of New South Wales at 14 knots, comfortably easing our sleek 112 feet over the long Pacific swells. Inshore they broke on reefs shining white in the sun, but they were no danger to us. Off-duty sailors were lounging around the depth charges or leaning against the guns smoking, enjoying the air and watching the coast slip by. All peaceful there too. But we were at war; the Japanese had torpedoed about thirty ships off this coast, including the hospital ship *Centaur*, not far from our present beat. At present, however, our Asdic was picking up no suspicious echoes. 'Captain' lit another cigarette, glanced at the compass, and swept the sea with his binoculars, lingering momentarily on a smudge of smoke on the horizon. The sub lieutenant joined us and, with his congregation doubled, 'Captain' began to preach from one of his favourite texts— 'Blessed are wary sailors, for they shall return to dry land.' He dwelt on the dangers of the sea rather than the violence of the enemy. That, he said, would be broken, but nothing could break the power of the sea. The signalman, arriving with three mugs of kai—chocolate melted in hot milk—stayed to listen. In a few weeks, 'Captain' said, we could be taught to fight, shoot straight and dodge torpedoes and bombs. We knew about guns, revolvers, rockets, signalling, smoke floats, depth charges, scrambling nets and morphine. We knew how to sink a submarine, and understood the rules of war. But the sea waged a ceaseless war against us and many of us were very ignorant of its rules. It took years, he said, to learn real sea-wisdom and, as for my remark about there being no danger—a quick wave of his hand over the sparkling sea—there was our real enemy and few understood that. Many people spoke loosely about 'freak waves'. Freak waves did not exist: all waves behaved in accordance with oceanic law. Every fisherman swept from the rocks by a 'freak wave', everyone drowned on a river bar during a strong ebb tide, had tossed a coin with Father Neptune and lost. And it was the same with swimmers caught in rips, sailors who used the wrong hitches, and officers who failed to check soundings and anchor bearings. They were all gambling with the sea and, the safer things seemed, the more likely they were to gamble. In gales men were on guard but, 'At times like this there's always danger, son.'

'Captain' walked aft to the wardroom leaving some thoughtful young men on the bridge. They had been sitting at the feet of a Gamaliel learning about the laws which governed their lives.

September 1944 marked the end of five years of the world's most destructive conflict. About thirty per cent of my class at school were already dead or soon to die. The war had also left its mark on the family: my cousin, Pilot Officer Peter Hordern RAF had been the first Knox old boy to die for his country in battle; other cousins, John and Henry Hordern, were prisoners of the Japanese; another, Anthony, had returned from the Middle East in a hospital ship and would never walk again; my brothers Hugh and John were in the RAAF and RAN respectively, and there were at least five other relatives in the army.

September merged into October. Having now spent six months in a temperate climate, I was again eligible for tropical service and, as good as his word, Peter Antill had me appointed first lieutenant of ML *817* in New Guinea.

Returned to HMAS *Rushcutter* to wait for transport to New Guinea, I spent my time carrying out odd jobs. The most memorable was to command the naval guard on board the American ship *Admiral Chase* in Sydney Harbour. Her captain—an old salt and born story-teller—welcomed me as a captive audience, feeding me well in his cabin and entertaining me with anecdotes of his adventurous life. Having first gone to sea in 1880 under sail, he had frequently rounded Cape Horn in windjammers, and once had wintered in Spitzbergen where he did not see the sun for months. It was so cold, he assured me, that the barrel of a gun, touched with the bare hand, burned like a red-hot poker. Several times he described proudly how in Spitzbergen, when rations were low, he had gone hunting on the ice and shot a polar bear at midnight by the light of the aurora borealis. In 1906, when his ship's engine had broken down in the Indian Ocean, he set off for help with five Lascars in a 30-foot lifeboat to sail the 700 miles to Africa. When almost there, he had been surprised to see the ship coming up astern over the horizon; refusing to be picked up, he had insisted on finishing the voyage under sail—'just', as he put it, 'to show them I could do it.'

On another occasion, when he was a young mate of a ship bound from Suez to Sydney, the captain, stricken with syphilis, had been too ill to navigate but had refused to be put ashore at Colombo or Singapore. Sitting in his cabin, glass in hand, the old salt's eyes lit up as he described how he had brought the ship alone from the Gulf of Aden to the Torres Strait, down through the Great Barrier Reef and put her alongside the wharf in Sydney. When I said that I, too, had been through the Great Barrier Reef and Torres Strait, and that it was well-charted with plenty of beacons and navigational lights, he replied, 'Ah, but in those days it was not like Piccadilly with lights all the way down on every corner.' Listening to that man was like hearing Conrad talk, and although I made notes on our conversations and we became such friends that I knew I could never forget his name, I did not write it down and have forgotten it. The *Admiral Chase* went on her watery way; my transport orders came through and, after eight months of easy living, I was once again off on my travels.

8 | TOUCHING NEW GUINEA

Anxious to join my new ship in New Guinea quickly I hoped to fly there, but war-time transport was seldom simple and the Navy decided to send me first to Brisbane by troop-train. Ordered to be prepared to leave at short notice and find lodgings in Sydney in the meantime, I returned to the bosom of the family at St Paul's Rectory and made the most of the last home comforts I would enjoy for some time. And they were even more enjoyable as I was paid 'lodging money' for my trouble.

A few days later my travelling orders arrived and, after a last family meal and a prayer for safe keeping and journeying mercies, I loaded my kit into my father's Willys-Overland and he drove me to Central Railway Station. Pushing through the crowd under the domed roof of the concourse I found the departure platform packed with servicemen and their families. I had seen something of troop-trains at Coffs Harbour, but my only journey in one had been my privileged ride down from Brisbane about eight months previously in a sleeper. Now I was to see the other side of the picture. The train was already standing in the station and, seeing no sleeping car among its carriages, I abandoned all hope of a bunk and headed for my allotted seat. Here again, the prospect was not promising. It was in a compartment already crowded with men and baggage, and as the trip to Brisbane would take more than twenty-four hours, I recognised that my chances of sleeping were slim.

While gloomily surveying my prospects for the journey, I was hailed breezily by a naval surgeon lieutenant clutching a bottle. Taking a long pull from it, he announced that he knew all about troop-trains and was fortifying himself for the journey. About five minutes before departure, marshals began barking orders at the troops on the platform to board. They were mostly gathered in little groups—some tearful, some passionate, perhaps making their last farewells—and the doctor was weaving among them, trying to steal a farewell kiss from the more attractive women.

The engine hissed, its whistle blew, and as we slid out of Central Station some old hands began staking out their sleeping berths on the corridor floors. Taking a tip from this, I also began looking for a place to sleep and pegged out a claim on a large wooden luggage rack which ran across the train at the end of the carriage about six feet from the floor. Next day, comfortably quartered in HMAS *Moreton*, I reported home on the journey:

Friday 27 Oct 1944
Dear Mum and Dad,

Well here I am at 10 AM still in Brisbane living in quite comfortable Naval Barracks. We had a good trip up here & I got friendly with a doctor on the train who turned out quite a blessing in disguise. He had some sleeping powders and I took one and he took two. He was quite merry when we left Sydney ... As soon as we got going he undressed in the corridor and put on some old clothes—then he got a bottle of whisky and with a couple of others drank it all and became fairly drunk. I had climbed up into that luggage rack that runs right across the train and had been sleeping quietly for an hour or so, when I saw a tottering figure trying to lever itself on to the rack too—and as you know they are not too big. With cries of 'hold on Tony Old

Man I'm coming up' he got safely up and then passed out on the rack and snored like a pig all night. He is a Naval Lieut. and really quite a nice chap. He slept for about 8 hours, and half the time my feet were in his face or stomach, but he didn't mind. It was crowded on the rack with two. I slept for about 5 hours intermittently & had to wake up the doc for breakfast at Coffs. I saw my old ship there and would have liked to visit her but no time.

There is a hold up in our air transport to NG ... tho' I met a Yankee Colonel last night who is trying to get me on Liberator so I may go tonight ...

The 'Yankee Colonel' had sat next to me at dinner and when I told him I wanted to get to Milne Bay as quickly as I could, he said he thought he could get me onto one of the American Liberators which were crossing the Coral Sea to Port Moresby all the time. Once there, he said, it would be simple to get another ride to Milne Bay. But, just as I was enjoying the prospect of flying on an American bomber, orders arrived for me to be at Archerfield aerodrome at 2 a.m. next morning to board a United States DC2 flying directly to Milne Bay.

Archerfield aerodrome was like a beehive on a summer's day, and nearly all the workers were See Bees, the black American navy construction-corps men. Most of the planes were camouflaged with green and brown paint and the air throbbed with the roar of engines as heavily laden transports lifted from the runway, lumbered into the sky and turned north. Other aircraft, standing in the glare of lights with their cargo hatches open, were being loaded from US Army trucks. I had never seen a fork-lift machine before and watched in amazement as men loaded the stores, arms and steel mesh for the muddy airstrips being hacked out of tropical jungles to our north. Each load was shoved through the door, dragged forward and lashed down to rings on the floor. The doors closed, and the heavily laden machine taxied onto the runway and disappeared into the darkness. Watching this display of power, technology and wealth, I marvelled that the Japanese had had the temerity to attack America.

A few DC2s also stood on the tarmac, doors open, boarding ladders down, ready for their human freight. I climbed into one, stowed my kit bag and seated myself on the bench running along the starboard side of its fuselage. Two airmen strolled across to the machine, climbed into the cockpit and started the engines, filling the cabin with noise and vibration. At 3 a.m. we trundled down the runway and as we climbed away the lights of Brisbane spread themselves beneath our wings like a vast sparkling carpet. This first night flight so fascinated me that I kept my nose to the Perspex window until all pinpoints of light had disappeared in the inky blackness below.

As we gained altitude it grew very cold and the almost deafening noise of the engines made even a shouted conversation practically impossible. After about half an hour the cabin began to glow with a strange light shining through the windows behind my back. I looked round and felt the now familiar sick feeling of fear in my stomach which I had first known in the *Abraham Crijnssen*. The starboard engine was on fire. Flames and bursts of light like small explosions were erupting from it a couple of feet behind the wing.

The pilot shut the engine down and the roar in our ears diminished as he made a flat 180-degree turn and headed back to Brisbane. We had no parachutes and I sat frozen, waiting for the other engine to fail. The DC2 felt squashy in the air and, although I had no way of judging its speed, we seemed to be flying quite slowly. When the lights of Brisbane reappeared ahead, my appreciation of them was even greater than before. After a very bumpy landing we rolled to a stop and I climbed down the boarding ladder grateful to feel solid earth under my feet again.

Within a few minutes of landing I was in another plane flying north again in inky darkness. Dawn's light allowed me a closer inspection of the interior of this flying troop-train, and one of the first things I noticed was that the Perspex windows along either side of the cabin had holes about four inches in diameter. Their centres were fitted with plugs attached by small chains to the fuselage. When I asked an American sitting next to me what they were for, he explained that if we were attacked by Japanese fighters we could fire through them with our pistols or carbines.

Landing in Townsville, we trooped out into the sticky heat, half dead from engine noise, and swallowed a warm meat sandwich and a mug of tea. Then, rejoining the plane, we droned on for hours over a blue-green sea blotched with cloud shadows until the dark spine of a New Guinea mountain range appeared ahead. Crossing the coast, we dropped down to about 500 feet and flew along the shore of Milne Bay, where the Japanese had been first defeated by Australian troops after savage fighting. Beneath us lay the debris of that battle—sunken ships, wrecked motor transport and aircraft, and roads and airstrips hacked out of jungle. As we came in to land I could see Jeeps and trucks slithering along muddy tracks flanked with bomb and shell craters. We banked steeply over what had once been a copra plantation; now, most of its graceful trees had lost their feathered crowns and their scarred trunks stood like rows of telegraph posts. We hit the ground hard, bounced very heavily a couple of times and rolled to a stop on an airstrip surfaced with the steel-mesh frames I had watched being loaded into aircraft at Archerfield. A crewman opened the door and I stepped into a blanket of sticky heat.

A Jeep collected me and we rattled along the rough track beside the bay to HMAS *Ladava*, the Milne Bay Navy depot, and thence down to ML *817* nudging the jetty in the flooding tide. At first sight she was something of a shock. Her faded jungle-green paint was shabby, and the rust on her depth-charge racks, gun mountings and guardrails spoke of hard service and low maintenance and, all fresh to the scene, I began making mental notes and plans to smarten her up. But that first shock was nothing to my next discovery. Close to the White Ensign just above the bridge, a man's skull with a bullet hole near his right eye-socket was wired to the mast and cross-trees.

The watch-keeper led me to the wardroom hatch and, descending the companionway, I breathed again that familiar sickly smell of fungus, bugs and cockroaches in the stuffy air. In the wardroom three men in sweaty shorts and shirts confronted me; the captain, Lieutenant

John Doyle RANR(S), told me they had been expecting me for weeks and asked me pointedly what had kept me. He introduced the first lieutenant, Sub Lieutenant Frank Horner, whom I was to relieve, and the third officer, Midshipman Clem McMahon. Then, over a round of drinks, I settled down to learn what I could about these men and what sort of war they were having.

Doyle—'Johnnie' to his friends—was a brown-haired man about my size with a sharpish nose and, notwithstanding the awkwardness of our first meeting, we became good friends. Like Chapman in the *Abraham Crijnssen*, he had been reared as a cadet in the Merchant Service and mobilised by the navy when war seemed imminent. Although he was a highly competent seaman and a first-rate navigator, Johnnie was not a popular captain: in a recent fracas on board he had been punched in the face by one of the men. Frank Horner, gentle and scholarly, left the ship shortly after I joined her, but we kept in touch for over fifty-seven years. Clem McMahon and I hit it off so well that when I later got a ship of my own, I arranged for him to become her first lieutenant.

While I had been enjoying easy living in the cool south, ML *817*'s men had been earning their few extra pence a day 'Hard Lying' money on New Guinea's hot north coast, patrolling westwards as far as Hansa Bay ahead of the 6th Division's advance along the shore. She had supported the Australian landing on Karkar Island, and worked with American PT boats at Mios Woendi off Biak Island, intercepting Japanese submarines evacuating senior officers at night. More recently ML *817* had been on what Johnnie called 'Samarai escort duty'—a cushy job, meeting Liberty ships arriving from America and leading them through the narrow, fast-flowing China Strait.

When I asked about the skull on the mast, the gentle Frank didn't want to discuss it, but I pressed the question and got a gruesome story. Fairmilers working with the army had often been ashore in recent battlegrounds where Japanese bodies still lay about. Apparently some of *817*'s crew had found this skull, brought it back on board, called it 'Percy', stuck it up on the mast and then forgotten about it. It disconcerted me, but further questioning produced such an awkward silence that I gave up. From the distance of about sixty years, the very thought of a man's head wired to the mast of a warship wearing the White Ensign shocks me. It shocked me then too, for I had had little experience of the aftermath of land battles. And when I later saw heads stuck up on posts in Hollandia in Dutch New Guinea and photographed one outside the RAAF headquarters there, I realised that such displays were not peculiar to any nation or service.

For to everything there is a season. In 1944 the most dreadful war in human history was raging, and many young men hung on to their sanity by assuming the armour of callousness. The American war correspondent Edgar Jones, writing after the event and quoted in the *Sydney Morning Herald*, recalled that 'In the savagery of the Pacific war neither side had a monopoly on barbarism' and he posed the question:

> What kind of war do civilians suppose we fought anyway? We shot prisoners in cold blood, wiped out hospitals, strafed lifeboats, killed or mistreated enemy civilians, finished off the enemy wounded, tossed the dying into a hole with the dead, and in the Pacific boiled the flesh off enemy skulls to make table ornaments for our sweethearts.

For two days Frank Horner and I worked together, checking stores and equipment and signing over confidential code books, binoculars, charts, rifles, revolvers, hand grenades, the medical chest[1] and a long list of other items from sextants to sandshoes. The night before Frank left, Johnnie threw a party. Soon after sunset, guests began arriving from other ships in boats; a Jeep-load of doctors and sisters from the hospital, well equipped with supplies, rolled down to the wharf and Frank's farewells continued long after he had retired to his bunk. Soon after, he left for Sydney in an American Liberty ship, but he might as well have stayed with us for shortly after his departure we were ordered to return there for a refit, sailing from Milne Bay on our long voyage home.

For some time I had neglected my journal but as we entered China Strait and passed the island of Samarai, Papua's spectacular scenery sent me back to my extravagantly descriptive scribbling:

> ... we sailed past picturesque little coral islands under towering mountains. White sandy beaches fringed the shore with tall palms swaying over the blue water. Dotted here and there were villages with natives walking and running about under the trees ... the South East Trades ... from May to November, keep the seaboard cool and refreshed. Twice during this part of our voyage we have seen natives sailing their outrigger canoes—and once, a long way from land, in quite rough sea. They manage them very well. The canoes are about twenty-five feet long and are fitted with a triangular-shaped sail with outriggers for stability. The ones I saw carried five men, all naked, and a dark coppery colour with frizzy hair. They had pierced the lobes of their ears and their noses and carried shells and other ornaments in them. The sailing canoes were very wet and low in the water, and running free, in a twenty-knot breeze, I should say that they would move along at about 6–7 knots ... The time is 1750 and the sun is just dipping, fiery red, below the rim of the sea. I am sitting on the quarter deck of ML 817 writing this in the cool of the tropical evening. We are rolling our way Southwards just below the Gulf of Papua in latitude 10 degrees 20′ South & Longitude 147 degrees East. It is now getting dark and the evening stars are coming out over the Coral Sea. Today has been very hot with the sun's declination 15 degrees South. But now it is fresh and cool ... I have the first watch tonight till midnight.

And as we rolled south Percy rolled with us, grinning grotesquely above our heads. No one seemed to spare him a thought: for them his novelty had long worn off, but not for me. In his Oriental History lectures at Sydney University, Professor Sadler had often discussed the

Japanese soldiery and I wondered about Percy's background, occupation and family life. There was also the thought that, as the Japanese were given to beheading people, if things had gone differently for us in Timor, my skull might now be some sort of a Japanese war trophy. I began to feel an affinity with Percy; whenever I stood watch on the bridge he was there above me, his eye sockets circling the Coral Sea with every roll of the ship. By day his gleaming dome reflected the harsh tropical sunlight; by night it glowed softly under the stars.

Six days after leaving Milne Bay we sighted Castle Hill and Magnetic Island and, running into Cleveland Bay, berthed at Townsville's Timber Wharf in Ross Creek. Everyone was sweaty and smelly, and after months of privation, ML 817's men were quick to savour some of the blessings of civilisation. First was the luxury of standing, lathered with soap, under the waterside workers' showers, watching the creamy suds run down their bodies and swirl extravagantly around their feet. Then there was the prospect of fresh food properly served in a restaurant, cinema shows, book shops, and the feeling of order, peace and quiet, associated with well-kept churches, public buildings and gardens. And there was the chance of meeting girls.

But there was another side to the story. Townsville was an important allied base, with senior naval officers on the prowl, and it was here that Percy got me into trouble. The Ross Creek tides rise and fall about 10 feet. At high water ML 817's deck was almost level with the wharf and at low water the cross-trees on the mast were six or seven feet above it.

It was low tide when Johnnie and Clem went ashore for the evening leaving me as duty officer, and I was reading in the wardroom when my peace was shattered by the sound of an angry authoritarian voice ordering the sentry to 'get the commanding officer at once'. Footsteps sounded on the deck above my head, and the watch-keeper, wide-eyed with apprehension, poked his head into the wardroom. There was some 'big brass up top', he told me in a low voice, asking for the captain, and up I went to find an outraged RAN captain with a US Navy commander. They had apparently dined well on Townsville's best and, deciding to take the evening air, had strolled down to the waterfront and met Percy, eyeball to eye socket.

When I told the captain that Johnnie was ashore, he shot an accusing finger at me, pointed at Percy and thundered, 'Get that thing down forthwith.' He turned away and the watch-keeper, shinning up the mast, unwired Percy and handed him down to me. I put him where we generally put things with no special home—in the locker under the wheelhouse chart table.

The rising sun gleamed on the crests of the white breakers bursting on North Head as ML *817* ran through Sydney Heads, turned south past the Sow and Pigs, passed through the boom gate, ran up the harbour and berthed at HMAS *Rushcutter's* Fairmile Base. Johnnie, Clem and most of the crew went off on well-earned leave and I was left with a couple of men to return the stores and hand the ship over to Poole and Steel's dockyard at Balmain for her refit.

The last sailors left, the tug arrived, and I took the wheel to keep the ship directly in its wake as it towed us up under the Harbour Bridge to Balmain. There the dockyard workers rigged a gangway, I collected the keys to the lockers, flats, hatches and cupboards and, before handing them over to the dockyard manager, had a last look around to say goodbye to ML *817*.

The bookshelf above the chart table looked bare without its *Australia Pilot, Nautical Almanac*, navigation books and logarithm tables. The chart table looked strange too, without its parallel rulers and dividers, though a pencil and rubber still lay in their groove at the back of it. Peering into the deep compartment under the table, I retrieved a crumpled chart. Then I lifted the lid of the locker under the table. Nothing there worth a second glance—only a few old signal flags. I touched them casually and felt something round and hard beneath them—Percy! Impossible to leave him there. Imagine the press headlines when the workers found him. That would look bad for the navy. I wrapped him in an old flag, stuffed him in my kit bag and went home to the rectory in a tram with Percy on my knee. There I put him in a wooden box, stowed it in the garage, and for the time being forgot about him.

But I had a man's head on my hands—a legacy which was to dog me for a quarter of a century—and as the story did not end until long beyond the scope of this memoir, here it is.

In 1953, when I married Lesley Spooner and set up house in Sydney, Percy, still in his box, moved in with us and was stowed in the laundry. The problem of his disposal oppressed me. There could be no thought of burying him in the garden or consigning him to the waters of Sydney Harbour; the possible subsequent discovery by a plumber, builder or scuba diver of a human skull with a bullet wound under the eye would raise questions I would be bound to answer. Nor was there any official machinery for disposing of the heads of former enemies; ours is not a head-hunting society. I could not discuss the matter with Johnnie Doyle, for he was dead, and although I considered taking Percy to Canberra and presenting him to the Japanese ambassador, the prospect of the complications that would flow from such action quickly put paid to that idea.

For twenty-five years the problem continued to vex me while the skull remained in the laundry, disturbing my wife and children, and I felt the irony of Percy's sleeping in his box under the house more peacefully than I sometimes slept in my bed above him. But, at last, on 5 September 1970, I found my peace of mind. Three hours before dawn, while cruising along the New South Wales coast, due east of Crocodile Head, I rounded the yacht up into the wind, backed the headsail, and hove to. And there, under the glittering southern constellations, as we gently rose and fell on the long Pacific swell, I let the mortal remains of one of the Mikado's men slip from my hands, bound on his own uncharted journey to the bottom of the Pacific Ocean.

9 | IN COMMAND

Returning to the officers' pool at HMAS *Rushcutter*, I cherished hopes of an appointment as first lieutenant of a Fairmile in New Guinea, Borneo or the Molucca Islands. And my chances were good: I had served in Fairmiles for nearly two years, had been first lieutenant of three of the ships, and knew them well. But on 5 December 1944, when the navy promoted me to the rank of lieutenant, these hopes faltered: there was another class of patrol boats in the Royal Australian Navy—Harbour Defence Motor Launches, or HDMLs, as they were often called. Smaller and slower than Fairmiles, these were generally commanded by lieutenants.

Shortly before Christmas 1944 my fears were realised when I was appointed to command the American-built HDML *1347*, then on the deck of a Liberty ship bound for Sydney. I was alarmed: being totally responsible for any ship was not on my agenda. I knew that first lieutenants slept more easily at night than commanding officers. Discussing my problem with friends, I heard of a naval tradition that an officer appointed to command a ship had a duty to decline if he believed himself unfit for the job. Here was my escape. Being something of a sea lawyer, I resolved to request an interview with Commander Harvey Newcombe RN, commanding officer of HMAS *Rushcutter*, and refuse to accept this command on the grounds that, as

I was irresponsible, it would be irresponsible of me to accept the appointment, and not in the interests of the Navy or the nation.

As I climbed the steep wooden stairs to Newcombe's office above the *Rushcutter* drill hall they creaked ominously. I knocked on the door, and although Newcombe greeted me kindly I was conscious that my two thin wavy stripes looked very puny beside his three thick straight stripes, World War I ribbons, and the gold oak leaves on his cap lying on the desk. He asked me to sit down and tell him why I had come, and I recited my carefully rehearsed statement about my unsuitability for command. I had come, I told him, to decline the command of ML *1347*. Surprised, Newcombe looked at me, raised his eyebrows and said nothing for a long time. Although nervous, I waited confidently for his response: there were dozens of young officers itching for command. I expected him to accept my decision promptly and dismiss me.

At last he spoke: 'Hordern, we are but servants of the State. It is not our prerogative to question its decisions.' He then asked me about myself: how had I come to such a decision, what did I hope to achieve in life, and what did I plan to do after the war? As I listened to this sensitive man he changed character before my eyes. Gone was the awesome Royal Navy commander: sitting there was a wise and kind avuncular friend.

In answer to his questions, I explained that I was already twenty-two, and that, if we won the war, I expected to spend three or four years completing my Arts and Law degrees at the University of Sydney. By then I would be quite old. Newcombe digested this irrelevant information in silence and after another long pause leaned forward over his desk and said very quietly, 'Hordern, I am not going to make a decision on this today, and neither should you. To command a ship is a challenge, and if you refuse to accept this one, you will run away from other challenges all your life, and you will suffer for that. I want you to go away and think about this, and come and see me in a couple of days.' I thanked him, walked down the stairs, out on to the parade ground, and sat on the stone sea-wall to think.

Commander Newcombe was right. I was at one of my life's cross-roads, and my choice would decide my fate. Again the creaking stairs, and another knock on his door. I accepted command of ML *1347* and thanked him for his advice. He smiled, shook my hand, and wished me good luck. As I walked down to the drill hall I no longer heard the stairs creaking for I was walking on air and Wordsworth's words:

But through the clouds I'll never float
Until I have a little boat ...

might have been written just for me.

Newcombe and I were to meet again as old men, and when we spoke about this, I thanked him for having given me a push along life's road.

As ML *1347* was not expected in Sydney until the end of December 1944, I was given leave and enjoyed my first family Christmas for three years. This was our sixth Christmas at war, nearly one million Australians were in uniform and long casualty lists were commonplace. The world was war-weary, and the Sydney churches were packed. In St Paul's I sat in the rectory pew and heard my father preach on the meaning of Christmas, and pray for peace and the safe return of our men who, in his World War I phraseology, were 'fighting at the front'. He read out the long list of parishioners' names who had either 'made the supreme sacrifice', were missing, wounded, or on active service. Among them were some boys I remembered from the choir and Sunday school, now suffering under the cruel yoke of the Japanese.

After the service we made the pilgrimage to 'Chislehurst' to join aunts, uncles and cousins in giving and receiving presents and greeting our widowed grandmother. After my grandfather's death in 1940, she had lived on in the big house with her sister Auntie Clara and a much reduced staff. The garden, croquet lawn, glass-house and tennis court were still well maintained, but manpower demands had left their mark. Much of the property's fourteen acres had always been timbered with big trees, but the orchard was now untended, the aviary birdless, the cowshed deserted and the poultry yard much diminished.

On 31 December 1944 I stood beside the crane, Titan, on Garden Island's Cruiser Wharf, watching proudly as ML *1347* was unloaded from her cradle on the Liberty ship's deck. Painted battleship grey, with the large white characters 'Q 1347' on either side of the fo'c's'le, she looked trim and business-like.[1]

The crane driver saw no difficulty in the 50-ton lift and in a few minutes I expected to see *1347* floating beside the Liberty ship. Dock-yard workers passed two large slings under her hull and secured them to Titan's great hook. It took the strain, lifted her from the cradle, swung her out over the side and lowered her into the water. But, as the crane driver slacked his lift, she listed alarmingly to starboard and I thought she was about to capsize. He raised her from the water again while the watching naval engineers conferred. Her builders, the Truscott Docking Company in Minnesota, however, knew their business. She had been designed to float level with all her stores, armament, equipment, fuel and water on board, but now she was empty. Back in the water, still listing heavily to starboard, she was towed to the eastern side of the island and her fitting-out berth.

I climbed aboard to explore my new kingdom. At first sight she looked like a small cramped Fairmile and, compared with their over-all length of 112 feet, her 72 feet seemed very short. Her power, speed and equipment, too, were on a smaller scale; but she had guns, and would soon have other teeth, Asdic and depth charges. And she had advantages Fairmiles lacked. At about 12 knots her twin Hercules DNX6 diesel engines gave her a much greater range and removed the fear of a petrol fire when fuelling, or if hit in action.

Because some HDMLs had been built in Australia and others in America and England, they had various designs. Comparing ML *1347* with a Fairmile, I thought the crew's quarters very cramped; galley, stove, refrigerator, heads and wash-basin all fitted together like a jigsaw puzzle with no inch to spare. The cabin shared by the coxswain and

motor mechanic, which in Fairmiles was in the mess deck, was down
aft and entered from a small foyer onto which the wardroom and the
wireless room also opened. I went through the door leading aft into
the wardroom to see what sort of accommodation I would be sharing
with my first lieutenant and was pleasantly surprised. The living area
measured 13 feet athwartships, 8 feet 4 inches fore and aft, and with a
headroom of 5 feet 8 inches. Two settees on either side of the wardroom converted into bunks and between them stood a folding table
2 feet 6 by 3 feet 6 inches. A bookshelf and pistol cabinet were fixed
to the bulkheads and below the pistol cabinet stood the safe for our
secret books. Near the safe a small kerosene-operated refrigerator
gladdened my eye: in the tropics our margarine would not become a
pool of yellow oil and we would be able to eat something cold. And
there was another welcome sight: beside a closed door leading aft
stood a polished writing desk with drawers and stowage for stationery,
pens, pencils and rubbers, and a fid to hold a bottle of ink. But when
I opened the door leading aft my heart lifted, for there was an *en suite*.
Not very large, perhaps—only 3 feet by 12—but it ran right across the
ship with a scuttle on each side to allow in light and a flow of air. The
American designers had shown their skills here. The head, on the port
side under the scuttle, was flushed by a hand-operated pump; the floor
of the fresh-water shower on the starboard side had a wooden grate
through which the water ran into the ship's bilge; and above the wash
basin was a mirrored toilet cabinet.

On New Year's Day 1945 I boarded the ship, and after hoisting a
commissioning pennant and the White Ensign, signalled the Port
Admiral and the captain of HMAS *Rushcutter*, Commander
Newcombe, informing them that ML *1347* had been commissioned.
She was now a ship in the Royal Australian Navy waiting to be
manned and equipped for war. But where would she be fighting it?

At first I had dismal visions of being kept in Sydney, Newcastle or
Port Kembla for harbour defence duties, but the bush telegraph at
Rushcutter assured me that we were bound for Madang on the north
coast of New Guinea for further orders, and that was cheering. The

AIF's 6th Division was attacking Lieutenant General Hatazo Adachi's XVIII Japanese Army in the Wewak area and that might mean army cooperation work for us.

Eight days later this was confirmed when the Naval Board sent a general signal 'anticipating' that ML *1347* would be ready to leave for New Guinea on 22 January 1945. Before she could be—in navy parlance—'in all respects ready for sea and to engage the enemy', however, there was much to be done. On her journey from Minnesota some of her planking had opened up, hatches and doors had become jammed and fittings damaged, and these had to be repaired. The electrical and pumping systems also needed attention and the Asdic had yet to be installed and tested.

The crew began trickling on board. First to arrive was Sub Lieutenant Clem F. McMahon, my former companion in ML *817*. We had got on well and as we wished to stay together I had asked for him. The rest were new faces.[2] The most senior of them were the coxswain, Leading Seaman Leonard Clarkson, and the motor mechanic, Petty Officer John Archibald Page. Len Clarkson, an extremely conscientious man, had a deep respect for bureaucracy but regarded it with wry humour. We made friends quickly and remained so for life. When we first met he saluted me; at his funeral half a century later I saluted him.

Jack Page was twelve years my senior, and I came to rely on his paternal advice. On one occasion, confronted by a request from a family doctor in Australia for compassionate leave for a crew member on the grounds that a woman in his family was 'playing up with the Americans'—which, the doctor volunteered, was probably associated with change of life—I was puzzled. Never having heard the term, I asked Jack what it meant. He looked at me quizzically, possibly asking himself how one so ignorant of human affairs could be responsible for a ship and its sailors' lives. 'Sir', he asked gently, 'didn't your mother ever tell you?' When I admitted to her neglect of my education in this matter, he enlightened me. Jack was self-effacing, and it was only when the following signal arrived from the Navy Board that I realised I had a war hero on board:

Motor mechanic 4th Class John Archibald Page O.N. 26044 has
been awarded the B.E.M. (military) for rescue work in ML *427*
on 31st March 1944. Award will be published in London *Gazette*
on 6 February. Rating serving in ML *1347*.

On 31 March 1944 while he had been serving in HMAS *Koopa* at
Milne Bay, Page, driving past the jetty where ML *427* was berthed,
had heard a loud explosion and seen flames pouring from her engine
room. Racing on board, he went below and dragged two unconscious
men up the ladder and onto the deck. Then, returning to the burning
engine room, he ran through it to the forward bulkhead, activated the
methyl-bromide fire-extinguisher, put out the fire and saved the ship.
Three of the men who had been in the engine room died from their
burns. Jack's citation was 'For great gallantry'.[3]

ML *1347* became a hive of activity as dockyard carpenters, joiners
and technicians prepared her for war. While they were working, stores
and supplies of all kinds arrived by boat and truck from the Royal
Edward Victualling Yard, the Armament Supply Store, and the Fairmile Base at HMAS *Rushcutter*. Among them were an Aldis lamp,
ammunition, awnings, bailers, batteries, bayonets, beeswax, binoculars,
blankets, charts, confidential code books, cordage, demolition and
depth charges, a dinghy, distilled water, fenders, fishing lines, fuel, hand
grenades, heaving lines, ink, a Jacob's-ladder, a copy of *King's Rules and
Admiralty Instructions*, lead lines, marline spikes, a medical chest, a megaphone, mess traps, navigation tables, needles, oars, oilskins, pencils,
pens, pillow cases, rafts, revolvers, rifles, rowlocks, sailmakers' palms,
sandshoes, sailing directions, a sea anchor, sea boots, semaphore flags,
signal books, signal flags, sou-westers, stationery, torches, twine, and·
many other items vital to our survival. All had to be receipted, recorded
and stowed in their proper place.

While civilian workmen were on board, I was told to keep valu-
ables locked away, and particularly cautioned about the morphine in
the medical chest. It came in small toothpaste-like tubes with attached
needles. I read the first aid book, checked the medicines, forceps,

surgical knife, bandages, eye-glass, tourniquet and absorbent wound pads, and hoped we would not need too many of them.

Although most of the orders and instructions made heavy reading, they were informative. Three years of jungle warfare had caused punishing casualties from tropical diseases and the navy was now taking preventative medicine seriously. In August 1944 it had published booklet AM 2Z: HEALTH. *Prevention of Disease in Tropical Climates*, and reading it, Clem McMahon and I found it full of potential horrors. Sailors, it said, acquired most of their tropical diseases while ashore, or—and this was for us—in small craft working along jungle coasts and in rivers:

> Every sailor must remember that the real dangers cannot be seen; for example, minute germs and fungi.
>
> Germs are the main cause of sickness, and usually come from diseased natives … Every drop of water that is taken should be boiled or chlorinated. Your Commanding Officer will give you instruction about the water and the method of making it fit to drink … Chlorinated water, or boiled water, will not hurt you, especially if you take salt several times a day with your food. Remember, unclean water is a deadly poison.
>
> Wash your hands before starting to prepare food or beginning to eat. A dirty body attracts flies and insects. It is essential that you:
>
> (a) Wash your whole body at least once a day, paying particular attention to the creases of the body, the clefts between the toes, the armpits and the crutch.
>
> (b) Use your own soap and towel.
>
> (c) Dry yourself well and dust the creases of the body, clefts between the toes, under armpits and crutch with powder.
>
> (d) That only clean clothes be put on after bathing.

My mother had taught me about washing hands, soap and using my own towel, but not how to purify water, so here was another thing to learn. How, I wondered, in small patrol boats, with limited fresh water and no showers for the men, could they wash their 'whole' bodies at least once a day and put on clean clothing?

HEALTH: Prevention of Disease in Tropical Climates was a mine of information on alcohol, dengue fever, malaria, diarrhoea, prickly heat ('Nearly every white man in the tropics suffers from this annoying skin complaint'), dhobie's itch, surfer's foot, tinea, hookworm, scrub typhus, tropical ulcers, Singapore ear, heat stroke and venereal disease. In malarial areas, it warned, 'Atebrin must be taken after sundown ... one tablet with a big drink of purified water on every day of the week.' And although, as a result of taking atebrin, 'certain people' developed the sallow colour I had noticed on Captain Tancred's body in Canonbury Naval Hospital, we were not to worry about that: 'This colour is not jaundice'. And there was cheerful news for the navy's Lotharios, frightened by rumours of possible impotence, *HEALTH* authoritatively stated: 'This drug has absolutely no effect on your sexual function.'

On venereal diseases the book was explicit: 'These diseases are very dangerous in the tropics. In many of the places 90 percent of the natives are infected, many of them with diseases which do not occur in civilised countries—for example ulcerating granuloma.' It ended with the direction, 'Leave native women alone.'

While we were busy at Garden Island, Johnnie Doyle was also fitting out a new Fairmile at HMAS *Rushcutter,* and through renewed association with him and his vivacious cousin, Robin, we became part of a social circle of servicemen and pretty girls. During the next few weeks, when we could get away, we would take them sailing in naval whalers and dinghies from Garden Island's boat pound. Sydney Harbour in summer, with its prevailing north-easterlies, is a sailor's paradise, and we made the most of it. We would sometimes head across the harbour to a deserted beach; Obelisk Bay and Grotto Point were our favourites, depending on the wind. After running the boats up on the sand, we would have a swim, get a driftwood fire going and soon, with appetites whetted by the smell of wood smoke and sizzling meat, settle down to a feast millionaires might have envied. At about dusk the dying north-easter would waft us home with flowing sheets. These daytime pleasures were frequently followed by cocktail parties on ships, cinema shows and dining out at Sydney's exclusive night spots, Prince's and Romano's.

On 28 January 1945 Clem and I took *1347* out for her first sea trials. Lightly laden and tender, we ran north along the coast to Broken Bay, rounded Barrenjoey Head rolling heavily and entered Pittwater where I had spent my schoolboy sailing days in Uncle Norman's *Temptress*. To try and repay him for that I had invited him to join us in Broken Bay, and I felt a touch of pride as I eased the ship's bow into Goddard's jetty at Palm Beach and he stepped aboard. Heading out to sea, we tested our Asdic equipment, fired all the guns and dropped a depth charge primed to detonate at 50 feet. The explosion of a quarter of a ton of amatol threw a tall white column of water high into the air and circling back over the disturbed water we were met by the sad sight of about 200 small fish floating on the surface of the sea.

Returning to Pittwater, we began testing the winch, cable and the two American 80-pound, close-stowing anchors. We dropped the starboard anchor first in 4 fathoms on a soft bottom of sand and mud but, when we went to weigh it, we struck trouble. The barrel-type winch was worked by two detachable hand-operated levers about 3 feet long which had to be inserted into slots in the winch and when the sailors began to turn it they found that the full movement of a lever only retrieved about three links of the chain cable. Fairmiles' winches were worked by two crank handles which brought the chain in quickly, but weighing anchor with this winch was a slow and back-breaking business, and we were later to suffer much for that. Deciding that to haul in by hand would be quicker, I manoeuvred the bow directly over the anchor and the fo'c's'le party began heaving it in. As it broke from the sand its weight suddenly lessened, and when the anchor reached the surface we saw that its shank had broken off

6 inches from the crown and that there was a flaw right through the casting. When we dropped the port anchor exactly the same thing happened and, being now unable to anchor, I returned to Sydney and reported the losses in writing to Commander Newcombe, requesting two new anchors—this time of the CQR (alias 'Secure') type, as supplied to the Australian-built MLs. They arrived promptly and never let us down.

Our preparations dragged on through February and it sometimes seemed that we were as much at war with the bureaucracy as with the Japanese. Its constant calls for reports, returns and explanations irked me. One of the many missives I received was Requisition P.R. 2430/44:

OVER ISSUE OF RATIONED FOODSTUFFS
1. Investigation of Form A.S. 462 Z—Provision Account—for the month of February, 1945, discloses that the item of Butter has been over issued to the extent of 1 lb for the month, vide C.N.O. 265/1944.
2. An explanation as to the over issue is required, and you are to make a compensating under issue in this item between this date and 30th June, 1945 to bring the total amount issued between 1st February, 1945 and 30th June, 1945 within the ration for that period.

This was the first special demand I received to account for stores or equipment, but it was not to be the last. About nine years after the war I was astonished to receive a letter from the bureaucracy informing me that during World War II, a gun, valued at £2000, for which I had apparently been responsible, had been removed from my ship, and I was required to state what happened to it. After Japan surrendered in 1945, my ship remained in New Guinea waters working with the army rounding up prisoners and, to make our conditions more comfortable, the depth charges and the biggest gun had been taken ashore. I replied that, when last seen, the gun, suspended from a long green pole, was being carried into the jungle by two natives. That apparently satisfied my inquisitors as I did not hear from them again.

But this demand about butter was much more serious. It was thrust into my hand while Jack Page was explaining a problem he was having with the super-charger chains and, reading about those 16 ounces of butter, I was incredulous: Europe and the Far East were in flames; in once-splendid cities, such as Dresden, rats were gnawing human bodies in the rubble of blasted buildings; ships were being sunk and men, women and children were dying on rafts and drowning in oil. Tokyo was being torched, and in the jungles and swamps to our near north, youths who might have been camping or fishing together were at each others' throats with knives and guns. This request was absurd. I should have filed the letter and forgotten about it, but I made an issue of it. The super-charger chains would have to wait.

Dividing the amount supposedly over-issued by the number of the ship's company, and that figure by twenty-eight to estimate the exact average weight of butter each of us had eaten each day in February 1945, I found the amount too minute for our scales to measure. With a sheet of carbon paper between two sheets of 'Commonwealth of Australia Department of the Navy' stationery, I dipped my pen in the ink bottle on my desk and wrote a wordy, pompous letter to my long-suffering friend Commander Newcombe.

February was the first month in which ML *1347* was in oper-ational commission with the ship's company continually living aboard. The coxswain of this vessel had never previously had any practical experience in the discharge of his office. It was accord-ingly found from the experience of February, that in the normal period of flux and adjustment which invariably occurs during working up and settling down in all new ships, certain adjust-ments in the administration of foodstuffs would be necessary if the demands of the rationing regulations were to be met in ensuing months.

It was under these circumstances that this extra consumption of butter occurred … amounting to approximately .06 ounces per man per day in excess of the rationed allowance. [It] was so small that it was not until the end of the month that it was noticed.

On reading this Newcombe may have questioned his judgement in persuading me to accept the command of ML *1347*. The navy now had a file on our butter consumption and, as Big Brother was watching and waiting to pounce, at the end of March I reported that butter had been under-issued 'to a more than compensating degree', and closed my letter to Newcombe with an encomium for Len Clarkson, who, although he had been guilty in the matter of the butter had also '… continually discharged his duties in a most reliable and conscientious manner; and has been found at all times to show an appreciation of the responsibilities of his office surpassing expectation in the light of his former lack of experience'. The victualling powers never wrote to me solely about butter again.

Our little family in ML *1347* settled down well. The men called Clem and me 'Sir', and we called them by their surnames or titles. Len Clarkson was 'Coxswain' and Jack Page was 'Chief'. When Len Clarkson told me that 'the lads had been talking things over' and thought we should have a personalised ship's letter-head I encouraged the idea. I had never seen this done in a Fairmile and felt that they were developing a sense of identity. Our artistic canteen manager, Richard Jeffs, began working on a design, and I looked for a motto. Remembering the venerable instructor at Flinders who had lamented that in his youth the navy had had wooden ships and iron men, but that now it was the other way round, I chose the words 'H.M.A.M.L. 1347, Naves Ligno et Homi Ferro', and Richard's neat design of an Admiralty crown garlanded with laurels completed our logo.

Expecting our sailing orders daily, Clem and I pored over the charts we would be using on our long haul to New Guinea, identifying

H. M. A. M. L. 1347

NAVES LIGNO ET HOMI FERRO

ML 1347's letterhead

safe night anchorages in protected bays. But we were again delayed by being assigned anti-submarine boom patrol duties. Sydney Harbour's defence included a system of loops—electrified cables—on the sea floor outside the Heads. These recorded on a screen ashore the position of any vessel passing over them. If a 'blip' appeared on the screen where no vessel was visible, a submarine was suspected and the boom patrol vessel would investigate. From our anchorage in Obelisk Bay outside the boom, at instant notice for sea, we kept watch on the South Head Signal Station. Our most exciting call came on the blustery night of 21 February when the Station flashed the Morse code message: 'Go to the assistance of yacht in distress off Ben Buckler. Don't endanger your own ship.'

Out at sea a strong southerly had raised an angry ocean and, as we rounded Hornby Light and turned into it we bucked and plunged, and the clatter and crash of pots and pans below told me that we still had much to learn about securing the ship for sea. As we neared Ben Buckler we could see foam and spray hurled high into the air by the big waves bursting on its cliffs, and closing as far as we dared and shining our spotlight along the rocks, I was vastly relieved to see no sign of a yacht or wreckage. Storm-tossed, we remained there until we were ordered to return to harbour.

Being at anchor in Obelisk Bay close to the beach reminded me of Coffs Harbour and we sometimes launched the dinghy and rowed in for a swim and a game on the sand. Apart from the occasional yacht which circled us curiously, there was always entertainment in watching the passing parade of merchant ships, destroyers, corvettes, submarines, and on one occasion a huge United States Navy aircraft carrier, passing through the boom gate a few hundred yards away.

When at last I heard from HMAS *Rushcutter* that we would soon be off, I had a new worry. Clem and I were working well together and I considered myself lucky to have him, but whenever he took off his shirt I could not help noticing the blotchy red lumps on his back. He consulted the *Rushcutter* surgeon, who said it was 'acne vulgaris', a legacy of tropical service, and declared him unfit for more of it. We parted sadly and as we had had many happy jaunts on the Waratah motorbike I had bought from Ray Penny, I sold it to him for £35.

As I farewelled Clem I wondered what sort of a man would be sleeping in the other bunk and sharing my meals. I was soon to find out when a stocky fair-haired youth with a sub lieutenant's wavy gold stripe on his epaulettes stepped jauntily aboard and introduced himself as Clif Wilkinson, my new first lieutenant. We shook hands and went below to find out what we could about each other.

The 21-year-old Thomas Clifton Wilkinson RANR was the son of Arthur C. Wilkinson, the wealthy and influential chairman and managing director of Globe Worsted Mills. After leaving The King's School, Parramatta, in 1941, he had applied to join the RAAF but as his maths 'were not quite up to scratch', he joined the Navy as an ordinary seaman. Quickly commissioned, he became the first lieutenant of ML *1322* and had served in New Guinea.

Clif invited me to visit his family at 'Radstoke', the impressive Wilkinson home on The Boulevarde, Strathfield. It sat comfortably on five acres of manicured gardens and as I walked up its drive and through the front door I could see that Clif had grown up in affluent surroundings. At twenty-one he already owned a 28-foot yacht and a motor car. In the wardrobe of his large bedroom he proudly showed me his fifteen suits. I had only ever owned one, and was duly impressed. This affluence had not given Clif airs, however. Athletic and exuberant, he was a good sailor and good company too, and ours was another happy wartime association which was to last a lifetime.

On 2 March 1945 we all filed ashore to the sick bay at Garden Island to be immunised against tetanus, cholera and smallpox, and while we were nursing our consequent headaches and sore arms, the longed-for signal arrived from the Flag Officer in charge of Sydney:

> When ready about 0800 Sunday 4th proceed to Brisbane via Port Stephens and Coffs Harbour along inshore route pass six miles off prominent headlands.
>
> Keep 500 kcs single [radio] operator periods.
>
> Acknowledge.

Next morning at 7 a.m. my parents, 15-year-old brother Ian and Mr Wilkinson arrived at HMAS *Rushcutter's* wharf and climbed aboard to see us off. We chatted awkwardly for a few minutes in the wardroom and received their parting gifts. My mother's was a framed coloured photograph of a very young-looking King George VI, cut from the *Women's Weekly*. I hung it above my desk in the wardroom, where it remained during the ship's entire service in the RAN. It now hangs in my library beside the fireplace, my mother's inscription, 'With every best wish for ML *1347*', still faintly visible on the back.

My father called for silence and, in the words of the Prayer Book's superb naval prayer, sought our protection from 'the dangers of the sea and the violence of the enemy ... and that we may return in safety to enjoy the blessings of the land and the fruits of our labours'. During the next twelve months, the dangers of the sea and my own frailty were to prove far more threatening than the violence of the enemy.

We shepherded our visitors up the steep companionway to the deck, guided them around the guns and depth charges, then onto the wharf, and I recorded the moment of departure in my journal:

The engines purred to life. 'Let go for'ard, let go aft, slow ahead together'; and we slid silently away from the berth and turned to run out past Clark Island. Looking back to my dear parents, they merged as dots on the quay side & we steered down the harbour for the Heads.

At last ML *1347* was off to war.

10 | ALL AT SEA

We ran north for Port Stephens in pleasant weather, clear visibility and a light north-easterly breeze. But as the day wore on the wind hardened, raising a short head sea and giving us a wet uncomfortable ride. Some of the crew were seasick and Clif lost his breakfast.

We secured to a little wharf there, having maintained a speed of 10.6 knots on the run and I was well satisfied with the ship's performance. Port Stephens, our first haven on the voyage, rated an entry: 'We tied up in a snug little cove against a wharf. The boys went for a swim and in the clear water off a sandy beach caught some fish. I stretched my legs ... A sleepy delightful little place with hardly a soul about.'

As our next leg to Coffs Harbour would take about seventeen hours and I had no wish to be running through that breakwater at night, we left Port Stephens at 2 a.m. next morning. The weather was gloomy; an electrical storm had crossed the coast and dark clouds hid the moon. But as we had calculated the various courses to take us through the channels between the sandbanks we ran safely out between Toomeree and Yacaaba Heads, the moon obligingly emerging to light up the shoreline. Once we had cleared the land Clif turned in and I stood my first night watch in command of a ship at sea. Beside me the quartermaster, shifting his weight from one leg to the other as the ship rolled, moved the wheel gently to keep us on course. The lookout, muffled in his duffelcoat against the morning air, had found himself a snug spot between the Vickers gun and the signal locker. Humming sweetly, the big Hercules engines pushed us along at 11 knots, and the low quartering sea rolled us a gentle 15 degrees. With the swish of the sea in my ears, over-confident and happy, I said another silent 'Thank you' to Commander Newcombe.

As we had no radar we had to keep a sharp lookout, particularly at night in shipping lanes. Abeam of Sugar Loaf Lighthouse I took the necessary compass bearings, noted the time and weather, and went down to the wheelhouse to fix our position on the chart, calculate our speed, the effect of any current, and make the hourly log entries. After poring over the chart under its spotlight, on returning to the bridge it took me some time to recover my night vision and, while regaining it, I spotted a ship steering straight for us out of the blackness ahead. We quickly altered course to starboard and passed safely down her port side. A trivial incident perhaps, like giving way to a car in a round-about, but night passages were to prove very dangerous for us. With the quartermaster's eyes fixed on the compass, the watch-keeping officer at the chart table in the wheelhouse and a tired bridge lookout half asleep, we could be at great risk. I decided that I would have to take more care.

Returning to Coffs Harbour was like coming home. The weather was calm and I berthed at the jetty. The harbourmaster, Captain Brodie, welcomed me back, and the publican at the Pier Hotel offered us his hot showers. I introduced Clif to 'Father' and 'Mother' Yoole and the girls; we dined on steak and eggs at Andy's Café, and invited Captain Brodie, Cathy Bower and a few friends aboard for a drink.

On the run from Sydney some transit bearings of objects in line on shore had differed from those marked on the chart by as much as 7 degrees. Such a significant error could wreck us, and I decided to make a new compass deviation card showing the proper allowances to make on different headings. Next morning we lined the ship up on the harbour's entrance leads and, with one engine going ahead and the other astern, moved her round through 360 degrees, taking bearings of the leads as we swung. After comparing these bearings with those on the chart I was able to make a new deviation card.

From Coffs Harbour we steered for the spot near North Solitary Island where we had caught all those fish in ML *823*, and hove to there in bright warm weather. For about half an hour, while some of us swam around the ship, others caught enough snapper to feed us all for the day. Then we pushed on and, after a run of thirty-three hours, reached the Fairmile Base at Colmslie in the Brisbane River.

Here we struck trouble with the super-charger chains. On the passage from Sydney they had stretched; Jack had adjusted them several times, but now, although he had tightened them as far as they could go, they were still so slack that he could depress them three-eighths of an inch with his thumb. If they stretched any more, he told me, they would cut the lubrication pipes.

My first thought was to press on, watch the chains carefully, and hope for the best. But, as three sister ships soon to leave Brisbane might encounter the same problem, I asked Jack for a written report and submitted it to the Naval Officer in Charge Brisbane. He referred it to the Naval Board in Melbourne who ordered us to carry out day cruises in Moreton Bay for a hundred engine hours, varying the tensions on the chains and to report the result.

This sounded almost too good to be true. We were being sent off for one hundred hours in a yachtsman's playground where ours would be the only footsteps on the sand of its clean white beaches.

In consulting *Australia Pilot* and the local charts to brush up on my knowledge of Moreton Bay, I learned that in 1770 Lieutenant Cook had named it 'Morton Bay', that strong tides setting across its sand banks could cause rips and a dangerous short sea, and that some of it was mined. Over the next few weeks we discovered for ourselves other features of Moreton Bay not mentioned in *Australia Pilot*.

Remembering the loss of ML *814*'s Asdic dome in the Brisbane River approaches, I called on Commander S. N. Cobbold DSC, RN,

Staff Officer Operations, to get permission to remove it. 'Cobby', as we called him, was an approachable man who had been through the bombing raids in Darwin and was said to be hard of hearing. I told him that our dome cost about £3000, that I had already been associated with the loss of one in Moreton Bay, did not want to lose another, and asked permission to remove it. Cobby approved. My next request was more delicate. Brisbane's naval depot, HMAS *Moreton*, was full of attractive young WRANs, and I thought it would lighten our work to have some of them with us on our cruises. I had floated this idea with a lieutenant in the next office, separated from Cobby's by a flimsy partition, and he didn't like my chances. Cobby listened carefully as I explained the advantages of this scheme. The girls would see something of the watery side of the navy, it would be a change from their sitting at typewriters and making cups of tea, and it would be good for their morale. After pondering for a minute, Cobby looked at me hard, and with the suspicion of a smile said, 'Rather irregular, Hordern, rather irregular. How many could you accommodate?' 'Ten, Sir.' 'Why ten?' 'Ten men in the ship's company, Sir.'

On my assuring him that there would be no 'funny business' and that the girls would be back in Brisbane each day before dark, he agreed. He could see no harm in it, he told me, and he would arrange for a roster to be drawn up with the names of the WRANs who would sail with us each day. I would have to take the ship up-river and embark them at the Nixon-Smith Wharf close to HMAS *Moreton*. I thanked him, and as I left, he commented smilingly, 'I wouldn't mind coming along myself'.

Returning to impart the joyful news to the lieutenant next door, I burst into his room and said, 'Cobby approved, we can take the girls, and, what do you think? the old bastard said he wouldn't mind coming along too!' I had barely blurted out the words when there was a knock at the door; a sailor looked in and said, 'Lieutenant Hordern?' 'Yes.' 'The commander's compliments from next door. He says to tell you "it's nice to hear your voice".' Why, oh why, had I not kept my big mouth shut? Crushed, I knocked on Cobby's door. 'Come in.' 'I'm *awfully* sorry, Sir, I didn't mean it.' The commander looked at me for a few moments, leaned a little over his desk and said quietly, 'It's all right my boy, I was young once myself.' Newcombe and Cobby were cast in the same warm-hearted mould.

I had just received a newsy letter from Norman Wallis in Darwin—now one of the war's backwaters. He was finding life dull, hot and dreary, and to ease the boredom among his men he had encouraged water sports. The dockyard shipwrights had built him an aquaplane board with a towing bridle and hand-rope, and they were finding it great sport skimming along behind the ship. At about 11 knots a Fairmile's wake produced a series of steep waves and a board rider, once he got the hang of it, could skim backwards and forwards over them. If someone fell off, the ship had to circle back to pick him up quickly, and they always had a man on the bridge with a rifle in case they saw a shark or crocodile. This letter had come at the right time and we left on our engine tests with a new aquaplane board and a new sport to learn.

Now began a period of naval duty better than any floating holiday I had known, with all expenses paid. With a bevy of bright young women we swam, sported and picnicked on deserted beaches and fished in waters so clear that we could often watch the sharks and rays gliding below our keel.

We would leave the Fairmile Base at 7 a.m., embarking the girls at the Nixon-Smith Wharf about six miles up-river. Then we were off on a three-and-a-half-hour run out through the dredged channel, past the Old Pile Lighthouse, St Helena and Mud Islands, and across the bay to Cowan Jetty on Moreton Island. Remembering my promise to Cobby that there would be no 'funny business', I laid down a few strict rules: the wardroom became the girls' changing room and while they were there no man was to be near the wardroom flat. Clif showed the WRANs how to operate the hand-pumped heads and spring taps on the shower and we made special efforts to keep the wardroom clean and tidy, polishing the furniture and brasswork, and washing encrusted salt from the outside of its glass scuttles. The sailors—equally proud of their quarters—also applied plenty of spit and polish to the mess deck where the girls ate.

From Cowan Cowan the beaches north to Comboyuro and south to Tangalooma Point are washed by 7-foot tides and Tangalooma, with the nearby Dring Bank, was one of our favourite anchorages. This sand spit, almost awash at low tide, was 400 yards from the beach, and its sides dropped steeply into 5 fathoms of water full of fish. As soon as we anchored there we would launch the dinghy and recreational parties would go ashore in turns.

The girls looked marvellous in their costumes; some were excellent swimmers, and good at games of deck tennis on the sand. The more adventurous of them soon mastered the art of aquaplaning and seldom fell off, even when we tried to dislodge them by throwing the ship at high speed into a tight turn, sending the board skidding madly sideways. There were games on board, too. One day, when the girls were ashore Dick Jeffs got into one of the larger WRAN's uniforms and when they returned along the wharf they were surprised to see an impeccably turned-out WRAN, hat slightly listing to starboard, and with rolled socks moulding her brassière into generous curves, on watch beside the machine gun. The attractive owner of the clothes posed with Dick on the fo'c's'le, kneeling beside him with her hand on his leg just below the knee to show the uniform's regulation hem length. Cobby would have loved it.

We drew extra rations for the WRANs, who peeled potatoes, scraped carrots and occasionally cooked the meals. Their forté was fresh fish and to catch enough for twenty people we occasionally used hand grenades for quick results. This was not always successful: on one occasion, when Clif had dived down to collect some stunned fish lying in about 7 feet of water, two tiger sharks appeared, and Clif struggled back into the boat, content to leave them our catch.

The cruising gave us a chance to practise the drills on which our lives might soon depend. With our guns, revolvers and rifles, we shot at boxes thrown over the side, and practised throwing hand grenades.

We dropped a smoke float, and rehearsed the drills for fire in the galley, fire in engine room, attack by low-flying aircraft, and man-overboard. This last exercise paid off quickly when shortly afterwards I heard the shout 'Man-overboard!' and, looking astern, saw our acting cook, Norman Whitehurst, swimming strongly in our wake. He had, I later learned, slipped while emptying a bucket over the side. The drill became reality: the bridge lookout heaved a lifebuoy over the side, kept his eyes firmly fixed on Whitehurst and his arm pointed directly towards his position, which was constantly changing in relation to the ship as we circled back. Nearing him, we dropped the leeward scrambling net, stopped engines so that he could not be cut by the propellers, slid alongside him and helped him on board in good time to cook the lunch.

During this cruising we covered over a thousand miles in Moreton Bay. At the end of the tests Jack Page submitted a detailed report to the Base Engineer Officer and, while our fate was being decided, we spent most of our time at the Advanced Fairmile Base at Bribie Island with our sister ships MLs *1341*, *1354* and *1355* who—also destined for northern waters—had been detained in Brisbane pending the result of our trials.

While we were lying at Kangaroo Point in Brisbane River, Germany capitulated in Europe and I made the entry, 'PEACE DECLARED IN EUROPE', in the ship's log. For the next forty-eight hours we relaxed and as the log reminds me, 'Worked Sunday Routine as celebrations of Victory over Germany continued.' In the city people flocked to thanksgiving services, bells pealed, and I joined a packed congregation in the cathedral.

But amid these celebrations we could not forget that, while we were enjoying ourselves in Brisbane attending cinemas and dances, war was still raging in the north and we were chafing to be off. Finally, acting on Jack Page's report on the super-charger chains, the navy came to a decision, and on 16 May we received the long-awaited signal marked 'Priority Confidential':

HDMLs 1347 1354 1355 1341 are to be despatched to New Guinea as soon as practicable.

Adjust super-charger chain tension for maximum of 1400 RPM this speed not to be exceeded except in case of emergency.

Issue full instructions to boats regarding procedure for running non supercharged if necessity arises.

FOIC [Flag Officer in Command] Sydney is requested to forward by priority air freight to Brisbane before departure 8 (repeat) 8 … chains if available, to be carried on board as replacement spares.

We left Brisbane on 19 May in company with our three sister ships and HMAS *Karina*, a small vessel attached to the Services Reconnaissance Department—the army's cloak-and-dagger organisation. Lieutenant Jim White, in ML *1354*, was senior officer of the flotilla.

The forecast for fine weather and a light south-easterly breeze augured well for the 300-mile run to Gladstone, but after we had passed Caloundra Point and were running northward along the coast of Great Sandy Island, the wind backed and settled hard in the south-west. This slowed the flotilla as *Karina* could only manage 8 knots in good weather, and we did not moor alongside Gladstone's main jetty until mid-morning on 21 May. We fuelled, went to a dance, and sailed at dawn for Mackay.

This 234-mile passage took us twenty-eight hours and during it we doubled Cook's Cape Capricorn, entered the tropics, and began following his 1770 track in the *Endeavour*. I had sailed this part of the coast before, but now, armed with a copy of Geoffrey Ingleton's *Charting a Continent*, which told the story of the men who had discovered and surveyed Australia, I looked at it with new eyes. I had bought this recent publication before we left Sydney little knowing how greatly it would influence my life, and Ingleton had inscribed it for me.

Now I was passing the capes, bays, islands, reefs and rivers which Cook, Flinders, King and their associates had discovered and named, and in the pages of *Charting a Continent* they came alive for me. When we first sighted Cape Capricorn's bold cliffs it was as though I was back there on board the *Endeavour* in 1770 and, by an extraordinary coincidence, we passed it about 9 a.m.—almost the same hour on the same day of the year as Cook had done. It lay before us, warmed by the same sun and cooled by the same wind and, but for its lighthouse, I saw it exactly as Cook had described it:

> ... at daylight the Northernmost point of the Main bore N.70°
> W., and soon after we saw more land making like Islands, bearing
> N.W. by N.; at 9 we were abreast of the point, distant from it one
> mile; Depth of water 14 fathoms. I found this point to lay directly
> under the Tropic of Capricorn, and for that reason called it by
> that name. Long. 209° W. It is of a moderate height, and looks
> white and barren.[1]

How like the practical Cook it was to have so named that cape lying almost directly under that tropic.

From Cape Capricorn we edged out to pass seaward of the Percy Islands, and as the day wore on the trade wind strengthened, raising a steep sea, and for the next twenty hours we ran on north yawing heavily and occasionally rolling far enough to dip the depth-charge racks in the water. We were stationed about 200 yards astern of Geoff Miller's ML *1355* and the seas were so steep that occasionally a big wave would throw her stern so high in the air that we could see her propellers racing in the sunlight.

Thinking of Cook sailing through this brilliant blue water with the trade wind drumming in his sails, I recalled a photograph I had seen of an English ML en route to Africa, fitted with a mast and sail to help her along and save fuel and, as this was perfect weather for a trial, I hoisted a canvas awning as a square sail. It only measured 60 square feet, but it gave us an extra .3 of a knot and it steadied our rolling.

After a day and a night pummelled by gale-force winds, we were glad to reach the protection of Mackay's breakwater, enjoy a long shower in the dockside changing rooms, and eat from a plate not in perpetual motion. We had arrived at the top of high tide and felt pretty cocky as we stepped down onto the massive jetty under the curious eyes of watchers on the wharf. But Mackay's big tide was a great leveller; when it bottomed it left us lying about 19 feet below the wharf with the trucks of our masts just above it and our only connection with the shore a long slimy ladder. Clif and I explored the town, dined at the Imperial Hotel, took in a cinema show and we sailed for Townsville at midnight.

This was my third transit of the Whitsunday Passage and as the south-east winds were blowing a gale we again hoisted sail, this time spreading 260 square feet of canvas. This was a great success: although we heeled over a lot, it eased our rolling, gave us a more comfortable ride and increased our speed sufficiently for us to reduce engine revolutions, save fuel, and still maintain our station in the flotilla.

In these conditions steep seas occasionally broke over our stern and rolled along the deck and one of them left an unusual gift. On my usual walk around the deck soon after dawn, I was astonished to find a huge squid—the largest I had ever seen—caught between the depth-charge racks and the guardrails. It amazed me to think that this heavy creature must have been swimming on the top of a wave at the exact moment, and in the exact spot in the ocean, where it had broken on board. We used it for bait and caught enough coral perch to feed us for two days.

After a rough 208-mile run from Mackay, we rounded Cape Cleveland soon after daylight and moored at the now-familiar Hyne's Timber Wharf in Ross Creek, Townsville, surrounded by pearling luggers, trading ketches and schooners with Torres Strait Islander crews. At the time my brother-in-law, Boyce Horsley, was a chaplain at HMAS *Magnetic*, the Townsville naval depot, and since sighting the town's lights that morning I had been anticipating the comforts of *Magnetic's* wardroom. I envisaged a long cold shower with plenty of soap to wash away the dried salt, a breakfast of crisp cereals, fresh cold milk, bacon and eggs, toast, marmalade and coffee. I knocked on

Boyce's cabin door. No answer, so I went in and woke him from a sound sleep. Having had no idea of my whereabouts, he was surprisingly civil, and looked after me splendidly.

It was Whitsuntide and Boyce held an early service of Holy Communion in a hut on the Townsville waterfront. The Elements were placed on a rough table covered with a spotless White Ensign, and above it palm fronds rustled in the breeze. A low surf broke on the sand, and North Queensland's dry-season sunlight sparkled on the sea—and when Boyce pronounced the Benediction at the end of the service, a great peace seemed to settle over the little chapel beside the beach.[2]

On 1 June, at 2.45 a.m., having been weather-bound for some days in Ross Creek, our flotilla left for Thursday Island. By midnight we were off Cape Tribulation in worsening weather and, on 2 June, after thirty hours in gale-force winds, we ran in under the lee of Lizard Island to find a snug berth 200 yards from a protected beach. Geoff Miller secured ML *1355* alongside us to save himself the trouble of anchoring, and we spent a pleasant day there swimming, fishing and exploring the deserted island.

Having no large-scale chart of the bay, my first care was to sound around the ships and make a sketch of its prominent features, which I transcribed into the log for the watch-keepers to use when taking anchor bearings to ensure that we were not dragging.

For me, Lizard Island breathed history. In 1770, after Cook had struck Endeavour Reef and repaired his ship in the Endeavour River, he had again become entangled in a coral labyrinth and had climbed to the top of the island to seek a way out. Absorbed in reading about his adventures here, Clif and I decided to climb to the summit and try to pick out with our binoculars the passage through the reef Cook had discovered with his spyglass.

The dinghy's keel grated on the sand and we splashed ashore on the island which lay as it had been, little changed for thousands of years, and crossing a little stream trickling down through the bushes we set off for the summit 1179 feet above. There were, of course, no tracks and it was hot going clambering up through the scrub and boulders. But when, puffing and sweaty, we stood on the rock where Cook had stood, we had our reward. Far out to sea we descried a blue break in the foaming reef—the passage Cook had seen and through which the *Endeavour* had escaped from the coral maze.

On the way down, slipping and sliding around rocks in the wiry grass, we were nearly knocked over by a very large lizard. Like a goanna, but more thick-set, it rushed past almost under our feet. Here was another link with Cook, who had had a similar encounter and had named the island for our lizard's ancestors.[3]

Next afternoon we reached the Flinders Group and anchored in Stokes Bay on Stanley Island where I made another rough chart for the watch-keepers. Geoff Miller went beachcombing with some of his men and returned with as many fish and oysters as they could carry. As we were now getting close to New Guinea and perhaps roaming Japanese aircraft, we held a shoot here. So far all our gunnery practice had been in bright daylight and this time we waited until nearly dusk, when the sun, shining low across the water, created conditions favourable for an attacking plane. For a target we chose a rock ashore and fired several hundred rounds of high explosive and tracer ammunition at it. The result was as spectacular as it was unexpected. We set the dry grass alight and started fires which raged through the night, illuminating the anchorage and the five ships in the bay.

Next day's run was like a harbour cruise as we headed north in bright sunshine through a calm sea to Portland Roads. Here Jim White led us into the substantial wharf built by the Americans to service their air base at Iron Range in Cape York Peninsula. The five of us berthed across its deep outer end and ran out long head and stern lines to hold us against the tide.

Like Lizard Island, Portland Roads was of particular interest to me for, primed by Ingleton, I was aware that this part of the coast was sacred to Captain Bligh who had landed from the *Bounty*'s launch on nearby Restoration Island after the famous mutiny. In the gold rush days Portland Roads had seen wild times and there were still some relics of its turbulent past lying around in the form of derelict mining machinery and rusting water tanks.

At our next anchorage, Margaret Bay, Geoff Miller and I went pig hunting. We trudged through hot scrubby country dotted with anthills, crossed a fine fresh water creek full of fish and saw a crocodile—but not a solitary pig. Leaving Margaret Bay before light, we rounded Cape York at 3 p.m., and three hours later berthed at the Engineers' Wharf on Thursday Island. The bureaucracy had anticipated our arrival, and among the official mail requiring action was a letter from the Base Supply Officer at Madang, once more demanding an explanation for our extravagant eating habits. It was just like old times down south and read:

Rationed Foodstuffs

The following item(s) of rationed food has been over issued during the month of March 1945:

Butter 25 lb

Bacon 9 lb

A report is to be furnished of the circumstances causing the ration to be exceeded, and Commanding Officer is requested to ensure that the instructions contained in C.N.O. [Commonwealth Naval Order] 265/44 are strictly observed in future.

This was serious stuff; Len Clarkson and I checked his March vouchers and found that the butter bonanza had occurred while we were feeding all those hungry girls in Moreton Bay. Back at my desk, with a piece of carbon paper between two sheets of naval stationery, I dipped my pen in the inkwell and, in long-winded official jargon, did my best to placate Madang's Supply Officer:

... with reference to your memorandum stating that Butter had been over issued to the extent of 25 lbs. and Bacon 9 lbs. during March, the following figures have been computed by me from records contained in Form A/S 77; and from the ration scale embodied in C.N.O. 265/44.

(a) Total butter allowance for ten men for 31 days   33.9 lbs.

(b) Total butter received on board ML 1347 in March   35 lbs.

(c) Total bacon allowance for 10 men for 31 days   29 lbs 1 oz.

(d) Total bacon received on board ML 1347 in March   32 lbs.

During March, for five days, the ship's company, and for two days, two officers, were victualled out during dockyard work.

It is pointed out [a useful phrase I had learned from 'Captain'] that during March this vessel was used for taking some sixty-four WRANs on recreational trips in Moreton Bay during engine tests.

These female personnel were on board this vessel on an average of 8 hours per day—in parties of eight. They were not victualled aboard, but carried picnic lunches.

It was found however, that circumstances rendered it desirable, and courtesy demanded, that they should at times be given food from the ship's supply. These rations were thus unofficially consumed and recorded as being issued to the ship's company.

It is not anticipated that any more WRANs will be carried on this ship.

Even in the light of the fact that, if rationed allowances of (a) butter and (b) bacon, to the extent (a) approx. 5.9 lbs and (b) 8 lbs. were deducted from the totals over-consumed for the time the personnel mentioned were victualled out, there is still a discrepancy between your figures and mine.

When this ship arrives at its base it is requested that a comparison between the two sets of figures may be made to determine where the mistake lies.

I never heard about bacon and butter again.

Now about to leave Australia it was time for me to take stock. Old age loomed. I was twenty-three and took the view that by the time the war was over and I had finished my university courses, I would be too old to achieve much in civilian life. And I was not alone in this. Towards the end of the war this prospect faced thousands of servicemen and women. I was therefore gratified to receive a letter from the University of Sydney saying that it had established a Department of External Studies to enable undergraduates in the forces to continue their work while on active service. Textbooks, copies of lectures and examination papers could be sent to me and at the end of the year I could sit for exams under supervision. If I had difficulties, I could write to a nominated tutor in Sydney about them. I responded, telling the university that I would continue the history section of my Bachelor of Arts degree.

From Thursday Island I wrote home about ship-board life and an ice-cream recipe my mother had sent. It relied heavily on Nestlé's Condensed Milk, custard powder, milk powder, sugar and water, and she had hoped that if this mixture could be induced to freeze in our kerosene-operated refrigerator, it would be a luxury for us.

7 June 1945

I made my first ice cream tonight and am waiting for it to freeze now. Have just taken it out and re-beat it before it set. The fridge is a great boon as it is very hot below here now—we wear few clothes and sleep with none and sweat a lot. Our food is not so good now and I am on the vitamin tablets ... 1 atebrin (anti-malarial) 1 vita. C, 1 vita. B and one vita. A unit per day ... our food is immeasurably better than [it was] on 814. Butter, occasional eggs, & greens at times. Don't send honey, we have plenty thanks. A cake would be acceptable ...

I am resolved to finish History III this year & have written away for University notes. Will you try and look for a book on Australian History by Wood in my room and send it to me together with any other 2 books on Australian or European History ... study will be sporadic ...

While I was writing this we were fuelling at the Engineers' Wharf with ML *1354* lying outside us and when we had finished I went on deck to talk to Jack Page. As we were passing the oil hose across to *1354* we noticed a powerful tug moving at high speed on a course which would bring her very close to us. She was acting in direct contravention of Thursday Island's Port Order No. 7, which set specific low speed limits for all vessels moving in the harbour. The tug's big bluff bows were throwing up an enormous wave, and her ugly wash was speeding straight for us. It caught *1354* beam on, lifted her about 3 feet in the air and, as she dropped, we shot upwards with sounds of tearing timbers and grinding steel. This violence continued until the last wave of the tug's wake had finished battering us. All our fenders had been torn away, some guardrails smashed, our deck split open, and two depth charges, each weighing nearly quarter of a ton, had been ripped from their racks. I signalled the Naval Officer in Charge Carpentaria, reporting the damage and requesting shipwrights to repair it.

This held us in Thursday Island for three more days and gave Clif and me a chance to take the dinghy sailing in Torres Strait and to learn something about its 10-foot tides. On our first excursion to Prince of Wales Island we found the wrecks of five pearling luggers and the grave of a Roatongan diver buried there in 1865. This expedition went off well but the next day's jaunt nearly got us into trouble.

Planning to sail around the island, we left the ship in a light southwest wind with a strong tide making, and were soon running at about 4 knots with the centreboard up, over a shallow coral reef. This was dangerous as the bottom was only a couple of feet below us and a protruding coral head could have holed our thin plywood hull and left us floundering in the water without a soul in sight. But we were lucky: after some anxious moments we shot out over the edge of the reef into deep blue water and returned to *1347* pleased with ourselves for having circumnavigated Thursday Island in three hours.

On 11 June we left on the last leg of our voyage to New Guinea via the Great North East Channel, Cocoanut, Roberts, Rennel, Dalrymple, Campbell and Darnley Islands to Bramble Cay. From that speck in the ocean our way lay eastward across the Gulf of Papua to Port Moresby. This was the parting of the ways for our flotilla. We waved goodbye to *Karina*, *1341* and *1354*, westward bound, and sailed eastwards with *1355* planning to anchor for the night under Cocoanut Island. This was an easy day's run, giving us time for water sports on the way. We glided along while some sailors, trailing lines baited with red and white bunting, caught enough fish for the evening meal, and others, riding the aquaplane, slipped backwards and forwards over the waves in our wake.

About 5 p.m. I edged in under the lee of Cocoanut Island to anchor, but could find no suitable ground in less than 12 fathoms, just outside the reef. Such a deep anchorage would mean hard work on the winch when weighing in the morning, but we had to make the best of it. As soon as the anchor had taken up, Geoff Miller secured alongside us.

With its thatched houses under the palms behind the beach the island was a pretty sight and Geoff and I went off in his dinghy to explore it. After we had rowed along the reef for about five minutes a black figure on the shore pointed to an entrance into the lagoon and in a few minutes he became our tour guide. He first showed us some large seagoing canoes pulled up on the beach and led us past piles of neatly stacked coconuts to the village where dogs barked and faces peeped shyly from behind trees and huts.

Now the little Pidgin English handbook issued to us in Sydney came into its own. With its help and by sign language, we learned that the islanders fished for pearls and trochus shell which they exchanged in Thursday Island for goods. They also traded with the New Guinea natives around the Fly River delta, which, they said, was a 'long long' way to the north. By our standards the Fly River was not far off, but in their canoes a voyage there and back must have been long and difficult.

At nightfall the sea, light blue in the afternoon, had become purple and we rowed back to our ships guided by their riding lights with the stars sparkling in a black velvet sky. As we climbed aboard the dying trade wind carried the villagers' voices to us over the water and the light of their cooking fires flickered among the trees.

While writing up my journal I felt a heavy bump alongside. Trading canoes had arrived and noisy wrangling began with our sailors about the relative values of tobacco, bully beef, conch shells and colourful 'cats eyes' from the reef.

Weighing anchor next morning was back-breaking. Thirty-five fathoms of heavy chain and an 80-pound anchor, buried in the sand 12 fathoms below, had to be hauled in with a windlass which could only gain a few links with each lever movement. It took us a quarter of an hour to get the anchor awash, but long before that the canny Geoff Miller had cast off and left us with a cheery wave.

For two days we ran north and east past Bramble Cay and across the Gulf of Papua sighting little but birds wheeling over a calm sea. At dawn on 13 June New Guinea's majestic Owen Stanley Range loomed on the horizon and every hour climbed higher in the sky. We passed 4 miles off Cape Suckling and about 2 p.m. slipped through Basilisk Passage and secured alongside Port Moresby's main wharf after a run of 248 miles in dream conditions. But things were not so easy for our mechanics. All the way from Brisbane our engines had run sweetly, with never a cough or rattle. But they had now done 500 hours since their last overhaul, and Jack Page and Ken Akers began this dreary maintenance, confined for several days below deck in the stifling engine room.

While we were stuck in Port Moresby Geoff Miller and our friends in *1355* left for Madang, and for once I was glad not to be going with them. For three days the winds had been light in the mornings, but as the sun climbed higher they had strengthened, blowing a perfect gale which roared on the reef and sent the sea boiling over it into the lagoon.

The engine overhaul left most of us with time on our hands. Clif and I enjoyed the comforts of the wardroom of HMAS *Ladava*, Port Moresby's naval establishment, swam at Ela Beach—patronised in the palmy days of peace by the 'White Mastas'—and drove out to the airfield to talk to American and Australian fliers on their way to places where the killing was still going on. Our appetites whetted by these jaunts, we begged a lift from the driver of a truck taking supplies up into the Owen Stanley Range.

After driving for about 20 miles through flat country with hilly outcrops, we climbed through thickening jungle to a plateau where the truck stopped for a few minutes beside a hallowed spot—one of the newest cemeteries in the world. We wandered there among palm trees, well-tended lawns and rows of new wooden crosses marking the graves of the men and youths who had halted the Japanese on the Kokoda Trail and turned them back from Port Moresby.[4] A monument had recently been raised to their valour inscribed with the emotive words set by Tennyson into Ulysses's mouth—'To strive, to seek, to find and not to yield'.

Rejoining the truck, we pushed on to Rouna Falls through precipitous jungle slopes where staghorns clung to trees choked with vines, and foaming torrents plunged into seemingly bottomless ravines. Here the heavy vehicle lurched and slipped on the rough track and at an altitude of 1700 feet the temperature had fallen to a chilly 68° Fahrenheit. Passing villages in clearings surrounded by extensive gardens we pulled up at the headquarters of the Royal Papuan Constabulary guarded by smartly turned-out police boys. Everything here was neat and orderly. A strong fence surrounded the grassy parade-ground and thatched barracks, and beyond them were fields of grain. A mountain torrent ran through the grounds where yet another monument stood—this time a block of granite with a bronze plaque and inscription commemorating the battle of the Kokoda Trail and the men who had died fighting there between July and November 1942.

Through steep gullies and under rocky crags, the truck climbed on up the range to MacDonald's rubber plantation. Its proprietor, an old soldier, entertained us with accounts of rubber-growing in Papua and his moment of glory there in 1942 when the Japanese attacked his plantation. Refusing to retreat to safety he stood his ground while field guns roared by the back door and machine guns hammered away in his garden. With wounded diggers dragging themselves painfully along his paths, he had stayed put 'to help the boys' and waiting, as he told us, for the chance 'to put a bullet through the skull of the first Jap he could get in his sights'.

MacDonald's plantation was the end of the run. Beyond this point the Owen Stanleys soar upwards to 10,000 feet in a cold misty world of moss and mud, lichens, trailing vines and slippery tracks. And when I thought of our soldiers fighting there and their Papuan bearers dragging their food, weapons and supplies up those cruel mountains, I thanked God that I was in the navy.

On our return to Port Moresby we visited a graveyard of abandoned aircraft littered with the wreckage of hundreds of planes. Most were American and it astounded us to learn that some, still in their packing crates, had been abandoned as the war had moved north. Some planes had their pilots' names painted on them and little Japanese flags to record their kills.

One morning during our engine overhaul in Port Moresby, a soldier rode along the wharf on a motor-cycle, stopped opposite the ship, and we began chatting. Since I had bought Ray Penny's little Waratah, I had longed to have a really powerful bike. The soldier told me it was a 3.5 horse-power Norton, captured by the Japanese from the British at the fall of Singapore and brought by them to New Guinea, where we had recaptured it. When he said that he was about to leave Port Moresby, I offered him £20 for it. We shook hands and the deal was done. He double-banked me to his barracks, showed me how the gears and brakes worked, and I rode it triumphantly back to the ship. We hoisted it on board with our depth-charge davit, I had a canvas cover made to protect it from the elements and stowed it on the quarter deck.

The Norton was a very different beast from Penny's purring Waratah. It started with a throaty roar, and on a straight gravel road could accelerate to 70 miles an hour in a few seconds. Every morning soon after dawn Clif and I took it for a spin. Our favourite run was along the road under the she-oaks to Ela Beach. Riding that fast bike through the warm morning air was a sensual delight with the wind tearing through our open shirts, cool on our chests and stomachs, and by the time we had finished our engine overhaul the Norton had carried us for more than 150 miles over some very rough New Guinea tracks. The engine always started at the first or second stroke of the kick-starter, it never let me down, and although it was to carry me on some foolish and dangerous adventures, I never had better value from any other £20.

On 17 June Clif and I went to church and heard a sermon by Padre Sherwin, a robust divine who had been formerly in charge of the Anglican Mission at Wau in the Bulolo Valley. After the service he invited us to tea where we listened, almost open-mouthed, to some of his stories. This aggressive priest, with the reputation of a fighting parson, was apparently equally at home in pulpit or pub. In New Guinea, when the Japanese landed, he had taken to the hills and joined the New Guinea Rifles, becoming adept at hand-to-hand fighting. He had us on the edge of our chairs describing how, in Salamaua, he had crept up to a house 'full of Japs' and hurled hand grenades through the windows; he could not say how many were killed or maimed. Once when half starved he had survived on rice taken from the pack of a dead 'Nip'. Padre Sherwin claimed to have been the first to hoist the Union Jack in Salamaua after its recapture from the Japanese, having kept the flag for months in anticipation of that event.

In peace time he had practised a hearty, physical form of evangelism suited to his powerful physique. One of his brother clergy, who later became an archbishop and whose veracity I therefore would not question, told me that Sherwin would go into a pub, front up to the bar, order a drink and offer to fight any patron who fancied a little holy war. If he won the bout the patron would come to church. If Sherwin lost, he would buy a round of drinks.

When he asked about our families and I admitted to being a clergyman's son, he nodded approvingly. But when he heard that my uncle was George Harvard Cranswick, Bishop of Gippsland, the gleam faded from his eye. Uncle George was also chairman of the Australian

Board of Missions, which held much sway in New Guinea, and Sherwin did not have a high opinion of him. Cranswick, he said, had made many statements which were, to put it mildly, 'far from the truth, misleading, and terribly harmful' and he went on to say that no one should be head of such an organisation unless he had spent years in the area where the missionaries worked and, in Sherwin's view, Uncle George 'had not the faintest idea of the conditions or problems in the islands'. Knowing nothing of all this, and not wishing to engage with this robust priest militant here on earth, I was relieved when he glanced at his watch and said 'Who's on for a cold beer?' And as Clif and I were about to resume our wanderings, we joined him in having one for the road to Hollandia.

11 | ROAD TO HOLLANDIA

On 28 June in boisterous weather we sailed for Milne Bay on the south-east tip of New Guinea. An old New Guinea hand in Port Moresby had told me that the prevailing south-east winds generally died away at night, but recently they had continued to howl, sending big seas crashing over the barrier reef along the coast. And there was another worry. The Naval Operations Officer had warned me that the weather was too wild for us to make the whole voyage outside the reefs, and inside them the largely unsurveyed water was full of coral outcrops. He had therefore arranged for a Papuan who knew the coast well, to sail with us and show me where I could slip through breaks in the reef and continue the passage in calmer water.

Our pilot, who introduced himself as Guba, arrived before day-break wearing a dirty pair of army shorts and a once-white singlet. He was about thirty, spoke fair English and assured me that he had made many voyages in lakatoi canoes along the coast. But I was still uneasy. For the first time I was to be alone in poorly surveyed waters with no help at hand and I knew that if, under Guba's guidance, we struck a reef and survived the wreck, I would be held responsible.

We cleared Basilisk Passage at 6.30 a.m. and altered course to run parallel with the coast, rolling heavily in the big sea. Before long Guba began looking for a blue break in the smother of foam on the reef to leeward. After about half an hour he pointed to one and nodded. I altered course directly for it but, as we got close, clouds obscured the sun, masking the colours of the water and making it very hard to judge the depths over the coral, or to spot isolated niggerhead formations just below the surface. Then the sun came out again and, partially blinded by the glare and haze, and scared by the crash and roar of the breakers to port and starboard, I lost my nerve and overruled Guba's directions, turned back out to sea, and continued our rough ocean passage eastward.

About an hour later Guba pointed to another narrow opening and again he nodded. It seemed to be about 100 yards wide but, although the gleaming breakers on either side looked alarming, the water in the middle of the passage was clear and blue. I took a deep breath and said 'OK'. Guba climbed the mast, perched himself on the cross-trees and fixed his eyes on the reef. Now there could be no turning back; we were completely in his hands. We communicated by sign language. If Guba moved his head a little to the right or left, or flicked his finger, I would order 'Starboard five' or 'Port five' as necessary, and the quartermaster would turn the wheel gently that way. To a nod of Guba's head I would respond, 'Steady as you go', and the quartermaster would hold his course. This was the informal 'Starboard easy' sort of pilotage so vital to small ship navigation in such waters and so ridiculed by the Court of Enquiry which had got Chips into trouble in Brisbane and lost Kennedy command of ML *814*. But for us it spelt survival: with the surf roaring on the reef either side, we twisted and turned and ran safely into the lagoon with Newcombe's words about challenges sounding in my ears.

Early in the afternoon we anchored off the village of Hula and, as the next stage of our journey had to be outside the reef, I anchored there for the night. And that was just as well. The trade wind strengthened into a full gale which pinned us weather-bound at Hula for two days.

From Cape Capricorn all the way up the Queensland coast I had been reading about Captain Cook's adventures in the South Seas, and although much had changed since his time, at Hula I felt we were in some way reliving his sailors' experiences in island anchorages. Perhaps influenced by this reading, I recorded my impressions at length:

So we came to Hula, a native village of about 100 buildings & 1200 people. I anchored in two fathoms about 200 yds from the nearest huts—which were built on piles out over the water. The people are maritime and own many lakatois & outrigger-canoes in which they put off to the ship to trade. They manage their canoes under sail or paddles with great skill.

The men are sturdily built with pierced noses & tattooed—the women we divided into two categories. The young & fair—from about 14–20, with pleasing open faces, clean limbed, and beautifully moulded bodies, & the worn, aged, decrepit & haggard, as Caesar would have put it 'defessus labore'.

After the ship had taken up on her anchor in the lee of the reef, about one cable's length S.W. of the village, Clif and I went ashore in the boat ... Behind this village of Hula are groves of waving graceful coconut palms—thousands of them—& native gardens growing yams, paw paws and bananas. On the beach, drawn up on the sand, were many lakatois, & hundreds of boys and girls all stark naked gambolling ... They were very shy of us & especially seemed to avoid me because of my beard I suppose, which made me look a more disreputable character than Clif. However after some little labour & distributing sundry sweets to them we won their friendship & began to enjoy ourselves immensely. Conducted by our laughing dusky guides we wandered through leafy lanes under the leaning palms with everywhere heavily scented brilliant tropical flowers & trailing sprays of frangi-pani—& finally we came to the home of Mr and Mrs

Short, Congregational missionaries with 25 years of service in New Guinea. Mr Short was a most interesting and hospitable host & a keen observer of humanity. He had travelled widely over the earth and hailed from Devon with naval tradition in his blood.

His wife a charming & gracious woman & a considerable scholar, was working on the final stages of translating the Bible into the local native dialect. We talked with them late into the afternoon—and I was surprised and pleased to find that they knew my uncle's brother, bishop Geoff Cranswick, & several other acquaintances. They gave us a fine afternoon tea of scones & cakes & fresh brewed tea—after which we took our leave & walked back through the village seeing the sights ...

In this place we again noted the disfigurement caused by the betel nut habit. The nut is about 2 inches long and shaped like a small pointed pear, inside the kernel is light brown—they chew this kernel which is an astringent & has a certain stimulating effect on people climbing in the hills. They mix the juice of the nut with lime obtained from burned coral, & they keep this in a gourd and dip into it with a stick which they suck. The cud turns a blood red colour, & in this unsightly state their mouths remain attacked by the action of the lime. Their teeth go very black & eventually fall out. The young children and girls, however have beautiful firm even white teeth. The betel and lime act as a soporific & the people sit around chewing & passing the lime to each other—rather like opium smokers.

This night a native dance was held and we were invited, & were carried ashore in the lakatois of our native friends and eventually all went to a house built on stilts out over the water. Once inside we were disposed around the walls and a space was cleared in the centre for the dancing girls. These houses are built up on piles in about 6 feet of water with palm-thatched roof and walls, a fire was burning inside and the smoke issuing as best it could through the many cracks ... All the time the circle of betel nut

Socially, the time we spent in Moreton Bay with dozens of exuberant young WRANs was fantastic (above, two crewmen with Dick Jeffs dressed up in a WRAN's uniform). But exciting things were happening in the tropics when we were ordered north and I was very happy to be off on the road to Hollandia (right).

The poorly charted Papuan coast was full of dangers, but our local pilot Guba, pictured above in his white singlet, kept us out of trouble and became one of our family. At Hula (below) I made friends with villagers who led me along paths bright with flowers winding through coconut plantations.

Our days refitting at the Alexishafen Fairmile base (above) passed pleasantly and our artistic crewman Dick Jeffs spent some of his time there painting this oil of the ship. But, considering our for'ard gun—a .50 twin Browning—to look insufficiently bellicose, he gave us a 2-pounder.

But life was not all flowers
and sunshine as this shot
taken up the Sepik River
(left) shows. In the top
left-hand corner, I am
interrogating two Japanese
officers, while one of their
dying men is being loaded
onto an Australian barge.
We escorted it to the Japanese
prison compound on Muschu
Island where their burial
parties were constantly at
work (below).

I had first been shocked at the sight of this skull wired to ML 817's mast, and it subsequently caused me sleepless nights. But the most dreadful war in human history was raging and to keep sane many young men assumed the armour of callousness and joked about these things. Such displays were not peculiar to any nation or service and the photograph above right shows Q 1347's coxswain, Len Clarkson, outside the RAAF Headquarters in Hollandia beside a skull on a post.

Fun and fright were constant companions. While cruising with Clif Wilkinson on my Norton motor bike along this deserted road, a sniper's bullet just missed my throat.

Clif Wilkinson with Abdul
Latif and Chint Singh—
Indians we rescued in the
Sepik River (above). Aboard
Q 1347 Abdul and Chint
were astonished to find a water
closet, and ate nearly all
our sugar.

Off Wewak, out in the
midday sun beside Q 1347's
wheelhouse (left).

The Imperial Japanese Navy's cruiser Kashima *arrives at Wewak to repatriate prisoners of war (above). This once proud fighting ship was now a toothless tiger, the breech blocks of her guns destroyed, and at the truck of her mast flew the pennant of General Douglas MacArthur, US Army— Japan's new Mikado.*

Back in Sydney in 1947 (right, with my sister Noel), I was to discover a very different world from the one I had known in 1939 and, for the first time in my adult life, was about to confront the perils and pitfalls of civilian life.

About 1945, dressed in the drab army/navy outfit we sometimes wore on tropical service, I was showing signs of three years' experience of war.

chewers was growing drowsier and drowsier as they sat engrossed in their unpleasant habit.

The head man then came and asked for the captain in pidgin English, & when I spoke to him he explained that we Australian sailors, from across the seas, were welcome to their hospitality.

Then the dancers came in—young men and young women not above 20 years of age and very comely—they were finely dressed in coloured grass skirts with leis of frangi-pani about their necks arms and legs & with their hair decked with beautiful flowers. The orchestra consisted of about a dozen people who beat upon some instrument like a timbrel producing a note like that of a guitar. They sang in unison with rhythm and melody while the dancers took the floor. They moved exactly as those movie shots of Samoan girls portray—gracefully swaying their bare hips & bare shoulders & limbs, keeping up an enlivening display of footwork, twirling their flower-decked bodies & hands in a most pleasing way. All this time, song and time keeping music was supplied by the girls and young men sitting outside the dancing circle.

Their songs were translated to us in Pidgin English & by signs—this way they hand down folk law from generation to generation. They also sang songs of their boys who brought the dying Australian soldiers out of the mountain fastnesses from the grim battles of the Kokoda Trail. They sang also of their boys who were taken to Salamaua but were unhappy for they disliked rice and were far from their loves. Then they sang a wistful love-song of one whose lover was far from her across the sea & her young heart was broken, weeping and full of sorrow ...

After their entertainment ... we felt it our duty to make some return in kind, & so we sang some of our songs for them, & then to their extreme delight we danced the Hokey Pokey, which is a modern counterpart of some of these ... people's dances. We must have presented a very strange spectacle, 2 officers

& 6 seamen of His Majesty's navy leaping and shouting, whirling and gesticulating in a smoky thatched hut surrounded by 40 or 50 natives beating time with their hands & throbbing out the rhythm to the dark New Guinea night—& all of this in the year of Grace 1945. I wondered what Their Lords Commissioners of the Admiralty would have thought had they seen us. The dancing and singing continued until nearly midnight when some native refreshments were offered and it was time for us to return to the ship ... They paddled us across the silver lagoon in their lakatois —the night being made radiant ... by the moon rising out of the sea & just peeping over the fronds of the coconut palms—the ocean swell was thundering and pounding on the reef, and once aboard the ship a gentle swell lulled me swiftly into a deep sleep —the last sounds I heard this memorable night were the creaking of the ship as she lay to her anchor & the trade winds singing softly in the rigging.

Soon after dawn Guba piloted us out through a break in the reef into the open sea. It was punishing; we ploughed into it, drenched with spray and occasionally digging our bows into the swells and taking green water over the fo'c's'le. During this passage we sighted three fellow-sufferers, Fairmiles, about 3 miles away, steaming in line ahead. Three hours later, Guba conned us through a break in the coral and we were soon gliding along in a picture-postcard South Sea island world. By now I accepted his directions without question; the more I got to know him the more I relied on his counsel and liked him.

Early that afternoon we skimmed close past Batumata Point and before sunset anchored under Ainioro Island. Again the villagers danced and sang for us, and this time we responded with a fireworks display, shooting red, green and white flares from our Verey pistol. But it was an anxious night. The wind shifted, throwing us on a lee shore; I was worried about the anchor dragging and at first light was glad to be at sea again on a six-hour run to Fife Bay.

Fife Bay's natives welcomed us to their sheltered anchorage and soon we were surrounded by canoes trading fruit and shells for bully beef and tobacco. While leaning over the wing of the bridge watching this floating bazaar, I saw man hold up a bird of paradise which he had shot with an arrow and given a basic curing. He unfolded its brilliant wings and spread out its tail to display the bird's flaming red and green plumage, muted here and there with soft pinks, yellows and blues. I coveted it and began to calculate how many tins of condensed milk or bully beef he would want for it. But this man was a canny trader who had done business with Allied servicemen before. He demanded cash.

Birds of paradise were rare curios and I had heard of Americans paying up to £30 for them from middle-men in Port Moresby. But Fife Bay was at the beginning of the distribution chain and he sold it to me for £2. I kept this silly purchase for years, occasionally unwrapping it and grieving to see its flaming feathers losing their lustre. Eventually I sold it to some equally silly buyer for £5.

Leaving Fife Bay early next morning, we had another rough passage until we entered the protected waters of China Strait. This was the peace-time short cut for Orient-bound ships from the south, and its furious tide, boiling around our bows, slowed us down so much that it was mid-afternoon before we moored to the US jetty at Milne Bay, at the end of a five-day run from Port Moresby.

Here we parted with Guba, the man of few words who had brought us through many dangers. Officially described as a 'native pilot', he had become one of our little family and, had I possessed Matthew Flinders's authority to sign on a native, as Boongaree had joined the crews of the *Norfolk* and *Investigator*, so Guba would have become one of my men.

In Milne Bay I literally bumped into Reg Lewis, my former captain in ML *814*, now commanding an Air Sea Rescue launch. These 'ASRs, as we called them, were lively little ships, and many young officers longed to command one. They were painted bright yellow and black, their two Hall-Scott engines gave them a top speed of

35 knots, and they were armed with four .50 Browning machine guns and two depth charges. And they had lovely names reflecting their purpose—*Air Hope*, *Air Mercy*, *Air Faith* and *Air Save*. I longed to have one of my own, and in 1946, after receiving an appointment to command HMAS *Air Speed* and it was changed, I felt deprived.

Reg and I had a happy reunion. We visited each other's ships and, in recalling old times and shared experiences in 'Darwin's Navy', we laughed about past differences and buried them.

My sailing orders, collected from the Operations Officer at Milne Bay, instructed me to proceed to Madang, calling at Oro Bay, Morobe and Langemak. But first we had to take on 300 gallons of fuel at Gili Gili across the bay. As we were pulling away from the jetty, a large rat scrambled up from below through a ventilator, ran along the deck, leaped into the water and swam ashore—for sailors, a portent of bad luck, which was not long in coming.

The steel oil barge at Gili Gili was rolling in a big surge and in spite of all our care with fenders, it holed us in four places above the waterline. We repaired the damage on the spot and thought about that rat. Returning to the US jetty I planned to berth immediately astern of Reg's ship and, as I was moving in too fast, I rang down on the engine room telegraphs for 'Half Astern' on both engines. But an electrical fault occurred in the indicators; the ship surged on and our bow struck Reg's stern, smashing his transom and jack staff. The crash brought him on deck pretty smartly, and after his initial shock, perhaps remembering some of his own ship-handling, we laughed about it and blamed the rat. We were never to meet again. He was killed in an accident soon after the war and this is the last warm memory of my captain in 'Darwin's Navy'.

Nor was this the end of our troubles in Milne Bay. While manoeuvring beside the jetty, a mooring line fouled our port propeller and Clif and I swam down under the ship with hacksaws and knives to clear it. This took more than an hour, and with our thoughts often on Milne Bay's many sharks it was anxious work which left us with sore eyes, scratches, barnacle cuts and smeared with oil.

At 11 a.m. on 5 July, ML *1347* sailed on what was very nearly her last voyage. After running down Milne Bay I decided to round East Cape by the shortest route, cutting through the Hornbill Channel, between the Cape and the island of Mei-mei-ara. The narrowest part of this 2-fathom channel—known locally as the 'boat passage'—was marked by a buoy to the west and a beacon on its eastern side. We went through early in the afternoon with the sun high in the sky and as we skipped past Mei-mei-ara's palm-fringed beach the coral outcrops were clearly visible in the water. Having cleared Hornbill Channel, we turned west and at 3 p.m. anchored off the village of Ibulai. This part of New Guinea's north coast is dominated by Mount Trafalgar and indented with narrow harbours. Near one of them, Tufi Harbour, two important navigational marks equipped with lights, called the 'Tufi Leads', guided ships passing between Ham and Veale Reefs near Cape Nelson. But, as I thought the lights might be obscured by rain, I decided to delay the passage for five hours at Ibulai, and navigate that stretch of water in daylight.

From the anchorage Ibulai presented a pretty picture, with its hibiscus, flowering vines, huts, dogs, pigs, palms and children frolicking in the water. But the closer view was not so enchanting. The betel-chewing villagers greeted us with blood-red smiles, their dogs were mangy and pigs scrawny. But they seemed pleased to see us and climbed trees for coconuts which they opened for us to drink their cool milk.

Later that afternoon I spent some time checking the courses we would be steering en route to Goodenough Bay and familiarising myself with the local topographical features. To the north loomed Normanby and Fergusson Islands, and 60 miles away a little above the horizon, Nimodao, the 7700-foot peak of Goodenough Island, hung darkly etched against the sky.

We weighed anchor at 8 p.m. and steered N 60 degrees W across Goodenough Bay. Clif turned in and I held the first watch. It had been a busy week and I was tired. At 9 p.m. I marked the ship's position on the chart and made the hourly log entry, recording that we were doing

11.5 knots, that conditions were 'slightly hazy', native fires were visible along the shore, the wind was increasing, and that nothing of note had been sighted in the previous hour.

To the north the Japanese held New Britain and I was apprehensive. From their powerful base in Rabaul Japanese aircraft had made night attacks on shipping along this coast, and a number of Fairmiles had had close calls when the planes dropped flares and then attacked them with bombs and gunfire. These enterprising airmen had flown along the shipping lanes, their sound drowned out by the roar of the Fairmiles' engines, and picked up their targets by the gleam of their phosphorescent wakes. Some Fairmilers thought that if the first bomb missed, it was best to stop engines, drift, and leave no tell-tale wake. But if there was a moon this could make them a sitting duck and I could not make up my mind what to do if we were attacked at night and as we ran on in the darkness, apart from the soft light in the compass binnacle on the bridge we were completely blacked out.

For the next two hours I stood beside the quartermaster, watching the glow from the compass card play on his face and his hands moving the wheel gently to keep us on our course. The weary watch wore on and as we had no radar, there was not even the diversion of glancing at its screen for navigational data or signs of other ships.

Shortly before 11 p.m. I suddenly felt an overpowering need for sleep. I went through all the usual motions of face-slapping, pinching, and waving arms about to prevent my dropping off on my feet, but they must have failed, for my head fell forward with such a jolt that I woke up and noted that in a few minutes it would be time to make the hourly entries in the log. Deciding to use that time identifying the stars and constellations, I looked at them and noticed what I took to be a planet shining with a steady light dead ahead about 25 degrees above the horizon, but in a part of the sky where I did not expect to see any planet. This was strange but, lulled by the steady hum of the engines and our rhythmic rolling in the gentle swell, I briefly forgot about it. When I looked again it was larger, much brighter, and now moving swiftly across the fixed stars towards us. I picked up the binoculars, focused on it, and cold fear gripped me.

It was the steaming light of a large ship rushing towards us head on and almost upon us. Away out on our starboard hand its port navigation light glared an angry red, and on our port side its green starboard light shone fiercely down upon us. A few yards in front of our flimsy wooden bow her huge steel stem towered over us like a sharp black cliff, and from its cutwater a plume of spray arched out on either side. We were rushing towards each other at about 30 knots and we were a split second from death.

I can still see Len Clarkson's shocked face as I snatched the wheel from his grasp and spun it clockwise. We were moving fast and that saved us. ML *1347* answered the helm immediately, heeling over in a sharp starboard turn, and as she swung the big surge of unbroken water displaced by the ship's bow picked us up like a chip of wood and pushed us clear. Her massive hull flashed past a few feet from my face and disappeared into the darkness astern. Faint with fright, I looked at my watch—11 p.m. Time to fix our position on the chart and make the hourly entry in the log. It reads:

> Log. 32 miles. Distance run 11 miles, Compass Variation 6° 12′ east, Deviation 1° west, Standard compass course N 56°W, Revolutions per minute 1100, Wind S.E. Force 3, Barometer 1015, Weather and visibility, C/5, Sea Swell 2/3.

In the log book there was also provision for a more general entry, headed 'Remarks on attacks, exercises, employment of crew, Detailed Navigational Information', and in that space I wrote, 'Passed ship very closely—head on, nearly rammed.'

Among the men on board ML *1347* that night were K. Akers, E. T. Barry, L. W. Clarkson, S. Edwards, R. M. Jeffs, J. A. Page, J. Dobbs, N. Whitehurst and T. C. Wilkinson. Their lives were in my hands. Some of them are now dead, and the rest are old men. They may never have known, but I can never forget, how close I came to killing them in Goodenough Bay shortly before midnight on 5 July 1945.

We picked up the Tufi Leads in broad daylight, ran safely between the reefs and in the afternoon berthed at Oro Bay, jostled there by the surge rolling in from the Bismarck Sea. The harbour was packed with American ships, and on shore troops, jeeps, trucks, earth-moving equipment, temporary buildings, and the wigwam-like Bell tents of the black See Bees covered the ground.

When I landed to report my presence to the navy, I encountered a flamboyant public relations exercise designed to boost American morale in the form of a giant billboard bearing President Roosevelt's words 'There are many roads to Tokyo: we will neglect none of them.'

New Guinea seemed to be a place for meeting former commanding officers. Returning to the ship, I ran into Ray Penny driving along the waterfront in a Jeep. He looked more worn than when we had first met in the wardroom of ML 823; his beard was long and unkempt, and his green army shirt stained with sweat. But he wore the same jaunty smile. After commenting uncharitably on my beard and enquiring briefly after the Waratah motorbike, he volunteered that he was feeling dehydrated and, rising to the bait, I asked him aboard for a drink.

In the wardroom, as he had done in ML 823, Ray enquired into the state of our liquor supplies. I told him that Clif and I hardly touched whisky or gin but, knowing them to be scarce commodities in New Guinea, we had stocked up well for our friends. To prove it, I lifted the wardroom bilge-boards and showed him our store of Invicta Gin and Corio Special Whisky. Ray's eyes widened, he begged half a dozen bottles and left the ship satisfied that at five shillings a bottle he had a bargain. The going price ashore, he told me, even for inferior stuff like this, was about fifty times as much.

We parted warmly, vowing to keep in touch, but this was to be our last war-time meeting. Our paths crossed again after the war, however, when he became the proprietor of a fashionable Sydney restaurant and, with his brother, Squadron Leader Warren Penny, invited me to become a partner in an air-charter venture, using a former RAAF Hudson to bring migrants to Australia. As with Peter Antill's offer to join his trucking business, this also tempted me but, cautious about squandering my war-time deferred pay, I declined. This was fortunate: although Warren Penny was a colourful pioneer aviator and an experienced airman the enterprise did not prosper.

From Oro Bay we ran westwards past Cape Endiadere—the scene of bitter fighting between Japanese and Australian troops—and in the afternoon found a quiet anchorage off the former German mission station at Morobe. Here we lay in 5 fathoms, our stern barely 20 yards from a beach of black sand backed by a row of deserted shabby native huts. Next day a nine-hour run brought us to Langemak Bay just south of Finschafen, and at 1.45 a.m. on 9 July we pushed on to Madang.

On our voyage up the east coast of Australia and across the Gulf of Papua we had been in waters sacred to Torres, Cook and Flinders. Now for the first time we were following the track of Dampier's HMS *Roebuck* when he had discovered and passed through Vitiaz Strait between New Guinea and New Britain, disproving that they were one land mass. Here I felt the gentle pirate's presence all around me, and as we passed Cape King William with the sun lighting the lofty mountains and smoke drifting from village fires, the scene appeared to me exactly as Dampier had described it 245 years before:

The Eastermost Part of New Guinea lies 40 Miles to the Westward of this Tract of Land; and by Hydrographers they are made joyning together: But here I found an Opening or Passage between, with many Islands; the largest of which lye on the North-side of this Passage or Streight. The Channel is very good, between the Islands and the Land to the Eastward. The East-part of New Guinea, is high and mountainous, ending on the North-East with a large Promontory, which I nam'd King William's Cape, in Honour of his present Majesty. We saw some Smoaks on it; and leaving it on our Larboard-side, steer'd away near the East Land

... no Meadow in England appears more green in the Spring than these. We saw Smoaks, but did not strive to anchor here ... I was well assur'd that we were got through [the strait], and that this East-Land does not join to New-Guinea; therefore I named it Nova-Britannia.[1]

Entering Madang harbour I saw at the wharf the familiar lines of the Fairmile ML *804*, and we berthed alongside her. My first sight of Madang, which had suffered much damage, recalled Darwin's devastation. But here the buildings had mostly been repaired; instead of blasted wharves and sunken ships, the copra plantations were the most visible reminders of war; their once graceful rows of palms now standing like broken columns in a cemetery, stripped, truncated and torn by shells, bombs and gun fire.

Lieutenant Keith Kershaw, the tall, cheerful Fairmile operations-officer ashore, limped to greet me. He had a great tropical ulcer on his leg and as I had seen what those ulcers had done to men in Darwin, I was surprised that he was still in tropical service. Having commanded a Fairmile himself he had anticipated that we would arrive with defects and immediately arranged to have the work done at the nearby Fairmile repair base at Alexishafen. He invited me to dinner in the wardroom and briefed me on the local situation.

Thousands of well-armed Japanese were opposing our men in the Torricelli Mountains and the Sepik River area and many more, isolated on Muschu and Kairuru Islands, occasionally fired their field guns at our patrol boats. The Japanese were thought to have mined the entrance to the Sepik River and had had guns at its western entrance on Cape Girgir, but no one had seen any sign of life there for months and they had probably been removed.

As soon as our repairs were done, Keith told me, I was to proceed to Hollandia (now Jayapura) to provide anti-submarine protection for the American base there where we would be maintained by the United States Navy, and paid in American dollars. This was good news. Hollandia, the former capital of Dutch New Guinea, was about 400 miles north-west of Madang, and on our voyage there we would be sailing further in Dampier's track. And as we would be coasting Japanese-held territory that would add an extra spice to it.

At Alexishafen we were hauled out of the water for repairs on a slipway built by German missionaries, and given a 'haircut and shave' —sailor-talk for the dirty job of cleaning the marine growth off the hull and painting it with anti-fouling. There we found another sister ship, ML *1343*, commanded by Lieutenant William Watts, with Sub Lieutenant Bill Raper as his first lieutenant. Shortly after we arrived Watts was ordered to land a party of soldiers on Karkar Island, about 26 miles from Alexishafen. The army was always looking for fruit and vegetables, and this excursion was to assess the native gardens on the island's east coast near Sculau Point. Dampier had been the first European to sight Karkar's 5000-foot crater-mountain Maubin, and to describe this fertile island and, as I was anxious to see something of it for myself, I begged a lift and went along for the ride.

Karkar's principal villages were marked on the maps, but the island's waters were poorly defined. The chart (Aus F. 047), published in 1943 and compiled from 'Air Plots and British, German and Australian surveys', showed the island's shape well enough, but not a single depth in its surrounding waters. And to add to this secrecy, in its left-hand bottom corner was the command that its contents were 'not to be communicated either directly or indirectly to the press or to any person not holding an official position in H.M. Service'.

As *1343* closed the shore with the leadsman calling the depths, we struck a coral reef and lay there with painful crunching and grinding noises under the bow. Everyone crowded aft to weigh down the stern and lift the bow; Watts rang down for full speed astern on the engines, we slid off the coral unharmed, and a somewhat sobered Watts then nudged his ship around the edge of the reef and anchored off the beach. That night in Alexishafen I recorded some details of the visit:

The beaches are of black volcanic sand and there is a very large coconut plantation by the sea. Here and there amid the trees little rivulets of sparkling water … wound down through the green grass to the sea.

The natives were a dirty unsavoury lot and smelt to high heaven—but this did not prevent us from bartering with them. I obtained a large bunch of beautiful bananas for a single razor blade, and some coconuts & bananas for a tin of pears and a packet of P.K. chewing gum.

On our return to Alexishafen that afternoon I heard that the destroyer HMAS *Stuart* was in Madang harbour with some friends aboard, and that evening Bill Raper and I set off on the Norton to visit them. It was a 13-mile ride to Madang and the road, running partly through the jungle, had been resurfaced with sand and crushed coral. It crossed a number of small bridges, and humps had been raised at their approaches to prevent vehicles speeding. There was no moon and, as the Norton had no lights, we took a torch. I approached the first bridge too fast, did not see the hump, the machine became momentarily airborne, and we narrowly missed a nasty spill. For the rest of the ride Bill regaled me with stories about Japanese snipers on roads like this looking for people like us. I had heard that after the Australians had re-captured Madang Japanese stragglers had remained in the jungle and crept up to an army cinema show and thrown hand-grenades into the audience, but this was the first I had heard of Japanese sniping at road traffic, and I foolishly dismissed it as rumour. Leaving the *Stuart* about midnight, we set off back to Alexishafen. The night was even darker now and, with visibility down to a few yards, the torch was almost useless. I did my best to keep the machine in the centre of the light-coloured road, but about halfway home we hit a mound of earth and bike, Bill and I, went sprawling into the scrub. We scrambled out, somewhat scratched, and after a hard struggle got the heavy Norton back onto the road and made it safely back to our ships.

The next night Clif and I went to a cinema show at an army camp, this time travelling more comfortably in an armoured weapon-carrier. The track wound through palm trees to a clearing in the jungle where a sheet strung between two coconut trees provided the screen, rows of palm trunks the seats, and the tray of a truck the projector platform. The memory of that scene stays with me: fronds rustled above our heads, bats wheeled among the trees, and the stars burned brilliantly above New Guinea's mountains.

Several days later, while the ship was still in dock, Clif and I decided to ride to Madang, collect the mail, lunch in the wardroom there, read a newspaper, and ride home in the afternoon. Although I had almost dismissed Bill Raper's tale about Japanese snipers, it still lurked in the back of my mind, and before leaving Alexishafen we loaded our .45 revolvers and strapped them round our waists in unclipped holsters.

At the first kick of the starter pedal the Norton woke to life with a growl which became a roar as I turned the throttle-grip, and off we went with a surge of power and the tug of warm air in our shirts. Clif, on the pillion seat, tucked his hands into my revolver belt, occasionally leaning forward to shout into my ear.

After cruising comfortably at about 40 miles an hour along a deserted road through fairly open country, we came to a place where the jungle closed in on either side, with trees only a few yards away. Suddenly I felt a little puff, something whizzed past about an inch from my throat, and above the sound of the engine we heard the decisive crack of a rifle in the bush to our right. Clif's grip hardened on my waist, I accelerated to about 60 miles an hour and sped on down the road for about a mile, stopping only when the country opened out to hold a council of war. Madang was still miles away down the empty track. Although we had just escaped one ambush there might be more ahead. Risky to go on, risky to return, and risky to stand still. We knew roughly where the sniper had been and, as he had revealed his position, we hoped he would now be heading back for the hills.

Forgetting Madang's fleshpots, we made a run for it back to Alexishafen: with Clif's revolver at the ready, we shot through the ambush area at over 60 miles an hour and came through unscathed. The excursion which had promised so well ended on a sombre note with two very lucky young men thoughtfully celebrating their survival over a lukewarm drink under the awning on *1347*'s deck.

On Monday 23 July 1945 we sailed for Hollandia and, as the Sepik River carried many large logs out to sea, left Madang about 8 p.m. in order to pass the river's mouth in daylight. By 11 p.m. we were in the middle of Isumrud Strait between Karkar Island and New Guinea. I had been looking forward to this part of the run as we would be passing Bagabag, Karkar, Manam, and other islands in the Schouten Group discovered by Dampier.

Manam's volcano rises from the sea in an almost perfect cone to 5500 feet, and its eruption in 1700 so impressed Dampier that he named it 'Burning Island', describing it with his usual flair:

March 25th 1700, in the Evening we came within 3 leagues of this Burning-hill, being at the same Time 2 leagues from the Main I found a good channel to pass between them and kept nearer the Main than the Island ... The Island all Night vomited Fire and Smoak very amazingly; and at every Belch we heard a dreadful Noise like Thunder, and saw a Flame of Fire after it, the most terrifying that I ever saw. The Intervals between its belches, were about half a Minute, some more others less: Neither were these Pulses or Eruptions alike; for some were but faint Convulsions, in Comparison of the more vigorous; yet even the weakest vented a great deal of fire; but the largest made a roaring Noise, and sent up a large Flame 20 or 30 yards high; and then might be seen a great Stream of Fire running down to the Foot of the Island, even to the Shore. From the Furrows made by this descending Fire, we could in the Day Time see great Smoaks arise, which probably were made by the sulpherous Matter thrown out of the Funnel at the Top, which tumbling down to

the Bottom, and there lying in a Heap burn'd till either consumed or extinguished; and as long as it burned and kept its heat,
so long the Smoak ascended from it; which we perceived to
increase or decrease, according to the Quantity of matter discharged from the Funnel. But the next Night, being shot to the
Westward of the Burning-Island, and the Funnel of it lying on
the South-side, we could not discern the Fire there as we did the
Smoak in the day when we were to the Southward of it. This
Vulcano lies in the Latitude of 5 deg. 33 min South …[2]

Since Dampier's day Manam has been described by many other
travellers. Of its recent eruptions, those in 1919, 1921 and 1936 had
been spectacular, throwing huge rocks thousands of feet into the air
and sending molten lava pouring down its sides. The *New Guinea
Handbook* records that the 1919 eruption dumped its debris as far
afield as 70 miles and that:

> The red stream of lava poured into the sea, causing the water to
> boil furiously and sending up huge volumes of steam and black
> vapour, which rose to a great height, covering the rumbling
> mountain and surrounding country. At night it was possible eight
> miles away to read a newspaper by the light of the reflection of
> the lava on the clouds. Gardens and houses were destroyed, and,
> for two or three days, the natives had to spread banana and bread-
> fruit leaves on the tracks to prevent their feet from being burnt.[3]

I longed to see Dampier's 'Burning Island' in convulsion but the best
it could do for us was a cloud of smoke pouring from its crater.

We passed the mouth of the Ramu River before dawn, fortunate
to avoid its floating debris, and when the sun rose and the blue
Bismarck Sea suddenly became muddy brown we were surrounded by
the Sepik's floating trees and islands rising and falling in the low swell.

In 1616 the Dutchmen Le Maire and Schouten sailing along this
coast, had witnessed this same sight and suspected a great river near at

hand; but it was not until 1885 that a German, Dr Otto Finsch, in the *Samoa* discovered it and rowed 30 miles up it in a whaleboat. The Sepik River winds for over 700 miles into the heart of New Guinea, draining the Victor Emanuel and Torricelli mountains but, unlike its counterpart, the Fly, on the south coast, it has no delta or shallow bar.

Apart from these historical associations, the Sepik had a more pressing interest for us. This was Japanese territory and, although there had been no recent sign of them, we knew they had had guns on Cape Girgir and, hoping to clarify the position, I edged in closer to have a look. The rising sun lit the jungle and muddy low surf with a golden light, and although we saw nothing suspicious, in case they still had an observation post there, I decided to run in closer and shoot the place up. We turned in, and with the sun behind us ran directly down its path towards the shore. I sounded Action Stations, we donned our Mae Wests and steel helmets and manned the guns. When about 400 yards from the beach, we turned parallel to it and raked the area. The crash of gunfire, exploding shells, and the flurry of leaves and branches torn from the trees startled the bird life. But there was no answering fire. During the next five minutes we shot off four drums of ammunition from the twin Vickers on the bridge, 500 rounds of .5 inch tracer, armour piercing and incendiary bullets from the Brownings, and 300 20 mm Oerlikon shells. In retrospect it was a silly, foolhardy act of youthful bravado; had we hit a mud bank, or had there had been a Japanese gun there, we would have been in deep trouble. But it made us feel good to have a shot at the King's enemies.

As we approached Wewak, about halfway en route to Hollandia, it was our turn to be shot at; bullets splashed in the water around us and whined over our heads. As on this part of the coast I knew the Japanese were mostly back in the hills, I suspected this to be carelessness on the part of our soldiers ashore and, turning away, ran directly out to sea, presenting a smaller target, and flashed our Aldis lamp at them. The shooting stopped. I subsequently reported the incident to the army at Wewak who said that the fire came from men testing their machine guns.

And so we came to Wewak, a place of contention not only between Australians and Japanese but also a cause of concern for many thoughtful people in and out of uniform. In the view of some, attacking the enemy here at this stage of the war was a wanton sacrifice of Australian lives. They questioned why the Japanese around Wewak—now without any outside support—could not be left alone in the jungle to starve or die from disease.

On 27 June 1945, about a month before we arrived at Wewak, the *Bulletin* had discussed this in a powerful editorial probably written by Malcolm Ellis:

Australia's own War. Tough Going in New Guinea.

The Wewak campaign is developing into a weary game of chase and extermination, in wet, murky hill country which seems to have been furnished by Providence with an endless helping of peaks and razor backs for the benefit of the enemy. There is a phantom quality about the whole business which makes it one of the worst experiences in campaigning which Australian troops have ever been asked to suffer. The campaign has no great strategic objective, no glorious victory in the offing to lend lustre to the fighting. The enemy appears to have no form and no location. Pieces of him come away in the hands of attacking units, but his residue slinks off, dividing or uniting as occasion demands, but always all claws.

The nights are noisy with mortars flinging destruction at some sawback or warren while the 'woodpeckers' spit defiance and their owners try all the seemingly stupid but nerve-wracking raiding tricks for which they have become notorious. Each encounter ends with a scramble, usually through mud and blood and lawyer vines, up a slope like a greasy pole, after which all there is to show as a symbol of victory is a foul enclosure trodden into wet pudding, with mangled and charred bodies flung about like old rags and the rain beating down on them.

The patrols go on to take another place of the same breed, certain only of one thing—that the Jap will be there, well armed with the kind of weapons which give him mobility, and loss of which doesn't mean much if he has another cache of them to run to further back, as invariably he seems to have …

Food is flavoured with the damp and fungus of the tropics and with the eternal reek set up by 25-pounders, bombers and flame throwers, which swathe the landscape in oily smoke for days, the humidity bringing it down to ground level and assuring that the troops will wade through it up to their necks, sleep in it, breathe it along with the odour of Jap camps and of Jap dead … There seems to be months of this bloody piecemeal campaigning still ahead, at least for part of the force …

We found the atmosphere ashore tense with sentries posted everywhere and nearly everyone carrying a weapon. The Japanese, desperately short of food and medical supplies, would sometimes come down at night to raid our stores. Two evenings before we arrived, after a savage mêlée, a raiding party of them had been driven back into the hills, and as we lay at anchor that night our peace was shattered by the crash of 25-pounders and the chatter of Owen guns and Woodpeckers in the hills.

We spent 25 July watering, exploring the foreshore and chatting with soldiers, some of whom complained to us about the futility of this campaign. Next morning a visit to a compound holding Japanese prisoners gave me something to confide to my journal:

> They were dressed in dry clean clothes, new boots—given dry beds and mosquito nets, atebrin, & ate the same food as our soldiers. One of these Japanese was a Sergeant-Major—a surly treacherous-looking brute, another a corporal who came from Tokyo and after the war hoped to live in Mosman, Sydney!! The troops here are very bitter towards the Nips & would far prefer to kill them than take prisoners …

Clif and I borrowed a Jeep and toured the Wewak battlefield. Wrecked Japanese barges littered the beach and blasted vehicles lay beside its muddy roads and tracks. The airfield at Boram was pock-marked with bomb craters and surrounded by wrecked Japanese planes. As we arrived there it began to pour with rain and we climbed into a Mitsubishi transport aircraft for shelter. After sitting for a few minutes dry and snug among dirty packages and bundles listening to the downpour thundering on the fuselage, we smelt the sickly sweet aroma of the mature corpse Clif was sitting on. As the rain continued to bucket down a soldier joined us and for the next half-hour treated us to an eye-witness account of his jungle war.

After a spell in action on a feature he called 'The Ridge' he had been brought back to Wewak for a 'rest' and was now road-making. The Japanese, he said, were in a hopeless position, but they still defended every ridge fanatically. Starved for meat, many had become cannibals. Recently one of his mates had been shot near 'Lazy Creek', and about half an hour later when he reached the body he found that the flesh had been stripped from its arms, legs and thighs, the head had been split open and the brains removed. I had heard second-hand stories of such things but this, my first eye-witness account of this horrible face of war, shocked me.

The downpour stopped, out came the sun, searing the wet earth and making it steam. Driving on from the Boram airfield towards Wewak Point we passed a number of small white crosses marking the graves of young soldiers buried where they fell. Our tour ended at Wewak Point, strewn with wrecked guns, abandoned equipment, smashed trees and bomb craters. Notices warned of booby traps and the danger of leaving the cleared tracks. We peered warily into the tunnels excavated under the cliffs on Wewak Point where our soldiers had incinerated the Japanese defenders with flame throwers.

While waiting for a boat to take us back to the ship we met a subaltern and invited him aboard for a drink. As we sat on deck watching the sun sink behind the Prince Alexander Range, he talked about 'his' war. He had left school to fight on distant battlefields, and had already campaigned against the Italians in the Libyan Desert, the Germans in Greece and Crete, the Vichy French and the Foreign Legion in Syria. Captured by the Germans in Crete, he had escaped, returned to Australia and fought on the Kokoda Trail. Now, worn down by hard campaigning, he was fighting in this pointless campaign. He repeated the story we had already heard that the Japanese were 'dying like flies from disease' and spoke sadly of his own battalion's losses. When it first went into action in New Guinea, it had seventy-two 'originals'—men who had fought in North Africa. Now, he said, there were only twenty of them left. His account of the jungle war-fare here bore out the truth of the article in the *Bulletin*. The Japanese tactics made patrolling a nerve-wracking business; their snipers would hide in the vines or scrub until a patrol was only a few paces away and then shoot for the throat of the leading man. He confirmed stories of their cannibalism of our dead and added that they were also eating the natives. He painted a terrible picture of the sufferings of the Japanese soldiers on their retreat from Wewak to Aitape. Their corpses lay all along the road where they had fallen, many with packs still on their backs. No wonder they called New Guinea the 'Island of Death'. Some, when captured, had counterfeit Australian pound notes in their pockets and thought they were in Northern Queensland and that their army had captured Sydney.

At 6 a.m. on 26 July 1945 we sailed from Wewak in flat calm con-ditions on the last stage of our long voyage from Sydney to Hollandia. Eight miles from Wewak we had to pass through Muschu Strait separ-ating the enemy-held Muschu Island from New Guinea. When about 500 yards from the island's Cape Samien, we saw several Japanese on the shore and opened fire on them. Our shells, bursting in pin-points of light, started a small blaze, but thankfully there was no flash of a gun returning fire.

After an uneventful 70-mile run to Aitape we anchored off the beach near a partly submerged Japanese ship, and in the morning, continuing westward past Cape Concordia and Mount Bougainville, entered Humboldt Bay—the end of our road to Hollandia.

12 | WORKING FOR THE
YANKEE DOLLAR

We were met by one of Hollandia's few RAN staff and, after being allocated a berth in Challenger Cove, I went off to report my arrival and be briefed on our coming role. With one or two other MLs and several American sub-chasers we were to provide anti-submarine protection for the port. Then, while the ship was being fuelled, watered, stored and re-armed, Clif and I went off in a Jeep to have a look, and marvel at the vast American base.

Hollandia, lying just south of the Equator on Humboldt Bay and capital of Dutch New Guinea, had for me been mainly associated with the voyages of early navigators. In 1827 the Frenchman Dumont D'Urville, exploring the north coast of New Guinea in the *Astrolabe*, had sighted the bay and named it for his idol Alexander von Humboldt, in the hope that 'M. Humboldt may find in this sort of homage a token of my gratitude for his services to the *Astrolabe*'s mission'.[1] Thirty years later the Dutch surveying vessel *Etna* had called there, and in 1875 Captain George Nares had visited it in HMS *Challenger* during her voyage around the world. Now it was the site of an immense American base and, with the exception of the White Ensign worn by ourselves, MLs *1354* and *1358* and HMAS *Martindale*, the Stars and Stripes reigned supreme. Everyone in Hollandia worked for the Yankee dollar and while we were there we were to be armed, entertained, fed, fuelled, repaired, provisioned and paid by Uncle Sam in US dollars.

Before the Japanese invaded the island there were only about 200 Europeans in Dutch New Guinea, but on 22 April 1944, when General Eichelberger's First American Corps stormed ashore at Hollandia, it was defended by 12,000 Japanese. Of these the Americans killed 3300 and captured 611 for the loss of 159 men.[2]

The Americans then worked around the clock with the most sophisticated earth-moving equipment in the world, transforming an area of swamps and jungles into a huge military base designed to be a springboard for assault on Japan. Eichelberger recalled:

> Road construction had proceeded simultaneously [with building runways] and this was a gigantic task. Sides of mountains were carved away, bridges and culverts were thrown across rivers and creeks, gravel and stone 'fill' was poured into sago swamps to make highways as tall as Mississippi levees ... Hollandia became one of the great bases of the war. In the deep waters of Humboldt Bay a complete fleet could lie at anchor. Tremendous docks were constructed, and 135 miles of pipeline were led over the hills to feed gasoline to the airfields. Where once I had seen only a few native villages and an expanse of primeval forest, a city of 140,000 men took occupancy.[3]

Clif and I drove around Hollandia taking in its docks, airfields, wharves, stores, chapels, and recreational facilities, awed by the power and money it represented. Even at this late stage of the war I counted fifty-five ships in Humboldt Bay, and later learned that before the invasion of the Philippines it had been packed with over 800 ships.

Everywhere we went we were surrounded by American culture, power and wealth. The Stars and Stripes, flying in the wind or hanging listlessly from masts and poles, proclaimed America's national pride and, as we drove along winding roads gouged through steep jungle slopes, billboards displayed quotations from speeches by

General MacArthur and President Roosevelt. The amenities for their troops here were beyond the wildest dreams of our soldiers in New Guinea: about a dozen cinemas, Coca-Cola bars supplying a variety of iced drinks, doughnut stalls and recreational halls. On the radio, hits sung by Bing Crosby or Hogie Carmichael were interspersed with patriotic songs, martial music, news items, and details of the weather in American towns and cities.

There was evidence too of the constant presence of death. Beside perilously sharp bends on the mountain roads, white crosses with names and regimental numbers recorded the fate of soldiers who had taken those bends too fast; and the Japanese skulls fixed to an occasional post along the way reminded me that the sailors in ML *817* had not been the only head hunters in New Guinea.

Hollandia had been established as an outpost of the Dutch Empire in the East Indies and although few signs of those origins remained, some traces of Dutch culture lingered on. Our local charts were Dutch and we found their language quaint. Humboldt Bay was 'Humboldt Baii', and the sea washing it bore the romantic-sounding title 'Stille Oceaan'. All measurements on these charts were metric, and I had to remind myself continually that the heights and depths shown were not the familiar fathoms and feet of our Admiralty charts. *1347* could just swim in a little over a fathom of water, but to venture into 2 metres would court disaster. The compass roses on the Dutch charts also took some getting used to. Sometimes, instead of the familiar 360-degree notation of our Admiralty charts, they were divided into thirty-two points of eleven and a quarter degrees, bearing such names as 'North by East' and 'South by West', reminiscent of the windjammer days.

As new chums we had much to learn about local conditions, and our first patrol was sobering. With guns loaded, depth charges primed, and Asdic set pinging away, we commenced work 5000 yards to seaward of Humboldt Bay, running north-west at 8 knots for thirty-five minutes before reversing course back to our starting point.

As this was our first assignment we were all on edge and when, at 10.45 a.m. the monotonous 'ping, ping, ping' of our transmissions was broken by clear sharp submarine echoes, I sounded 'Action Stations', increased to full speed and altered course directly towards the target. The men tumbled up on deck, donning life jackets and helmets, and ran to their stations. On the bridge Clif and I listened intently to the echoes coming through the amplifier. The target was not moving and, assuming it to be a stationary submarine, I attacked at once. The ship had now gained its maximum speed and as we ran in, the interval between the transmissions and echoes shortened. When they were almost instantaneous, indicating that the object was immediately beneath us, we dropped two depth charges set to explode at 50 feet.

The detonation of nearly 1000 pounds of high explosive hit the ship with sledge-hammer blows and columns of white water soared into the air astern. With our binoculars trained on the boiling patch of sea, we circled back to renew the attack. A few dead fish floated on the surface but there was no tell-tale oil or debris and, as there were no more echoes I concluded that our target must have been a sub-merged tree trunk which our charges had pulverised into fragments too small to send back an echo. Such flotsam from New Guinea rivers was to become a thorn in our flesh. Some logs lay awash and were sometimes visible, others sinking slowly into the depths of the Stille Oceaan were invisible.

Rolling gently in a low swell we continued our beat with the Asdic's 'pings' sounding regularly through the amplifier. We trailed fishing lines astern and the watch-keepers on deck ate their lunch-time sandwiches and drank their mugs of tea under the bridge awning. But this holiday mood was interrupted at 1.10 p.m. when the ship was shaken by a heavy shock as our cutwater struck a massive log lying inches below the surface. It bumped along the side of the hull and hit the starboard propeller causing heavy vibrations and making a sound like a circular saw cutting through wood. This pushed one end of it deeper into the water and, as we watched, the other end of a huge tree rose from the sea and slowly sank from sight. I stopped both engines and Clif, generally the first to volunteer for jobs like this, dived over to assess the damage. After what seemed a long time he surfaced red-faced, and said the blades seemed a bit bent. But when we started the engine it did not vibrate badly and we continued plodding along our beat.

During these patrols, although most of the crew worked the 'three-watch' system—four hours on and eight hours off, and were able to enjoy long sleeps—the engine-room staff of two, and Clif and I, worked 'watch and watch' with four hours on and four hours off, and never had more than three and a half hours of unbroken sleep. When I was off watch in daylight hours, I would generally find a seat under the bridge awning and study the books and lecture notes now regularly arriving from the University of Sydney. I also had a few volumes I had brought from Sydney, or picked up in second-hand bookshops along the way. These now formed the nucleus of a small ship's lending library and I put this list of them on the notice board:

> *The Log of Christopher Columbus' first Voyage to America in the year 1492* (illustrated)
> Dampier's *Voyage to New Holland*
> M. Uren's *Sailormen's Ghosts*
> *Coast of Tragedy*
> Geoffrey Ingleton's *Charting a Continent*
> *Tokyo Record*
> Freud's *Dreams and Sex Theories*
> *David Copperfield*
> Trevelyan's *History of England*
> Wood's *History of Australia*
> *The Lives of Wellington, Napoleon and Abraham Lincoln*
> *Efficiency in Speaking and Writing*
> *The Poems of Francis Thompson*
> Evatt's *Rum Rebellion*
> Captain George Shelvocke's *A Privateer's Voyage*.

Whenever we returned to Challenger Cove one of my first chores was to read the official mail. Most of it was dreary administrative stuff but the Allied Intelligence Reports, marked 'secret and confidential', were an absorbing read. By now, Japan's merchant fleet, navy and air power had been largely destroyed, her armies isolated, and her island garrisons left to wither on the vine. Her strongholds of Iwo Jima and Okinawa had fallen, American Superfortresses were torching Tokyo and reducing other Japanese cities to ashes and the Soviet Union, at long last, was about to claim her pound of flesh. But, as with Nazi Germany when all was lost, there was still no public clamour for surrender in Japan, and America was preparing a vast operation to invade its sacred soil. In her desperate hour Japan's valiant kamikaze pilots were taking a fearful toll of our ships and that was a bad omen for any allied landing there.

As Professor Sadler had impressed on me in 1940, the Japanese valued life so differently. After the American invasion of the island of Saipan, when they had killed or captured the last of its 32,000 garrison, hundreds of Japanese civilians had fled to the northern end of the island where for two days they:

> ... embarked on a ghastly exhibition of self-destruction. Casting their children ahead of them, or embracing them in death, parents flung themselves from the cliffs to the jagged rocks below. Some waded into the surf to drown or employed other gruesome means of destroying themselves. How many civilians died in this orgy of mass hysteria is not known.[4]

From the intelligence reports I gathered that the first landing on Japan could take place in early November 1945 and already, in response to this threat, thousands of boats, packed with high explosives, were being prepared in creeks, harbours and rivers all around the coast of Japan to make suicide attacks on our shipping. Ashore, too, the allies could expect to face hordes of civilians with grenades, guns, knives and even sharpened bamboo stakes. Some speculated that the conquest of Japan might cost us a million lives and there were gloomy prospects of the conflict dragging on until 1947. After nearly six years of war most of us were looking homeward and were appalled at the thought of having to fight yard by yard for our wretched enemy's homeland.

It was therefore with a feeling of elation and relief that one morning, as we were listening to Hollandia's radio report on the weather in Detroit, Michigan and Kansas City, we heard an excited voice break in to announce that a bomb of awesome power had been dropped on Hiroshima. It killed more than 140,000 people and many thousands more were to be disfigured and suffer and die from lingering radiation illnesses. The announcer gave us a vague description of this terrible weapon, grossly understating its size, and an assurance that there were more to come.

That evening, in an emotional mood and drawing from the radio reports which had continued throughout the day, I recorded our entry into the nuclear age:

At sea on anti-submarine Patrol off Humboldt Baii—Dutch New Guinea.

The Americans are now dropping Atomic Bombs on the Japanese. These new and terrible bombs are said to be the size of a medium parcel, & yet have the explosive force of 24,000 tons of High Explosive. One is sufficient to completely wipe out a whole city or island—the steel in buildings in the explosion area is said to be vaporised by the terrific force of the explosion. Russia has declared war on the crumbling Japanese Empire who now have the whole world arraigned against them. She now faces the prospect of being torn to pieces and her cities ... ravaged. It seems certain now that ... within a few weeks she must surrender or commit her misguided millions to drown in a bath of their own blood. This is the pass to which this proud, arrogant and bestial enemy has now been brought. Her soldiers were merciless and cruel in victory, & we expect that they will be subservient and humble in defeat. It remains to be seen however, whether the

tens of thousands of well-equipped soldiers that Japan still has in
the many island strongholds ... will refuse to surrender. Their
native fanaticism ... may urge them on and they may continue
to fight ...[5]

And this seemed to be borne out. After the second atomic bomb had
been dropped on Nagasaki, killing 70,000, the Japanese fought on,
with her brave suicide pilots taking a terrible toll on our ships. In the
face of such devoted fanaticism the prospects of the forthcoming
invasion and one million allied casualties haunted me.

Meanwhile, we continued trundling up and down off Hollandia
searching for submarines. But the end was near. On 15 August a triumphant American voice announced that Japan had unconditionally
surrendered.

In war, momentous events are sometimes uncomprehended by
those who observe them. But hindsight clears the air and, in 1996, the
military theorists Harlan Ullman and James Wade spelt out the real
impact of these two bombs on Japan: 'The Japanese ... were prepared
to fight a suicidal battle to ward off the invasion of their home
islands. Then we drop two bombs and they quit ... that was shock
and awe.[6]

Immediately after the surrender announcement the 'Star-
Spangled Banner' blared from the loud-speaker on our bridge, and
then 'From the Halls of Montezuma to the Shores of Tripoli'—the
battle hymn of the United States Marines, who had indeed fought
their country's battles on the 'land and on the sea'. Ashore, news of
Japan's capitulation sparked hysterical celebrations. Humboldt Bay was
full of American destroyers, oilers, Victory ships, Liberty ships, tugs
and other vessels. None would now be needed to assault Japan: all had
been reprieved, countless lives had been saved, and Hollandia threw a
wild party.

Brilliant bunting blossomed along the waterfront and from the
ships in the bay gunfire erupted as rockets, flares and star shells soared
into the sky, and we heard next day that several men had been killed

by shell splinters in their triumphant hour. I made a beer issue to the crew and when pressed, doubled it. That night I described the scene:

> ... as darkness fell the fireworks broke out again ... such a display. Scarlet orange and white magnesium flares & parachutes and rockets blossomed in the starry tropical night, & tommy gun, rifle, machine gun, Bofors and general gunfire broke out in a pandemonium of noise ... Sirens hooted & bells rang & we joined in this general jubilation, firing our rockets & sounding our horn ... tracer shells soared into the air ... pieces of burned out shells and rockets fell hissing into the water about us ... and the words of the American anthem
> > 'And the rockets' red glare,
> > Bombs bursting in air
> > Gave proof through the night
> > That our flag was still there ...'
> were vividly interpreted for us this night.

The celebrations became wilder and when an unexploded shell splashed into the water a yard from our bow, I realised that we were not out of danger and ordered everyone below. Our troubles were not yet over: home was thousands of miles away and a long and uncertain voyage still lay ahead. Subdued by these thoughts, I left the fireworks to others, went below, donned my steel helmet lest a shell came through the deck, and read myself to sleep.

Next day we returned to war routine. Many Japanese in New Guinea who did not yet know, or could not believe, that their Emperor had quit, were still at war and we were directed to be alert for treachery. Arrangements were being made for Japanese aircraft to fly members of their Royal Family to island garrisons to convince them that Japan had really surrendered, and the planes carrying these envoys were ordered to trail streamers. On 18 August a signal arrived from the Naval Officer in Charge New Guinea couched in capitals for emphasis:

ALL R.A.N. SHIPS AND AUTHORITIES N.G. AREA.
JAPANESE HEADQUARTERS HAS ADVISED THAT AIR-
CRAFT ARE CARRYING MEMBERS OF IMPERIAL
FAMILY TO VARIOUS THEATRES OF OPERATIONS TO
PROMULGATE SURRENDER. NO ITINERARY HAS YET
BEEN TRANSMITTED FOR THIS AREA. MARKINGS
OF AIRCRAFT ARE SIMPLY STREAMERS OF POINT
DECIMAL 55 METRES LENGTH. ANY JAPANESE AIR-
CRAFT APPROACHING IS NOT TO BE FIRED ON
UNLESS IT OBVIOUSLY SHOWS HOSTILE INTENT.
182326Z

Then came a series of official messages, the first being from the enemy.
The Commander-in-Chief of the Japanese South-Eastern Army and
Navy signalled his congratulations to the 'Commanding General of
the First Australian Army' and added a cautionary note:

> We pay our respects to your brilliant fighting to this day. According
> to the order of HIS MAJESTY THE EMPEROR THE JAP-
> ANESE ARMY AND NAVAL FORCES on NEW BRITAIN
> BOUGAINVILLE and NEW IRELAND are by every means
> endeavouring to accomplish the cessation of all action as soon as
> possible. As yet there has been no clashes of any kind between
> your forces and ours but in BOUGAINVILLE on account of the
> dense jungle it has not been possible yet to deliver the order to
> cease fire to those forces which have penetrated deep into your
> lines. Therefore the commander of the JAPANESE ARMY in
> these areas has sent an emissary to your front lines and has com-
> menced negotiations for your co-operation regarding the con-
> veyance of the above order. We will appreciate if you will kindly
> render assistance in this regard. The JAPANESE Commanders of
> these islands have not been authorised as yet to commence direct
> negotiations with your Command except concerning the cessation
> of hostilities. Therefore until we are so ordered from TOKIO we

wish to have you understand that we cannot open up further negotiations but these regarding the 'Complete' delivery of the stop fighting order to all men.

But orders are not always received, or obeyed; many Japanese in New Guinea were to retain their weapons for weeks and we were to play a part in disarming them.

As a suicidal attack on Hollandia's shipping was still possible, the anti-submarine patrols off Humboldt Bay were actually increased and MLs *1347*, *1354* and *1358*, and US sub-chasers *699*, *736* and *742* were placed on high alert. We patrolled as usual, fully blacked out at night, with our depth charges primed and guns loaded. Convoys still arrived and departed and we continued challenging all approaching ships and recording their names and destinations.

Then came a series of official messages, the first from the Naval Board relaying a message from General Douglas MacArthur:

I have received the following inspiring message from His Majesty King George the Sixth of England and am proud and happy to forward it through you to the forces.

I send you my heartfelt congratulations on overwhelming success which has crowned your efforts. From the first day of the treacherous attack on the Philippines to this last glorious moment, your military skill, your dauntless courage and your inspiring leadership have gained universal admiration and esteem.

On behalf of all my people I would ask you to convey a special message of thanks and congratulations to the forces of the British Commonwealth who have had the honour to serve under your command in the series of operations which you brilliantly concluded. 201318Z.

Another was an Order of the Day of 15 August 1945, from General Sir Thomas Blamey, Commander-in-Chief of the Australian Army:

SURRENDER OF THE JAPANESE

The Japanese have surrendered.

Our long and arduous struggle has ended in complete victory.

The climax has come at the time when all six Australian Divisions are fighting strenuously, each on its own area, in the far flung battle line … formed into a magnificent army to the pride and glory of Australia.

We have fought through the burning days and freezing nights of the desert. We have fought through the ooze and sweat of tropical jungles. We have defeated the Italians and the Germans and we would soon have destroyed completely the Japanese before us.

We are now to go to our homes, having done our part in ensuring freedom, for which we have fought so long and successfully …

General Blamey made no reference to the thousands of our soldiers with no known graves, or who were still lying under such little white crosses as Clif and I had seen beside the muddy Wewak tracks. They would never be going back to their homes.

The surrender of the Japanese forces in New Guinea and the islands did not occur until 6 September 1945, when the following Instrument of Surrender was signed on board the Royal Navy's aircraft carrier, HMS *Glory*.

In Hollandia our contacts had mostly been with our sister ships and the small RAN unit ashore, and we seldom had much to do personally with the Americans. But one day during this twilight time between peace and war, the captain of the US sub-chaser *736* came aboard to see me. He had just arrived from the coast of France and had been ordered to inspect a local native village near Germania Head. He knew nothing about coral waters and as the charts were sketchy, he asked me to accompany him in *1347*. This was a change from monotonous patrolling; I welcomed it, received permission to accompany him, and off we went together.

Instrument of Surrender

of

Japanese Forces in New Guinea, New Britain, New Ireland, Bougainville and adjacent Islands

I, the Commander in Chief of the Japanese Imperial Southeastern Army, hereby surrender to the General Officer Commanding First Australian Army all Japanese Armed Forces under my command in accordance with the Instrument of Surrender issued by the Japanese Imperial General Headquarters and Government and General Order Nº 1 Military and Naval issued by the Japanese Imperial General Headquarters.

I will henceforth and until otherwise directed by you or your successor carry out the orders issued by you or your staff on your behalf to the best of my ability and I will take action to ensure that my subordinate commanders carry out the orders issued by your representatives.

General, Imperial Japanese Ar.

COMMANDER IN CHIEF
JAPANESE IMPERIAL SOUTHEASTERN ARMY

草鹿任一 匹
(南東方面海軍總指揮官)

Received on board H.M.S. Glory off Rabaul at 1130 hours sixth day of September 1945.

LIEUTENANT GENERAL
GENERAL OFFICER COMMANDING
FIRST AUSTRALIAN ARMY

'Instrument of Surrender' for the Japanese South-Eastern army signed on board *HMS Glory*, 6 September 1945

As we drew less water than SC *736*, we led the way in and anchored off the village. In landing, both our boats were half swamped and we all got a good soaking. The villagers were a dirty-looking lot; their scruffy dogs were covered with sores, and the children ran away from us. Their huts, however, were neat, well made, and surrounded with flourishing gardens of taro, yams, and bananas. After we had inspected the village and returned to our ships the SC's captain rowed over for a glass of beer, which he rated a 'real treat'.

Here was a man I had only just met, and probably would never see again. But war brings men quickly down to basics and almost immediately we began talking about our homes and families, our philosophies and beliefs, and after six years of war, our apprehensions about returning to civilian life. He asked me back to dinner in SC *736*, but as the rising wind had thrown us on a nasty lee shore I declined and he had a hard row back to his ship. It was one of those war-time moments where strangers meet, share intimate thoughts, move on, and never meet again.

On our return to Hollandia when Jack Page asked to see me I had to make an unwelcome decision. He had received a letter from his family doctor about home problems which, the doctor thought, required his immediate presence, and he advised him to apply for compassionate leave. This was very bad news for the ship. Jack was a skilful engineer; he had been with us from the beginning, understood our engines perfectly, kept them in top condition and I had been comforted by the thought that on our 3000-mile haul back home, they would be in his hands. But the big run-down in the navy had begun; he had long been separated from his family and I recommended his application for leave. We had a farewell drink together, shook hands, and he left promising to call on my parents in Sydney and deliver an oil painting of *1347* painted for me by Dick Jeffs. I prepared the family for Jack's arrival:

> Jack Page … is such a good type and was a very steadying influence on the crew. He is [leaving] on the 'Manoora' now going to Morotai, Balik Papan, Sydney and Hobart where he will be

demobilised. He will be in Sydney between the 14 & 20 Nov. He is taking down an oil painting of this ship ... he has been a great comfort & help to me during ... trying times.

His replacement, Motor Mechanic G. J. Russell, was to be unlucky— and in joining us he very nearly shipped out on his last voyage.

The Americans in Hollandia wasted no time in winding down their affairs and began ditching much of their unwanted equipment. One morning, as we were returning from patrol we passed an outward-bound tug towing a large pontoon packed with brand new Jeeps; an hour later the tug returned to Humboldt Bay with an empty pontoon.

Smaller items—typewriters, electric fans, watches, binoculars, cooking equipment, and some weapons—were freely available. Soldiers went round the bay in boats exchanging them for liquor, and Clif and I traded several bottles of whisky and gin for a typewriter, wrist watch and two .30 calibre carbines with 5000 rounds of ammunition. These light and versatile semi-automatic weapons were much superior to our heavy Lee-Enfield rifles and served us well.

We continued patrolling off Hollandia on a full war footing until 4 September 1945 when we were ordered to Madang. On the way we called at Wewak and were astonished to hear that General Adachi had not yet surrendered his army, sporadic fighting had continued and that two days earlier the Japanese had attacked, killing some of our men, and our 25-pounders had shelled their position in the hills.

At Madang we expected to receive sailing orders for home but were told that much work remained to be done in the islands. After the Japanese had all surrendered and been disarmed, they would have to be guarded and supplied until they were repatriated. A few MLs would have to remain to help the army in these operations and we were to be one of them soldiering on in the islands.

13 | SOLDIERING ON

The Japanese presence in the islands remained formidable and we
now had a difficult job on our hands. As well as the Japanese
army in New Guinea, there were about 139,000 men in New Britain,
New Ireland and the Solomon Islands, and more of them in Balikpapan, Morotai, Labuan, Timor, Malaya, Ocean Island and Nauru—in
all, about a quarter of a million men, the last of whom were not to surrender until 1 October 1945.

And they had not been honourable foes. Many of us distrusted
them and, as we learned more of their horrible cruelty to the natives
and war prisoners, we came to detest them. We neither understood
nor sympathised with their philosophy that:

> The greatest honour a soldier could attain was to die for the
> Emperor. A soldier who was taken prisoner was an outcast, a
> Commander whose force suffered defeat should ... commit
> suicide.[1]

Soldiering on suited me: there was a taste of adventure in it, and when
I was given the choice of working with the army in New Britain or
Wewak, I chose Wewak. First we had to prepare the ship for our new
role. We landed our depth charges and unshipped the Asdic dome at

Madang and that was a load off my mind. Without it we drew much less and could venture into shallower water. We were then sent to the Alexishafen Fairmile Base for an engine overhaul and the removal of our 20 mm gun, and that was a boon too. We still had plenty of firepower for police work and, as it was very hot and sticky below deck, we rigged an awning over the gun platform to provide a shady place to sit by day, or sleep at night. I also managed to persuade the Alexishafen shipwrights to cut a hatch in the deck above the wardroom to let in more light and air. This greatly improved our living conditions below but got me into hot water with the authorities. The outraged Base Engineer Officer, Jim Moore, told me bluntly that I had no authority to alter the design of one of His Majesty's ships without official approval, and that he had a mind to close off the hatch and make an official report on the matter. He was, however, a good-hearted Scotsman, and when I pleaded with him over a drink he softened, said that I was an 'irresponsible young bugger', and that in future, if I had any ideas of changing the design of 1347, before taking the law into my own hands I must submit an 'A&A'—an application for an alteration or addition to a ship.

In September 1945 Alexishafen was like a holiday resort and one of its luxuries was to shower under a 44-gallon drum near the wharf. In its soft sweet water—a far cry from the heavily chlorinated water in Hollandia—we could work up a rich soapy lather and wash it off extravagantly, and then, after a heavy dusting of Johnson's Baby Powder, return fragrantly on board.

Removed from Madang's officialdom, life at the Fairmile Base was relaxed and at times delightful. On Sunday 16 September 1945, I stood on deck in the cool morning air and watched dawn break. Around us, except for a rat gnawing in the bilge of a ship alongside, all was still and quiet. Just after 5.30 a.m. the sun lifted out of the Bismarck Sea, flooding the lagoon and flame trees around the blasted mission station with a golden glow; 30 feet below me in the clear water fish glided around a sunken Japanese barge, and 27 miles away to the north, the peak of Karkar Island gleamed with a royal blue light.

As we would probably be operating in areas with few port facilities or roads, I decided to sell the Norton motorbike and learned something about the laws of supply and demand. Hoping to get my money back, I asked £20 for it, but everyone in Alexishafen was looking homewards and there were no takers. Just when I was planning to dump it at sea, I jumped at an offer of £5.

The engine overhaul and repairs kept us at Alexishafen till 24 September; the days passed pleasantly, fishing, sailing, swimming and reading recent additions to my small library. One of these, Frank Greenop's *Who Travels Alone*—the story of Baron Miklouho-Maclay's fifteen-month residence in this part of New Guinea in 1871—had a topical interest. He had been landed from the ship *Vitiaz* in Astrolabe Bay about 40 miles from Alexishafen and, surviving many adventures, died at the age of forty-two.

It was equinox time, and although the noonday sun burned in the sky about 84 degrees above our heads, the sea breeze cooled us and gave us splendid sailing weather. Occasionally I would go off alone in the skiff to a village on the lagoon for fruit. Approaching the beach I would raise the centreboard and run the boat up on the sand near the huts. These people had lived through the Japanese occupation and greeted me with waves and smiles. With a little help from my basic Pidgin English, but mostly by sign language, we would exchange limes, pawpaws and bananas for tobacco, chewing gum and perhaps a razor blade. On one occasion Clif joined me on a jaunt to deserted Sek Island. Pulling the dinghy up on the beach, we dropped the sail and followed a path leading under a canopy of trees and vines into the jungle. Before long we stumbled upon a well-constructed Japanese bunker with a cleared line of fire from its weapon pit to Alexishafen's wharf just across the water. Its deep, sandbagged fox-holes had platforms for machine guns, and positions had been constructed for snipers in some of the surrounding trees. With our American carbines we shot down a few coconuts, drank their cool milk and lunched on local bananas and pawpaws sprinkled with the juice of limes picked from a nearby tree. Then, after a swim in the lagoon, we sailed back to

Alexishafen after a day almost as good as those we had spent with the girls on the beaches in Moreton Bay.

After six years of crippling war expenditure the Australian government began tightening its purse strings. In 1939 Australia's population had been about seven million and in 1945 nearly one million of them were in uniform—possibly the greatest percentage of militants of any country. To restore the economy Australia had to get her fighting men home quickly and off the pay-roll. For six years marriages had been postponed and it was now vital to re-establish the nation's family life and breed the Baby Boomers' generation.

The government's efforts to save petty cash led it to a pinch-penny meanness resented by the sailors in small ships soldiering on in the islands. In addition to their ordinary pay, men in MLs on tropical service had drawn 'Hard Lying' pay, a few pence a day, to compensate them for harsh living conditions. At the stroke of a bureaucratic pen this was now was halved and called 'heat money', making us wonder what sort of people down in the cool south were running our lives up in the steamy north.

Our rations too, were much worse than they had been under Uncle Sam's generous catering in Hollandia, and on 23 September I muttered in my journal:

Our food has been very poor of late—for several days at a time no bread, and not much of anything else except a little tinned food—we have been in a more or less semi-hungry state for some time and, but for the native fruits, it would have been much worse. Since we arrived in New Guinea some of my crew have lost more than one stone in weight, and developed sores and tropical ulcers and other ailments indicative of a vitamin-deficient diet. The coxswain is issuing more lime juice.

Towards the end of September, however, things looked up when a ship arrived with 'eggs, sausages, and the first fresh meat we had had for weeks'. Food was always in our thoughts, and we could not understand why it was not more varied. A Liberty ship had recently unloaded a cargo of what we called 'yippee beans and goldfish'— baked beans and tinned herrings in tomato sauce. It also brought a consignment of tinned mackerel. Some of the fish, in tall round tins, were 'fish standing up', and others, in long flat tins, 'fish lying down'.

On 26 September we sailed for Wewak to come under the operational control of Lieutenant General Sir Horace Robertson and joined our sister ships *1342* and *1356* at Wewak Harbour. This is one of the four bays—Boram Bay, Wewak Harbour, West Harbour and Dallman Harbour—lying along the 7 miles of coastline between Cape Moem and Cape Wom. We came to know them well and, although they received some protection from the nearby Muschu Island, we were to suffer in the wet season for their being open to northerly weather.

1342's captain, Lieutenant Keith Englert, briefed me on the situation. For weeks his had been one of the MLs patrolling Muschu and Kairuru Islands, which were still garrisoned by thousands of Japanese, who had occasionally opened fire on the MLs with their field guns. On 13 September he had attended the Japanese surrender at Boram airstrip near Wewak. There, in the presence of 3000 6th Division soldiers and a few Fairmilers and airmen, General Adachi, commander of the Japanese 18th army, had been made to march between rows of specially chosen tall men right up the airstrip to General Robertson, and lay his sword on a table in front of him.[2] This historic table from ML *805* is now in the Australian War Memorial, a reminder of the part played by the MLs in the war against Japan.

The Wewak campaign had cost both sides dearly and our troops had suffered the highest disease rate of any campaign in New Guinea. The 6th Division's horrific casualty returns speak for themselves: although 442 young men were killed and 1141 wounded in this obscene campaign, 6227 went down with malaria, 1386 with skin diseases, 1229 with dysentery, dengue fever and scrub typhus, and 7370 more became casualties from other afflictions. Without proper food and medicines the Japanese had suffered dreadfully too, dying like flies from wounds and disease.

We also learned from Keith Englert that there were probably about 3000 well-armed and equipped Japanese along the Sepik River still holding allied prisoners of war. F. O. ('Derick') Monk, an Australian New Guinea Administrative Unit (ANGAU) lieutenant, had led a patrol on a dangerous mission to contact them. As we shall meet Monk and these prisoners shortly, here are some details of Monk's adventures as he described them to me.

The day after Adachi's surrender, he left Wewak accompanied by 'an army medico', Lieutenant Jim Goreham, Warrant Officer P. F. Feenberg and ten native police boys. There were also a 'couple of adventurous passengers, Captains Arthur Pepper and Don McCrae, who went along for the fun'. Part of Monk's mission was to contact the enemy in the Sepik area, tell them that the war was over, and order them to lay down arms. He took with him with a piece of paper signed by General Adachi, to show to the commander of any Japanese post he might meet, ordering him to let Monk pass.

The patrol marched eastwards from Wewak for about 2 miles partly along a beach known to be covered by a Japanese machine-gun bunker. As they neared it, Monk could plainly see the camouflaged weapon pit and when, as he put it, they were 'uncomfortably close' he left his police boys and went on alone—a courageous act which he dismissed as 'routine'. But it also would have been routine for the Japanese to open fire, and Monk was a brave man.

When he was about 20 yards from the muzzle of the gun, a Japanese corporal 'stood up behind the sand bags and scratched his head'. Monk walked closer, waving Adachi's piece of paper, and the soldier signalled him to stop. Monk describes the moment:

> The Japanese N.C.O. came forward, read the note, bowed, and said 'Ah so', and bowed again. We established that he could speak enough Pidgin English for us to be able to converse quite freely.

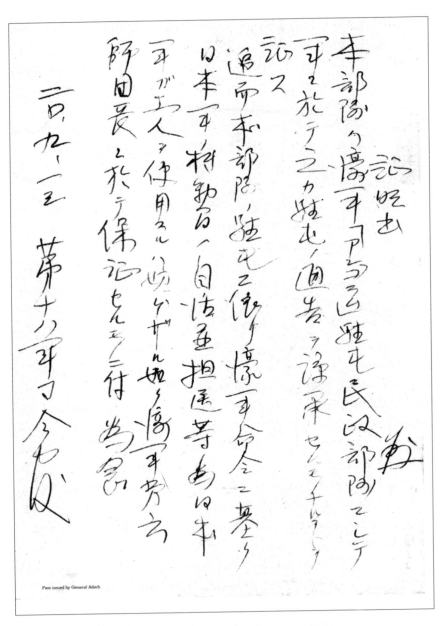

本部隊ノ俘虜タル「フランシス、ヲルター、モンク」氏ハ部隊ニ於テ之ヲ収容シアリタルモノノ通告ヲ諒承セラレタキコトヲ認ス

記ス

追而本部隊ノ撤退ニ伴ヒ俘虜ヲ本隊ニ会スルコトニ基キ日本軍ノ将勢力ノ自活ヲ全ク担遇等ヲ日本軍ガ正ニ人ニ依用スル助ケザル地ノ俘虜ノ労力ヲ野田長ニ於テ保証モノニ之ニ付当該

二〇、九、一二 第十八軍司令官

Pass issued by General Adach

The pass given to Lieutenant F. O. Monk by General Adachi

I told him peremptorily, that I wanted one of his men to hurry on ahead and warn all the other troops that we were going right through to Angoram [Japanese headquarters on the Sepik River]. I detailed the track we intended to follow and hoped that the runner he sent off immediately would follow it carefully.

I asked him had his party not been warned that we were coming, and on his answering that they had not, I asked the further question 'How then is it that you didn't fire on us?' His reply was to the effect—'Well, when we all saw you wandering along like that ... we couldn't believe it. We were still arguing about it when you and your kempi came right up here'.[3]

Some days later Monk reached Angoram and confronted the commanding Japanese general there, informing them that their Emperor had surrendered and they had 'lost the war'. He found the general:

a very withdrawn remote sort of man obviously disdainful and resentful of this large uncouth Australian lieutenant, sent out to co-ordinate the dishonour of his troops. He appointed a couple of liaison officers, Captain Namura, who seemed a nice sort of fellow, and a ratty little man, Sergeant Kita who was later either executed or gaoled for a very long time, for his war crimes.

When asked, the Japanese denied that they had any prisoners, but on being told by the natives that they were lying, Monk demanded to see them. The meeting, he told me, was 'heart wrenching'. He found about fifteen Indian soldiers, captured in Singapore; with thousands of others they had been shipped to New Guinea as slave labourers and these were the pathetic survivors of that force. Monk gave them what little food and care he could and continued his patrol, leaving them in the power of the Japanese some of whom, in the event of defeat, planned to kill their prisoners lest they should testify against them.

About a week before we had arrived at Wewak, Fairmiles *805* and *809* had been sent up the Sepik River to Angoram to also tell the

Japanese that they had lost the war. Keith Englert in ML *1342* had followed them escorting three army barges fitted with pre-fabricated bunks to evacuate the worst Japanese sick and wounded to their hospital on Muschu Island.

While the faster Fairmiles went on ahead to instruct the Japanese to have their sick ready to leave next day, Keith followed, leading the barges. Not far from the entrance a Japanese mine exploded underneath the barge directly astern of him, disabling it and leaving it drifting out to sea. Turning back, he tried to tow it up river but was unable to make any headway against the current until the other barges had been lashed alongside the cripple. Next morning, with the river shrouded in dense fog, about a hundred Japanese sick were carried on to the barges and with *1342* towing the breakdown, they left on the painful voyage to Muschu Island.

This then was the picture when we arrived in Wewak to become an odd-job ship for the army.

The Wewak hospital—a canvas affair—was always looking for fresh food, and our first operation was a fruit-run of about 70 miles to the mountainous island of Vokeo in the Schouten Group. The Schoutens, about 3 degrees south of the Equator, were once mostly active volcanoes, and the natives grew splendid fruit and vegetables in their rich soil. The trip was like a picnic cruise: two soldiers, Captain Brian Fogarty and Lieutenant Don Stevens, came along to do the trading, and two army nursing sisters came along for the ride.

Vokeo was poorly charted and I nosed into the shore gingerly, anchoring in a bay on its south-east side. Soon we were surrounded by canoes loaded with bananas, pawpaws and coconuts. Fogarty and Stevens quickly got down to business. Both were fluent in Pidgin English and sign language, and before long they had bought everything on offer for a few tins of bully beef or, as they called it, 'bulmakau'. The next trading post—a village on the island's western side—was a nasty place for a sailor with a lee shore and a surf breaking on the beach. It was also too deep to anchor and, as I would not risk the ship close in, all we could do was to steam slowly up and down well offshore, and when the canoes came out, heave-to and trade. But the wind kept pushing us closer to the surf and we frequently had to start the engines and move further out to sea. For two hours this anxious cruising and drifting went on while the black and white businessmen jabbered and gesticulated at each other. Here twenty-four tins of bully beef were exchanged for three-quarters of a ton of pawpaws and bananas which we stacked around the gun platform and depth-charge racks.

This was the first time I had heard Pidgin English spoken by competent linguists. Before we had left Sydney the Navy had issued me with Captain John Murphy's *The Book of Pidgin English*, to guide us in dealing with natives. Most of us did not understand the vocabulary or grammar and, at best, used what Murphy deplored as 'the broken English and English words tricked out in Pidgin-English forms … an unsatisfactory medium for representing the sounds of Melanesian Pidgin-English'.

Fogarty and Stevens indicated numbers by signs directly opposite to those we would have used. Had we wanted five pawpaws, we would have held up a thumb and four fingers but, in Pidgin, quantities are indicated by the number of fingers turned down, and they showed a clenched fist.

Our next duty was to patrol Muschu Island. Occasionally we would land army teams to inspect the Japanese establishment on the island and I would sometimes go ashore with them:

> The Japanese are very servile to us now and bow and scrape whenever we go among them—we always go armed, none-theless. An order has been issued that all Japanese officers, irrespective of rank, must salute Australian officers. All Japanese soldiers must salute all Australian soldiers. This regulation is to impress on them that no longer do they enjoy the prerogative of being the master race.

The Japanese had little idea of hygiene and in the hospital—little more than a long open-sided hut—I was nauseated by the stench of excreta and decay. Death was everywhere:

> The Japanese ... are very thin—just skin and bone. I walked through the ward of their hospital & was horrified at what I saw. Three men were lying together on a large litter or bench—the centre one had his head covered with a dirty rag and a cloud of flies hovered over him—he had been dead a long time—with the other two struggling for life lying shoulder to shoulder with his stiffened corpse.

Across Muschu Strait in New Guinea, our burial parties were busy digging the bodies of our soldiers from their battle graves and interring them in a military cemetery. The strain of this hot heavy work was exacerbated by lack of proper food. In far-off Sydney, surrounded by cool comforts, waterside workers were staging a series of strikes and refusing to load food for their countrymen soldiering on in the islands. With this industrial action tightening our belts, New Guinea became a political issue in Canberra. On 13 October 1945, the *Sydney Morning Herald* had run an article entitled 'Half Ration for Wewak Troops M.P. Quotes Army Signal': 'An Army signal, ordering the reduction of certain rations to half the usual issue and the substitution of vitamin tablets, was quoted by Mr Abbott, MP, to support the claim that the 6th Division A.I.F, in the Wewak area of New Guinea, are short of food.' The article went on to state that the 'failure of shipping' to supply the army had led to drastic rationing—particularly of tinned meats, milk, beans and margarine, and that until full rations were restored Vitamin B and C tablets would be issued in lieu.

Confronted by this issue in the House, Prime Minister Chifley called for inquiries, but the situation hotted up when the Deputy Leader of the Opposition quoted from a letter from a soldier in Wewak:

The position here is serious. Do you know the 6th Division is almost starving? They announced last night that we have enough food for one and a half days' issue. At present we have a meal at 9 a.m., two vitamin tablets for lunch, and a meal at 4 p.m. Is this the thanks we get from a grateful country? I'm fed up, and to top it off I'm hungry.

On 13 October the *Bulletin* published a cartoon under the caption 'Whacko in Wewak', showing the corpulent Minister for the Army, Frank Forde, in a cooking pot at Wewak about to be fed to the hungry diggers.

Early in October I was summoned to 6th Division Headquarters and told that MLs *1347*, *1356* and four barges from the 43rd Army Water Transport Division were to proceed up the Sepik to Angoram where there were about 3000 Japanese and hopefully, the Indian prisoners Monk had discovered in September. The Japanese were to be disarmed and their worst sick taken in the barges to Muschu Island. ML *1347* would escort the barges while ML *1356* would go on ahead to Angoram and instruct the Japanese to get their sick ready. As it was expected that we would find Japanese barges in the river, but without enough fuel to return with us to Wewak, several 44-gallon drums of it would be sent in our barges. As Monk would be coming with us to re-establish the Australian government post at Angoram I looked forward to learning more about the Sepik and its people from him. And, with the possibility of encountering another Japanese mine, this was going to be an adventure.

Among the many orders, instructions and memoranda I had received since the war's end was one tailor-made for this operation. I had so far only glanced at it and filed it away, but now I dug it out and read it carefully. Dated 22 August 1945, it came from Acting Commander J. B. S. Barwood RAN and had been sent to all the RAN ships in New Guinea, Biak, Balikpapan and the Moluccas.[4]

Transporting Japanese Prisoners—Liberated Asiatics

The capitulation of Japan will probably necessitate H.M.A. Ships transporting Japanese and liberated personnel. Commanding Officers are to see the following instructions enforced as far as is practicable.

Diseases

These personnel may be expected to be suffering from one or more of the following diseases.

Malaria, Hookworm, Dysenteries, Scabies, Pediculosis of the pubes, head and body hair, Ulcers and Tineas.

A possible case of latent cholera and small pox may be found, and pulmonary tuberculosis may be present though not obvious. This list is not exhaustive but these are the conditions which may be transmitted to the ship's company or to the camps ashore.

Months before, the navy had foreseen such health risks and given me some tips. Before coming on board all prisoners were to be stripped of 'dirty, verminous or smelly' clothing, which was to be thrown overboard. They were to be segregated on the upper deck and, as some of them would have dysentery, the area where they squatted should be hosed frequently:

Sanitation is the most difficult question. Asiatics will spit, urinate and defecate promiscuously. A hose running in the scuppers is probably the best solution for heads. No paper need be provided —the running water is used.

Additionally, 'Orientals' on board were to have all 'head and pubic hair' clipped, and to prevent our being infected with typhus, they were to be made to clip each other. We were to give them drinking water in buckets and after they left the ship we were to wash down the decks with a solution of 'about 10 scoops' of chlorine to a kerosene tin of water. We were not to use Dettol and must boil all mess traps they had used or touched. Sobering reading this: I left Wewak sincerely hoping that I would not have any spitting, urinating and promiscuously defecating Japanese on my ship.

Early on 10 October Lieutenant Monk joined us and later that day we led the four barges into the mouth of the Sepik River. Its swirling 4-knot flow caught their bluff bows squarely and slowed them down so much that it took us about an hour to reach the village of Kopar a little way upstream. This was the area where the mine had exploded under one of Keith Englert's barges and I felt pretty tense. There may be some alchemy between the mind and body, and as I stood on the bridge conning the ship, my feet tingled. I don't understand these things, but even as I write this now, my feet tingle.

Now we began to sense something of the magic of this mighty river running 700 miles into the icy heart of New Guinea in the Victor Emanuel and Torricelli Mountains. From its entrance, in latitude 3° 51′S, we followed it south-south-west when it sinuated back like a great brown snake, almost touched itself, and then ran north without a bend for 4 miles. The muddy water gave us no indication of depths, but the deep channels, sometimes disturbed by big whirlpools, were close to the steep timbered banks, and the shallows lay off bends backed by low land.

The clumsy convoy plodded on, twisting and turning to avoid the logs and floating islands so well described by Patrol Officer J. K. McCarthy as: '… huge masses of earth and roots, floating down the river to its mouth … Half-an-acre in area, the earth was firmly held by the twisted vines and roots and even trees still grew on them. Sometimes an unlucky pig would be an unwilling passenger on a voyage to the sea.'[5]

These islands scared me. If one caught our bows it could swing us side-on to the flow and smother us and, as there would be no night navigation for us here, we began looking for somewhere to spend the dark hours. Eventually we found a likely place; our barges were secured to trees on the bank and we moored outside them.

This was the first time the ship had been in fresh water and, in spite of its muddy colour, it tasted sweet and was so soft that in our bucket-baths on deck we were able to work up a rich soapy lather. The halt gave us a chance to meet the soldiers in the barges. Most were old New Guinea hands, and a detachment of armed Papuan police boys gave the expedition something of a Stanley and Livingstone flavour. They told us that the Japanese had controlled all this area, that there still might be some straggling snipers about, and that the natives had cooperated with them and might be untrustworthy.

A few yards upstream from our berth a path led into the jungle and, as an hour or two of daylight still remained, Clif, a sailor and I, went off to explore it. Mindful of the cautionary tale about Japanese stragglers, Clif carried a Thompson sub-machine gun, the sailor several grenades and I buckled my loaded .45 revolver around my waist. Then, additionally armed with two tins of bully beef, off we went.

The track led us through the jungle for about quarter of a mile to the edge of a clearing. Men had been killed before by a sudden burst of fire from a native hut and I wondered if these huts contained suicidally minded Japanese snipers. While nervously fingering my revolver and wondering what to do next, I noticed a movement under one of the houses. A domesticated black pig wandered out into the open: men were not far off. Then a black face appeared at the entrance of the nearest hut; I beckoned, and two nearly naked men climbed down and walked warily across the clearing towards us, stopping about 10 yards away. Holding up a tin of bully beef, I said in my worst Pidgin, 'Bulmakau number one kaikai. What you got?' This was supposed to mean, 'I have food of the best quality, what have you got to trade for it?' They understood and by sign language, told us to wait, then, returning to the house they brought back a carved wooden figure of a man with an erect penis, an unnaturally large head, beetling brow, and with his little ears pricked forward. A bun-like protuberance, hollowed through from left to right, crowned his head and a brown circular shell adorned his right arm. He had no feet, but just below his knees where his legs joined the base of the sculpture, four finials rose towards his thighs.

In 1945 I knew nothing of Sepik art, but this grotesque figure attracted me and I offered a tin of bully beef for it. The man took the tin eagerly, but held tightly to his figure, looking for something more, and I noticed that his eyes were glued to the gold button, embossed with the Admiralty crown and anchor, on my right epaulette. A flick of my knife freed it and clinched the deal. He grasped the button, thrust the figure into my hands, the five of us smiled, and the men walked back to the houses. It was now almost dusk and remembering the sniper near Alexishafen we hurried back to the ship.

I stood my Sepik man on the wardroom desk where he stared at me accusingly as though passing judgement on me. And I deserved it. I had left the ship with no thought of the consequences of an accident which might have removed both her officers. I had originally refused to accept command on the grounds that I was irresponsible, and this proved it. In calling me an 'irresponsible young bugger', Jim Moore had hit the nail on the head. As I write this nearly sixty years after the event, my Sepik man still glowers at me from a bookshelf in my library—this time, perhaps, in reproach for my having removed him from his Sepik spirit world. That night, despite my earlier cavalier attitude to security, I felt apprehensive, and ordered the sentries to stand their watches with rifles loaded and hand grenades ready. After doing midnight rounds, I stayed on deck for a few minutes, listening to the Sepik's voices before going below to bring my journal up to date:

> The night is dark and moonless—full of river noises and the stars are bright. I saw a strange light flicker and disappear in the jungle accompanied by an eerie gurgling sound, as though someone was being strangled—the sentries are all armed, and I have cautioned them to keep a keen watch and call me if there is the slightest disturbance. There are fireflies trimming their tiny lamps along

the banks and huge bats are flitting about in the trees. This then is the setting as we take our rest tonight—the dark and impenetrable jungle on one side, and the mighty Sepik on the other, murmuring and sighing, as it rushes out to join its muddy torrent to the blue Bismarck Sea.

At 4.50 a.m. we were off, heading for the Japanese base at Marienberg where we hoped to find the Indian prisoners, and on our journey we began to learn more about this vast river. In cutting its way to the sea it made deep loops, turning almost back on itself. At these places the natives had occasionally cut shallow canals, short-circuiting the main stream and saving themselves miles of poling and paddling on their journeys.

As we moved upstream the jungle thinned out and we began passing meadows dotted with clumps of sago palms and stands of tall timber. This park-like appearance was deceptive, however, for what looked like lawns were really stretches of kunai grass, wild maize and long reeds, and in the river's backwater we could see lagoons covered with water lilies and crowded with herons, ducks and other aquatic birds.

Now and then we would pass a village in a clearing or overtake canoes crawling along this ancient highway. We kept the lead line coiled on the fo'c's'le ready for instant use and sounded frequently. On some bends we found as much as 11 fathoms close to the steep banks, but opposite them where reedy banks ran back to kunai country, the water was shallow.

About midday we passed the village of Bien and a couple of hours later reached Marienberg and moored to the bank close to several Japanese barges, three of which were in good working order. Then with a sergeant from one of our barges, two soldiers and a police boy, I went off to look for the Indians. Warned by Commander Barwood's memorandum on Asiatics and my experience on Muschu Island, I was prepared for ugly sights, and they were there:

... here was a Japanese Army post with about 300 troops—most of whom were very depleted and ill with beri-beri & malaria. Many lay about under miserably constructed shelters, their bloated and pestilent-ridden bodies as disgusting as the scenes of indescribable filth which surrounded them. Some were obviously dying, and a foul stench of death and disease invested the whole place. The fitter ones bowed and scraped to us ... as we inspected their lines. I was shocked that human beings so close to death could be allowed to lie in pools of stinking urine, surrounded by their own excreta, and covered by swarms of flies. Their food (sac-sac, the extract vegetable from the sago palm) was there too in the midst of all this horrible filth. Those of the Japanese who were fit and able to shift for themselves had apparently been so brutalised by their experiences of the last six years, that they had ceased to care for their compatriots who could no longer shift for themselves.

The sergeant summoned a Japanese soldier and in Pidgin English ordered him to bring his commander to us at once. A haughty officer arrived wearing his sword and stared at us disdainfully. The sergeant told him that we had come to remove the Indians from his control and to take his sick to Wewak, and then asked 'Where are the Indian prisoners?'

'I don't know', the Japanese officer replied.

The sergeant persisted. 'Some weeks ago the Australians found about a dozen Indians here under your control. Where are they? Tell me now or we will kill you now.'

A strange look clouded the Japanese officer's face as though it had just perceived a great truth. 'Ah! Perhaps there may be some Indians with our troops at Angoram, I will send our barges and bring them to you.'

The sergeant pondered. It was now mid-afternoon, our barges could not travel at night and he did not want the Japanese going on ahead to make their own arrangements. 'We are giving the orders here now. You will do as you are told. Our barges will leave at first light in the morning for Angoram.' He then dismissed the officer with a peremptory wave of his hand and we set to work disarming the Japanese. That night I noted:

> We took here a good haul of rifles, bayonets, ammunition, machine guns, electric generators, and other equipment. We dumped all the arms into the middle of the muddy Sepik River. We kept some Japanese revolvers and also sixty Samurai swords.

At 5.30 next morning, 12 October, we led the barges upstream from Marienberg and shortly after 9 a.m. secured alongside ML *1356* at Angoram. Here we found about twelve Indian prisoners in a pitiful condition, diseased and undernourished with wounds, sores and ulcers all over their bodies. Their officer, Jemadar Chint Singh, who wrote an account of his 'deliverance', later commented that we looked a pretty ragged group too:

> I saw here a launch ML No. 1347, very nicely painted. There were men with long beards on the quarter deck. Sepoy Chain Singh who was standing near to me asked, 'Are those men Prisoners of War recovered by the Australians?' I gazed again and again and was inclined to agree with him. They were dressed in only short pants but had long beards the same as we. After a short time one, Sub Lieut Wilkinson, came to me, talked for a while, and then guided us to the launch. He introduced me to one of those bearded men as the Captain and the others as the crew of that boat. Here my guess failed, but the impression was still on my mind, so I asked the Captain, 'Were you Prisoners of War sometime before?' He is a keen witted man and replied, 'I keep the beard to keep prestige over the crew and also to frighten the Japanese.' His answer pleased me very much. He is only twenty-three years of age, thin, but strong, with a very cheerful and intelligent disposition.[6]

Notwithstanding Commander Barwood's warnings, we took the Indians on board and fed them. Singh recalled: 'The crew gave them very new things to eat and packed them (not like the Japanese) with bundles of chocolates, biscuits, milk and so many things. They all went happily to their barges.'

That night in the wardroom, while constantly dipping his finger into a bowl of sugar, and sucking it greedily, he poured out the story of their sufferings, talking wildly of anything that came into his mind: now weeping for the fate of his murdered friends, now laughing uncontrollably at his deliverance. He had often contemplated killing himself and thanked God he had not done so. Singh had a profound sense of divine protection and wept when I told him that, at whatever times he wished to pray, Clif and I would leave him alone in the wardroom. He thanked me repeatedly, saying the Japanese had never allowed the Indians time to pray and had mocked them when at prayer by snatching their holy books, desecrating them, and ripping out pages for cigarette papers.

Frequently his face darkened as he relived some particular brutality, and in a flood of words he would blurt out its details. Stories, such as this which he recorded for the war crimes trials in Wewak, appalled us:

One day Pte Maida (Jap nursing orderly) was suffering from dysentery and his boots became dirty with his uncontrollable motion. He ordered one of our officers Jem. Kitial Singh to clean his boots. The officer cleaned the boots but did not carefully examine them and a little dirt remained. Pte Maida took a big stick and mercilessly beat the officer over the head. Kitial Singh became unconscious but the Jap did not stop beating him. His head started bleeding and blood flowed over his face and shirt. The officer remained very ill for over one month and then died ... One day Lt Murai caught Sepoy Ram Singh with four lemons in his possession. He tied him to a tree and then the whole guard, in turn, started beating him. They beat him for a day and a night until he became unconscious. The following day he was untied and put in the sun. In the morning the Japs ordered us to dig a grave for the man, which we did. Sgt. Kibbe, L/Cpl Iga Rashi, Pte Tokura and Lt Murai took him to the grave. L/Cpl Iga Rashi and Pte Tokura bayonetted and buried him.[7]

On 30 September 1945, the day Monk had found Chint Singh, he said he had been 'reborn'; and his first act had been to call his scarecrows to attention and give three cheers for the King-Emperor of India and the Australians. And on the banks of the Sepik at Angoram, he did that for us too.

Next morning the barge crews unloaded the stores for the government station and began disarming the Japanese, dumping many of their weapons in the river. We had a busy day too. Twice we escorted barge-loads of Japanese prisoners from Angoram to Marien-berg, where we ordered their three serviceable barges to be ready to leave for Wewak with us at dawn.

At 5 a.m. on 13 October, Jemadar Abdul Latif, the other surviving Indian officer, who was too weak to walk, was carried aboard ML *1347* in a litter and the other Indian soldiers boarded one of our barges; then towing one of our broken-down barges loaded with sixty Japanese sick, we led the motley convoy down river and out into the Bismarck Sea. Many of the wretched Japanese soldiers we were towing were bloated and dying with scurvy and beri-beri, and conditions on board the barge must have been dreadful. When the wind was from astern we floated along cocooned in a nauseating stench.

On board we did our best to pamper our two Indian guests. As Singh had told me he was a Hindu and cows were sacred, and as our rations were mostly tinned bully beef, I gave him the choice of 'yippee beans and goldfish' or scrambled eggs—a tasteless concoction of powdered eggs, powdered milk and water.

For him being aboard and the trip down river was a voyage of discovery, duly recorded in his official report:

I found myself in an entirely new world ... I went down to the cabin and went into the dressing room which is adjacent to it. I used the latrine but could not manage the mechanical apparatus for disposing of the excreta. Lt. Hordern was watching me and came smiling and demonstrated its function. That was the first lesson I had in mechanics that morning ... Then I had breakfast. Everything on the table was strange to me. When I put four teaspoonfuls of sugar in my teacup, my hosts laughed, and Lt. Hordern smilingly said, 'Don't finish all our sugar, we have not got enough now.' After this the second lesson in mechanics took place and I learned all about the new Tommy Gun and a few new pistols. Then firing practice took place, logs in the river being the targets. I fired about 100 rounds.[8]

Approaching Wewak, the Indians recognised painful signposts along their Via Dolorosa and became agitated. There were the hated marshes where they had slaved more than twelve hours a day without food, waist-deep in slime, and there was the place where the Japanese had executed their Australian and American prisoners and—perhaps most poignant of all—there was the spot near Waringe Creek where the Indians had burned their dead.

As soon as we had anchored, an amphibious 'duck' came alongside to take Chint Singh and Abdul Latif to the hospital but before boarding it Singh paused at the gangway to make an impromptu speech:

Sir, I thank you from my heart at your kindness and for what you have done to give me rebirth. I can never repay you & wherever I go memories of you & your kindness I will always carry in my heart. I hope to be in India soon to see if my wife is alive—she has heard nothing for four years nearly & she must think that I am dead ... When you come to India here is my address, Jemadar Chint Singh, Village and Post Office Jalari, Via Naduan, District Kangra, the Punjab, India. My home will be yours. You have made me a happy man, and I will take you to the interesting places of India, and to the sacred places of my religion in which you have said you are interested. Goodbye, goodbye.

He then came to attention, gave me a Sandhurst salute, and shook my hand. I fumbled a few words about our debt to him for his lesson in endurance. His men, already in the 'duck' alongside, smiled, nodded and waved goodbye, counting the days until they would see their homes again.

Singh quickly responded to hospital food and care and, a few days later, when I was ordered to take a Captain Petersen and a party of soldiers to inspect the Japanese hospital on Muschu Island he arrived on board with them. I edged the ship alongside Muschu's rickety jetty, picked up my camera and revolver, and was about to step ashore when Singh asked to have a private word with me. He said that these Japanese were a cruel, suicidal and treacherous people and, as everyone except him was armed, before he ventured among them he wanted a gun. I gave him a fully loaded .5 Smith & Wesson six-chambered revolver, and he buckled it round his waist proudly. This was the first time he had met the Japanese face to face with a gun in his hand since the fall of Singapore. Now for him the tables were turned at last.

Close to the jetty we came upon a party of Japanese soldiers working on the road. All but one, who stood glaring sullenly at us, laid down their tools, bowed obsequiously and saluted. Outraged by this defiance of orders, Singh shouted at him in Japanese which he later translated for me:

> You fool, have you no eyes? Do you not see these officers pass you by? For long years American, Australian and Indian soldiers, and officers, have been forced to salute you bloody little soldiers —even when we were diseased you treated us worse than wretched animals.

The man just stood there staring sullenly into Singh's face and something snapped in his brain. Tearing a pick handle from the grasp of a

Japanese standing a yard from me, he struck the staring soldier hard, first on the left leg and then across the side of his face and ear. As hard wood hit hard bone I heard a loud crunching sound. Then, dropping his cudgel, Singh fell upon the man, punching him in the face and shouting abuse. The soldier did not fight back but tried to protect his face from the flying fists by covering it with his arms and moving backwards. Petersen and I grabbed Singh and dragged him off, and Petersen told him forcefully that we were under strict orders not to punish prisoners, and that he must never lay hands on a prisoner again. This ugly face of war had happened in a flash and taken us by surprise, but Singh was unrepentant. He claimed that the man knew the rules and that the Japanese treated their own men like that. And he was content; after years of torture and cruel abuse, he had enjoyed his moment of revenge and got it off his chest.

Walking on, we came to another gang with picks and shovels digging a large hole. Swarms of flies hovered around it and the sickly stench of death rose from about a dozen bodies lying in the sweltering sun. Some were partly clothed, some naked, sprawling grotesquely where they had been dumped, with flies crawling through their nostrils and open mouths. This was no place to linger, and as we walked on to the hospital a truck lumbered up the muddy track with another load of corpses. From these scenes of filth, litter, decay and death, we returned gratefully to the ship floating in sweet warm air on the clean salt sea.

On 15 November 1945 Singh stood beside the transport plane on Wewak airstrip to farewell Abdul Latif and his men, about to take off for Rabaul and join a ship for India and a hero's welcome home in their towns and villages. But he would not be going with them as he had been called to give further evidence at the Wewak war crime trials. As the plane sped down the strip, lifted into the air and climbed away, Abdul Latif and his 'boys' peered down through its Perspex windows, looking for the last time at the harbour and swamps where they had suffered so much. Then, as it headed out to sea, they settled back in their seats and thought of home. That day, New Britain's mountains were partially shrouded in cloud and, as they approached Rabaul, the pilot began flying blind, relying on his instruments. But they could not navigate for him. The Sydney *Sun*'s reporter Noel Ottaway described the last act in this Indian tragedy:

> Wewak, Monday.—One Indian Officer survives today of 2600 soldiers captured by the Japs at Singapore in 1942 and shipped to New Guinea for forced labour.
>
> All had refused to enter the Japanese-sponsored Army being raised to fight against the Allies and were sent to New Guinea as punishment. Disease, hunger, mutilation, beatings and cannibalism reduced their number from thousands to hundreds and then from hundreds to scores. Finally, when Japan surrendered, 13 scarecrows (of whom two later died) staggered into the Australian lines.
>
> The eleven survivors told their story to the Allied War Crimes Commission, naming scores of alleged war criminals and identifying them in line ups. Having signed their depositions ten of them set off last Thursday by transport plane for Rabaul to take a ship home. The plane crashed into a mountain and all perished.
>
> Prayers were said for them and one minute's silence observed at church services at Wewak yesterday. Sole survivor Chint Singh, said: 'I think that what were, in effect, their dying depositions, will ensure that the sufferings of my comrades will not go unpunished.'

For several weeks we continued escorting Japanese barges, freighting stores and food from Wewak to Muschu Island, patrolling it and making fruit runs to the Schouten Islands. On 24 October we were lucky to survive a fruit run to the island of Blup Blup with two nursing sisters aboard. About 2.30 p.m. we approached the reef protecting its lagoon in flat calm conditions but, before attempting the narrow entrance, I decided to circle round and study it through my binoculars to look for isolated coral outcrops. We were moving at about 3 knots, 150 yards from the reef, and running parallel to it. All seemed clear and as we turned away from the reef to circle back to the entrance I glanced casually to seaward and felt that sick sensation in my stomach which always came with sudden danger. A tsunami was racing silently towards us.

Somewhere to the north, perhaps on the floor of the Bismarck Sea, there had been a seismic movement and its waves, now almost upon us, were rising steeply from the flat sea. Though not huge, perhaps a little lower than our cross-trees, they had enormous power and, as they entered the shallow water near the reef they reared up and seemed to gain speed. We were moving side-on to them and if they caught us like that they would pick us up like a chip of wood and throw us on to the reef. Our survival now depended on the power and speed to push through them. I rang down for full revolutions on both engines and altered course directly towards the waves, shouting 'Hang on!' to the coxswain and the two sisters on the bridge.

The engines responded immediately: we turned directly towards the tsunami and the ship was gathering speed quickly as we hit the first wave. She rose to it buoyantly. It slowed her down, but our speed was still building up, and as she slid down its reverse slope she regained some of her lost momentum and we were still moving ahead when we slipped off the tops of the second and third waves and were again floating in a calm sea.

We turned to watch them rushing shoreward astern of us. They reared higher and higher and crashed onto the reef with a tremendous roar, smothering it with foam and spreading a carpet of froth across the lagoon. Then, when all was quiet, we went in and bought our fruit.

On 31 October we struck trouble on another fruit run, this time to Koil Island in the Schouten Group. We had left Wewak early that morning in company with ML *1356*. Soon after midday we reached the island and, relying on the sun and the breeze ruffling the surface to pinpoint its dangers, felt our way through the narrow entrance into the lagoon and anchored off the village of Setette. The soldiers buying the fruit planned to visit several villages and before they went ashore we impressed on them that we had to be out of the lagoon by mid-afternoon while the sun was still high enough to reveal under-water dangers. Uneasy that the sky might cloud over, I took compass bearings to fix our position in the lagoon and plotted the course to steer to take us safely through the entrance and out to sea.

The trading was slow; the canoes arrived late at the ship and the fruit took a long time to unload. About 3 p.m., when the soldiers had not returned, *1356*'s captain and I were becoming concerned, and at five o'clock, with the sun now very low in the sky and under-water visibility poor, there was still no sign of the soldiers. We conferred again and decided reluctantly to wait a little longer, and it was well after 6 p.m. when they arrived with a large load of fruit, so the two ships did not weigh anchor until five minutes to seven. By this time the lagoon was leaden-coloured, with nothing visible below the surface.

ML *1356*, being the senior ship, led the way to the entrance and we followed in her wake. Within about a minute she was stuck fast on a reef with her bow in the air and the water boiling under her stern as her engines roared in reverse to get her off. But she did not budge and we nosed our bow up to her stern, passed her a heavy line secured to our windlass and then, with both ships' engines running full astern, we pulled her off undamaged. Her shaken captain then suggested that, as I had taken bearings of the entrance, I might like to lead on. But we had now strayed from my plotted course, and after our manoeuvrings I only had a vague idea of our position and the course to steer for the entrance. However, I foolishly agreed, and off we went with *1356* following in our wake.

At ten minutes past seven, our starboard screw struck a coral out-crop with a sickening crunch. The engine stalled, the wheel spun in the coxswain's hands, and became partially jammed; then, with a bump and a scraping sound, we cleared the entrance and were out in the open sea. It was now dark, and my first care was to find out if we were leaking. We cleared the pawpaws and yams from the hatch and a torch-light inspection revealed no leak there. Our port propeller had not been damaged and, although we could only move the rudders through about 20 degrees, the weather was fine, we had company, and I saw no difficulty in making the 35-mile run home to Wewak.

Once well clear of the reef, *1356* came alongside to discuss the situation. I said we were not taking water, and on my assurance that we were all right, he waved cheerily and shot off into the darkness for home. We reached Wewak about midnight and next morning the officers of both ships held a post mortem. As *1356* had received no damage, from her point of view, the less said about it the better, and her captain said he was not going to submit a Collision and Grounding report. But when I pointed out that King's Rules and Admiralty Instructions required me, and my damage compelled me, to submit one, he asked me not to mention that he had also hit the reef. I thoughtlessly gave him my word and was soon to suffer for that.

S23 *Report of Collision or Grounding*—a four-page document— required sketches and a track chart of the ship's movements, and asked many leading questions. I completed it as best I could and sent it to Acting Captain E. S. Stewart, the Naval Officer in Charge of New Guinea, at Madang.

For a few days we continued on one engine, running errands for the army to Yuo and Kairuru Islands, and searching for a missing Japanese barge, before sailing to Madang to report to Stewart and have the ship repaired at Alexishafen. Stewart was hostile. A career officer, who may not have been enchanted with his sticky billet ashore in New Guinea, he appeared to have no great opinion of reserve officers in general, and of me in particular. And as I had promised not to mention that *1356* had caused my troubles by hitting the reef first, I simply stated that we had been delayed in the lagoon until nearly nightfall by the soldiers, and in getting out had tipped the coral. Stewart dismissed me bluntly saying that he would report to the Naval Board that I had shown poor seamanship and hazarded my ship, and I left him fearing that my naval service would end ashore in some jungle backwater like Madang.

The thought haunted me until I received the Naval Board's response to Stewart's report, dated 12 December 1945, and marked 'Confidential'.

Grounding of H.M.A. M.L. 1347
1. With reference to your N.G. 400/83 dated 15 November, 1945, I am directed to inform you that the Naval Board have given consideration to the report of the grounding of H.M.A. M.L. 1347, on 31 October, 1945, and concur with your remarks.
2. In this connection I am to request that the Commanding officer of H.M.A. M.L. 1347, Lieutenant M. C. Hordern, R.A.N.V.R., be directed to take more care in such waters in future.

> (Sgd) THOS J. HAWKINS,
> for Secretary, Naval Board.

This was almost a pat on the back. I had half expected to have been relieved of my command and the best I had hoped for was an official reprimand.

During the next half-century I became increasingly curious about what Stewart might have said about me, and how the Naval Board came to this decision. After fifty years had passed I wrote to the Navy, mentioning the circumstances and saying that I felt I owed a debt of gratitude to someone, probably now long dead, who had considered my case sympathetically, and I asked for copies of the minutes of the Board's relevant meeting.

And there it was. Captain Stewart had reported that convening a Board of Inquiry would not 'serve any useful purpose as the cause is apparent. It would appear that the Commanding Officer showed poor judgement in remaining in such an anchorage after sunset.' The attached Minute Paper, with comments by four members of the Naval Board, however showed that I had had at least one friend at court. In a small neat hand, he had written, 'The C.O. appears to have got under way as early as possible ... Propose NOIC NG be informed that C.O.

ML 1347 should be directed to take more care in navigating in such waters in future'.

But Stewart had been right. I had indeed shown 'poor judgement', and particularly in giving my word not to mention the real cause of the accident.

After our repairs at Alexishafen I was given the option of returning to Wewak or going to Rabaul to work with the army around New Britain and New Ireland. But the chance of another Sepik adventure won the day and mindful of the poor rations at Wewak, before we left we traded heavily with the natives and sailed with boxes of limes, pawpaws, yams, melons and pineapples stowed wherever we could find space for them. It was an anxious voyage. We were now in the wet season; the Ramu and Sepik rivers, swollen by heavy rains, discoloured the ocean for miles offshore and the water was thick with half-submerged logs and trees.

Unwelcome news awaited me in Wewak. Clif Wilkinson had been appointed to command the 56-foot HMAS *Gumleaf* and this was the parting of our ways. Clif had been my first lieutenant and friend since we had left Sydney. For nine months we had shared our cramped quarters with never a strained word, never an awkward silence. He had given me loyal and cheerful support and his going would leave a big gap.

His replacement, Sub Lieutenant Peter Noad, a stocky dark-haired doctor's son from Melbourne, had served in the flagship HMAS *Australia* and passing from that spacious world of protocol and gold braid into our small sweaty outfit must have been a sobering experience for him. Aboard *1347* there were no iced pink gins, crisp white sheets or laundry facilities. Our men bathed naked on the fo'c's'le with a bucket of salt water, and considered themselves well-dressed in a pair of shorts pleading for a wash. But Peter settled in quickly, took it all in his stride, and everything went smoothly between us.

On 26 November when the cruiser HMAS *Shropshire* arrived off Wewak en route from Tokyo to Sydney to repatriate some

6th Division soldiers, I was ordered to take Brigadier M. J. Moten to confer with her captain. Moten—a legendary warrior of the New Guinea campaign—had commanded the 17th Brigade and Kanga Force, and distinguished himself in battle at Salamaua and Nassau Bay. It was an honour to have him aboard and we enjoyed it. He showed such an interest in everything—how we weighed anchor, how the bridge telegraph operated, what went on in the engine room, and in the general working of the ship.

I followed him up *Shropshire's* steep landing steps to her huge deck high above our mast, and there, standing in the shade of her 8-inch guns, was a face from the past—Cyril Alcorn, the chaplain who in 1943 had given ML *814's* men pieces of melting chocolate, and taken letters to send to our parents if we had not come back from Timor. He asked me about conditions at Wewak and, on hearing that I had not attended a church service for months said, 'Come down to my cabin now and attend one'. And there, as I wrote that night:

> Kneeling in his cabin I received the Communion. Through the port, the early morning sunlight shone on the green misty hills of New Guinea where so many of our countrymen are lying. It was at once a sad and beautiful situation, & the first service I had attended for three months, it refreshed my spirit as much as roast chicken, potatoes, green peas, fruit, cream, and ice cream would have refreshed my body.

Another naval cruiser also arrived off Wewak that morning—the Imperial Japanese Navy's *Kashima*, one of the few of its major warships still afloat. *Kashima*, which had come to repatriate Japanese prisoners from Muschu Island, had been Vice Admiral Inouye's flagship from which he had directed the fateful battle of the Coral Sea. But now she was a toothless tiger, with the breech-blocks of her guns destroyed, and stripped of her weapons. To add to her shame, her name was painted in English in large white letters on her sides, and in place of the proud

Imperial Japanese Navy ensign, she now flew the flag of Japan's devastated merchant marine, which was also painted on her sides. But perhaps the greatest humiliation suffered by her men was when they looked aloft; for there, from the truck of her main mast, flew the pennant of Japan's new Mikado, General Douglas MacArthur, United States Army.

We were ordered to patrol the *Kashima* continually to prevent her from taking on board unauthorised Japanese prisoners who might escape from Muschu Island to her in boats, and this caused her further humiliation. As laid down by MacArthur, she was required to pay us courtesies without receiving any acknowledgement, and every time our scruffy little tub came close to her, she had to sound off and send a man running down the deck to dip her flag to us. She had anchored several miles from Muschu Island, but to embark the prisoners she was ordered to a closer anchorage in Dallman Harbour, and I was instructed to board her, give the captain his orders, and lead the *Kashima* to the anchorage there.

Hoping to make a favourable impression, I donned a fairly clean green army-issue shirt fitted with my best epaulettes, a pair of green army trousers, combed my hair and beard, buckled on my loaded revolver, and hoped that I looked the part. The *Kashima* lowered a gangway with a landing stage to water level. Its steps rose at an easy 45 degrees to a canvas-roofed platform at deck level. Peter brought *1347* in slowly, I stepped on to the stage, he turned away and I started up the companionway feeling very much alone.

Compared with our cluttered little deck, the *Kashima*'s was like a tennis court. I ignored the sentry's smart salute and followed him down a series of companionways and gloomy passages to the wardroom. It was large and airy, comfortably furnished and fitted with a fan, radio and a big clock. A handsome mahogany sideboard with a bevel-edged mirror stood against one bulkhead and opposite it a striking picture of Mount Fujiyama covered with snow reminded me of a Hokusai woodcut. Leather-upholstered chairs lined the sides of the wardroom, and in the centre a long polished table with eight chairs was set with dishes of food which the Japanese prisoners on Muschu Island might have killed for.

The cruiser's balding captain and a lieutenant-commander acknowledged my existence with slight but dignified bows and, not-withstanding my dislike of the enemy, I felt sorry for them. This war, which had devastated their empire and destroyed their hopes, had left me almost unscathed. They did not speak, and a seaman standing beside them explained in an American accent that they did not under-stand English and that he would interpret for me.

The captain motioned me to a chair at a table and the two officers sat down opposite. The lieutenant commander stared aggressively straight into my eyes. It disconcerted me. I wondered what was going on in his mind.

I told the interpreter that the *Kashima* must move to Dallman Harbour. There were reefs about 3 miles south-east of Muschu Island which would be invisible in the overcast weather and, as I knew where they were, he was to follow directly in my wake. He translated this into Japanese, the captain nodded and, having ascertained how much water the cruiser drew, I told him to weigh anchor in fifteen minutes and follow *1347* and that if I had any instructions I would send them to him in English by Aldis lamp in Morse code. He then pointed out that his clocks were set to Tokyo time and that the operation could require our clocks to be synchronised. I hadn't thought of this and told him to alter *Kashima*'s clocks to Sydney time. A little win for the home side.

The interview ended, he tinkled a small brass bell and a steward appeared with two lacquered bowls of sweet black tea which we drank in deathly silence. Had we been able to communicate this would have been the moment to thank him for his courtesy and perhaps exchange a few human thoughts. But a great gulf lay between us: his face remained impassive, I stood up and a seaman escorted me to the gangway.

With the *Kashima*'s deep draught in mind I planned the courses to Dallman Harbour carefully giving a wide berth to dangers, and

ML *1347* set off with the cruiser following directly in our wake. But as we were rounding a spur of a submerged reef she suddenly veered off on a more direct course for Dallman Harbour which would take her perilously close to the reef. Our Aldis lamp blinked, 'Obey instructions, follow exactly in our wake', and the *Kashima* swung back directly astern of us to be led safely into her anchorage.

The *Kashima*'s arrival in Wewak coincided with the end of the first war crimes trial in Wewak of a Japanese lieutenant for cannibalism and the mutilation of a Queensland soldier in July 1945. Singh had attended it and came aboard to give me an account of the proceedings. The accused, he said, had admitted stripping the flesh from the soldier's arms and legs and eating it; the meat had tasted good, he told the court, but now, realising his crime, he expected death and asked to be shot. An Australian officer, who defended him vigorously, said that the lieutenant had been racked with fever, weak, starved of protein, shaken by bombardment and temporarily insane. But the court found him guilty and condemned him to death by hanging. This vigorous defence had so alarmed Singh that as soon as the verdict was announced he had hurried to congratulate the President of the Court and shake his hand.

On 5 December, while patrolling Kairuru Island, we anchored in Victoria Bay close to the shore. Puzzled by the sight of steam rising from the rocks, three of us set off in the dinghy to investigate. As we rowed in, the water became warm, and then so hot that it scalded our hands and the air so stank of sulphur that we pulled further along the beach until we could step out of the boat and wade ashore. We walked up into the humid shadowy jungle where vines entwined themselves around trees covered with lichens and exotic blooms. I found an immense cluster of orchids clinging to a tree and took it back for the nursing sisters from the hospital who were having a day's outing on board. Continuing our patrol around Kairuru Island we landed on a beach to examine two Japanese ships which had been strafed by our fighters and run ashore. One was still loaded with new vehicle engines and land mines and on its fo'c's'le we found an 80-pound anchor.

We carried it back to the ship and it proved a short-term treasure. At this time of the year the north-west monsoon sent a swell into our anchorage at Cape Wom. It did not worry us much by day as the wind held the ship pointing into it and, although we pitched, we did not roll. But at night, when the wind dropped and we swung beam on to the swell, we rolled heavily, with crockery rattling and doors banging to disturb our sleep. But when we laid this Japanese anchor out astern, it kept our bows pointing into the swell and we slept in peace.

Hearing that the army was planning to send stores to an ANGAU post up the Sepik River, I volunteered to take them there, got the job, and on 9 December we began loading up. Although we had all been taking our anti-malarial atebrin pills, remembering the Sepik's ferocious mosquitoes I inspected the crew's nets and found six so holed that they had to be replaced. In calm weather in harbour, we often slept under our deck awnings to escape the airless, sticky heat below. But this presented problems when rain squalls swept in under the awnings. In my jaunts around Wewak I had seen the silk parachutes used to drop supplies to our soldiers still lying in the jungle. We collected about a dozen of these and made side-curtains for the awnings. Although flimsy, they deflected driving rain and kept us fairly dry when sleeping on deck.

This time we would be going much further up the Sepik than before, and going alone. And we would have a passenger, Major Milliken, a former Sepik District Officer who probably knew as much about the country as any white man alive. We left Wewak at 2 a.m. on a bright starry morning with a light southerly wind and a calm sea, aiming to be off the river's mouth early in the morning, but late enough to have light to see the floating logs and islands. I had stopped worrying about the minefield. Only one mine had exploded there, and I reckoned that by now the rest would have been swept out to sea by the river's debris.

At 8 a.m. we entered the river and I began to realise how lucky we were to have Milliken aboard. His knowledge of the Sepik, its valley and its people, transformed our progress into an educational Cook's

Tour. He was a fountain of information on the local culture, crocodiles, cassowaries, cuscus and the natural history of New Guinea. In the twentieth century, the patrol officers Champion and Karius had ascended the Fly River, crossed the freezing roof of New Guinea, and descended the Sepik. Men like them, and Jack Hides, O'Malley, Adamson, Monk, McCarthy and Milliken, are to New Guinea what Mungo Park, Burton, Speke, Stanley and Livingstone are to Africa.

Wishing to share some of my experiences with the family, I began a serial letter describing our adventures:

> I am writing this sitting on deck. Peter is on watch, & we are keeping to the centre of the river. On either side dark impenetrable jungle & steamy swamps stretch away to the Ramu River in the east and the mountain ranges in the west ... we are doing 10 knots against the current, v. pleased. Tonight we will be at Angoram about 68 miles up ... [and there is] some talk of us pushing on to Ambunti (as far up the river as Sydney is from Gunnedah) ...

We passed Marienberg about noon and a couple of hours later reached Angoram. Since our last visit Monk had worked wonders there and I hardly recognised the place. This time instead of mooring to the bank and tying up to trees, we secured to a brand-new wharf, and the filthy Japanese camp full of sick, desolate and dying men had been transformed into an ordered government post manned by healthy, disciplined native police.

The airstrip, which had been used by Japanese Zeros, was still surrounded by bomb craters filled with water, and the Sepik's big brown mosquitoes were as large and vicious as ever. They tormented us day and night, and the only way we could escape was by going below deck and activating Freon 'bombs'—an insect repellent supplied to us by the Americans in Hollandia. Although these killed clouds of mosquitoes they affected us too, leaving us with headaches and nausea.

At daybreak on 11 December Monk joined us with an armed detachment of native police, and we set off to show the flag at villages up-river which had for years been in Japanese-controlled territory. Like Milliken, Monk was full of information and anecdotes about the country. About mid-morning, we pulled into the bank at the village of Kambrine and when Monk went ashore with his police to re-establish Australian authority, we landed to see the sights. The mosquitoes here were so relentless that, even though the natives followed us whisking the sweaty patches of our shirts with bunches of cassowary feathers, we were still stung through the cloth and in spite of the pills most of us eventually went down with malaria.

Pushing on up-river, weaving about to dodge floating logs and islands, we passed basking crocodiles and villages set in groves of coco-nut, sago, and nipa palms. About midday we tied up to some trees at the village of Kanduonum, 130 miles from the sea. From here we could see the mountains clear and bold shining in an intense blue light. The mosquitoes rated a special mention in my serial letter to the family:

> Here for the first time ... I saw the remarkable sleeping bags, kalanbus ... they are made out of woven reeds more closely meshed than our mosquito nets and are like a giant sausage, open at one end. There are cane hoops inside to keep the belly distended & allow more stowage space for the human stuffing. The mosquitoes are so ... voracious that they would almost eat a human body alive if exposed all night. Four or five men or women, dogs or pigs, crawl in and the end is closed; and there they sleep all night; it is a sealed stinking bag and the heat must be terrific. Neither mosquitoes nor air can get in. We opened one and about 40 mosquitoes flew out!!

At Kanduonum I saw for the first time one of New Guinea's huge longhouses and marvelled at the skill of its architects and engineers. It could accommodate about eighty people, was built up on piers with its floor about 15 feet from the ground. The gloomy interior was fitted with cubicles facing the central aisle and, when I put my arms around one of the massive upright pillars supporting the ridge-pole, I could barely touch my fingers:

> The roof, heavily thatched with Nipa fronds tapered steeply. Running fore and aft along the ridge was a pole about 5 feet in diameter and about 120 feet long—it was about 45 feet above the ground; and must have weighed tons. I was astounded, and wondered how such a primitive society could erect such an immense building—&, in Pidgin English asked how they got the huge ridge pole up there. It was evidently managed by lashing many smaller poles together & using them like giant scissors, & levering the big one up in their forks with the strength of 200 or 300 natives. Detailed carvings of crocodiles eating snakes, gods, animals, some several feet high, adorned other large poles which were stuck in the ground and rose to 30 or 40 feet. Everywhere was an atmosphere of industry and accomplishment. Their canoes are made of straight, hollowed-out trees, up to 100 feet in length with no outrigger, as is found in the canoes of the coastal tribes … They require 20 or 30 paddles to propel them … Miserable dogs roamed around … feasting on portions of a recently captured crocodile.

Having shown the flag here Monk turned for home. I dropped him off at Angoram and sailed for Wewak, hurried along by the river's swift flow. Now the logs and islands were all going our way and we could pick and choose how to pass them, but they still bothered us. Rounding one bend we were confronted by an immense natural boom of logs and debris stretching across the river from bank to bank. I stopped the engines to think about it. The centre seemed to be moving fairly fast and, selecting what appeared to be its weakest point, we nosed through it. During this shoving and pushing our starboard screw fouled a length of vine and vibrated so badly that I shut the engine down. This reduced our speed, but as I had no wish to dive into that muddy crocodile-infested water, we continued on one engine out to sea where one of the sailors joined me over the side with a hack-saw; we cut the vine away and reached Wewak without further trouble. That night, however, we were tormented. The ship swarmed with fat brown mosquitoes—Sepik stowaways—and every one we squashed was full of our blood.

We had barely returned from this operation when there was talk of yet another. A man in a village further up the river than Kanduo-num had apparently been running amok and killing people. A patrol officer with native police was to go and get him, and they were expected to leave about Christmas Day. Here was the chance of another adventure and I decided to volunteer, but before any plans were finalised a signal arrived recalling us immediately to Australia—we were to sail for Brisbane almost at once.

We spent our last days at Wewak running errands for the army and attending or giving farewell parties, one of which might have ended in tragedy. On 15 December, two army doctors and two sisters arrived in an army launch to enjoy some fishing and dinghy sailing. About 10 p.m. they recalled that they had to be back on duty by mid-night and, as there was now no launch to take them off, they pressed me to row them ashore in the dinghy.

That afternoon the wind had raised a short sea in the anchorage and a sizeable surf on the landing beach. The dinghy had been secured astern; we dragged it up to the Jacob's-ladder and I climbed down and sat on the rowing thwart. The four of them fumbled their way aboard and we pushed off low in the rough water. Today, everyone in that situation would have worn a life-jacket, but in 1945 many of us in small ships were not meticulous about such safety precautions and none of us was wearing a Mae West. As I rowed in, partly across the waves, an occasional crest broke on board and slopped around our feet. Near the shore the seas grew steeper; we weathered one breaker but the next picked us up, shot us forward, and dumped us in about 5 feet of water where my passengers, in long-sleeved shirts, trousers, and heavy army boots, floundered nearly up to their necks in the surf.

But we all struggled ashore, manhandled the boat on to the sand and emptied it. Then the soggy foursome pushed me out through the surf for a hard row back to the ship.

We had had a very lucky escape, but with the exception of Sister Kay Murch, a vivacious young woman from Cloncurry, the others seemed unaware of their danger. I had been very foolish not to have made them stay on board for the night or to have worn life-jackets in the dinghy. Had it been swamped in deep water, some of them must have drowned and, had I survived, the subsequent inquiry must have found me responsible for their deaths.

After the war Kay and I continued our friendship and wrote regularly. She married and raised a family in South Africa, and in 1979, when dying of cancer, wrote a poignant farewell:

> Tony I want you to know how much pleasure your cards and letters have given me all these years, to say nothing of the days at Wewak. Yes I have even forgiven you for tipping me into the surf—a demonstration of your fine seamanship and my will to survive that enormous surf. I remember you saying then that we would remember those days as an experience that millionaires would envy, and you were so right.

That was my last memorable incident while soldiering on in New Guinea. But some pretty nasty ones lay ahead of us on our hazardous long haul back to Brisbane.

14 | SEA OF TROUBLES

The voyage began auspiciously. We weighed at dawn on 16 December with light music from Wewak radio station 9A flowing through the amplifier on the bridge, and as we gathered way the announcer interrupted the programme to wish us a safe voyage home and play the popular hit 'How About a Cheer for the Navy?'. This farewell salute from the soldiers touched us. Now our long-cherished hopes of spending the first peace-time Christmas for six years in Australia seemed about to be realised and as the Prince Alexander Mountains dropped below the horizon, I wrote up my journal in cocksure mood:

> At sea ... our hopes are coming true ... we are about to commence our island and reef cruise through the beautiful waters of Torres Strait and the east coast of Australia.

But my euphoria was short-lived. Before us lay a chain of mishaps which turned the 'island and reef cruise' into a nightmare. The first came quickly. That night as we lay rolling at anchor in Hansa Bay, the auxiliary engine, which had been thumping away noisily, suddenly shattered a piston and stopped with a bang. We needed it, not only to pump the bilges but also to charge the batteries on which we relied to start the engines and work the lights, fans and radio transmitter. Peter and I discussed the problem with motor mechanic Russell and our cheery stoker Ken Akers, and decided that, as we would be running night and day for weeks, the main engines should keep the batteries charged and we could pump the bilges with the 24-volt electric petrol pump Jack Page had cut from the wing of a crashed American fighter at Port Moresby. But from now on, to save electricity, there were to be no fans, and no unnecessary lights.

Then Russell reported that we had run out of distilled water for the batteries and that their plates were becoming exposed. While I was struggling with this problem the heavens opened with a torrential downpour and we caught enough water in a canvas awning to supply our batteries for weeks.

That night the surge running into Hansa Bay rolled us heavily, and to ease our discomfort we laid the Japanese anchor out astern and heaved on it, hoping to bring our bows into the swell to steady us. But we were on poor holding ground and the anchor kept dragging. All night we slid about in our bunks while cups rattled and doors banged. The anchor had been a cumbersome thing to stow on deck anyway, and in the morning, judging it useless, I cut it loose and left it on the bottom—a find, perhaps, for some future marine archaeologist.

We sailed in pre-dawn darkness and at 2 p.m. reached Madang, the seat of naval government in this part of New Guinea. I hoped to push on quickly but feared that the Naval Officer in Charge would find work for us. On reporting to him my fears were confirmed. The Supply Officer handed me a packet about the size of a shoebox, which he said contained £656—the Christmas pay for HMAS *Ping Wo* lying in Langemak Bay, and I was to deliver the packet personally to her Supply Officer. As I signed for the packet, containing more money than I had ever handled in my life—equal to about two years' pay— the Supply Officer made it abundantly clear that it was now my personal property and that I was accountable for every penny of it. I was also given six very heavy 44-gallon drums of lubricating oil for the *Ping Wo*.[1]

After taking on bread, a few vegetables and our beer ration, we sailed for Langemak Bay as the first stars glittered over the Bismarck Sea. I was now more worried about the oil than the money, fearing that if we hit bad weather the lashings around the drums might loosen, and we would be in trouble. But the sea slept, the lashings stayed bar-taut, and about four in the morning we entered Vitiaz Strait between the mainland and mountainous Umboi Island, with the dark shape of New Britain looming on the eastern horizon and New Guinea's rooftop etched against the southern sky.

Approaching Dampier's Cape King William we had some anxious moments when our navigation lights, glowing on the dark water, picked up a huge tree trunk flashing past a few feet from us. It would not have worried Dampier: the *Roebuck*'s bluff bows would have nudged it safely out of the way. But our bows were flimsy, we were travelling at about four times the *Roebuck*'s speed, and a trunk like that could disable or sink us. We slowed down, sharpened our eyes, and reached Langemak Bay without further incident.

When I finally located the *Ping Wo* I found her supply officer seated at ease under a fan in freshly laundered shirt and shorts. He took in my grubby appearance and unwashed clothing at a glance and asked warily what I wanted, but when I handed him the money and said, 'To get rid of this and six drums of oil', he became affability personified. His men, he said, had been demanding their pay in time to send a Christmas pound or ten shilling note to their families in Australia, and he added that had my beard been white and my clothes red, I might have doubled for *Ping Wo*'s Father Christmas. He signed for the money, the ship's derrick hoisted the oil from our deck and we left at mid-night for Samarai Island in China Strait.

Everything was now going swimmingly. I had hoped to reach Samarai in twenty-three hours and, for the last time on this dreadful voyage, my hopes came true. Soon after daylight we skipped past Mitre Rock, which had so reminded Captain Moresby of a bishop's head-gear and, although in crossing the Huon Gulf a strong westerly current pushed us uncomfortably close to Mambare Shoal, we made good time.

On this run we passed rocks, reefs, capes and headlands named by, or for, men I had met in Ingleton's *Charting a Continent*, and one by one we ticked off the signposts and milestones on our passage—Red Rocky Point, Spear Island, Ham Reef. At noon on 20 December we skipped a mere cable off Cape Vogel and, pushing on at top speed, doubled Capes Rawlinson, Mourilyan and the island of Meimeiara. From there it was only a short hop through Jack Daw Channel and round East Cape to berth at Samarai, with the China Strait's blue tide boiling round our bows.

With only five days to Christmas and the prospect of ham, turkey and iced drinks with friendly Queenslanders, we had no time to waste and only lingered in Samarai for three hours to stretch our legs and look around. For months, every human, vehicle, building, gun, ship or aircraft we had seen had been dressed in drab military browns, greens and greys and Samarai, with its brilliant vegetation, brightly painted buildings and gaily dressed people, dazzled us with a riot of colour:

> Neat government buildings & a ... meek-looking little church in a grove of casuarina trees ... When the Japanese landed in Milne Bay the 'scorched earth' policy was put into execution here. The hotels were burned down, the gardens abandoned and the area largely desolated. The civil administration is however now resurrecting the place ... called 'The Pearl of the Pacific'.
>
> A civil administrator here—Mr Middleton—had two of the most beautiful pink-faced children aged 7 & 10. The youngest had the very excellent name of Owen Stanley Middleton. The sight of these children made us realise how much we had missed in not seeing them for so long. Native children can be very winsome but our own kind awake ... feelings for home.
>
> Mr Middleton generously gave us two large bunches of bananas—about 100 on each. We hung them from the guardrail

& ate unsparingly of them. He expected nothing in return and indeed we had little to give. It was a delight to have him on board & chat quietly with him in the cool shade of the awning on deck. He very much appreciated the iced bottle of beer we shared together. His wife joined us, a pleasant woman wearing a yellow cotton frock and a spotted blue scarf about her head.

At noon we waved the Middletons goodbye and left on the 230-mile leg to Port Moresby. After an uneventful run against a west-south-west current with glimpses of the Owen Stanley Range drenched in heavy rain, we berthed there at the government wharf alongside the three-masted trading schooner *Eva*. In contrast to our outward passage—five days inside the reefs—we had covered the same distance in exactly twenty-four hours.

The next leg of our voyage to Cairns was over 900 miles. We were now in the cyclone season; this was a long run, and as it might be drawn out by bad weather we filled our tanks with 700 gallons of fuel and lashed another four drums on deck, filled our water tanks to the brim and also every bucket and container we could find.

That evening I borrowed a Jeep from the motor pool and, after driving to a film show at Murray Barracks, went aboard HMAS *Poyang* to collect the charts I would need to navigate in the Great North-East Channel and Torres Strait areas.[2]

The *Poyang*, like the *Ping Wo*, had been built for service on the China coast and fitted out for captains who expected comfortable quarters. Invited aboard by her captain, Lieutenant J. W. Edwards, I could not help comparing his large airy stateroom furnished with fans, a polished table, writing desk, leather armchairs, gleaming lamps and shining brass with our cramped accommodation. His crisp, freshly laundered clothes made me feel awkward and dirty. Over a cool drink I confided my fears to him about crossing the Gulf of Papua and we discussed the weather and the Gulf's shifting currents. Then, as I got up to go, he said, 'Hang on, how about a bath?' and pointed to a door. Beyond it I found a spotlessly clean bathroom with a white bath and taps marked 'Hot' and 'Cold'. I had not had a bath for eleven months and for most of that time mildew, mosquitoes, cockroaches and the stink of stale sweat had been common companions. I filled the bath, lathered myself with his scented soap and luxuriated in the warm water. The physical delight of that bath, of drying myself afterwards with a newly laundered white towel and dusting myself with Johnson's Baby Powder, is one of my most enduring war-time memories. I had never met Edwards before, nor have I heard of him since, but I remember him gratefully.

Generally I drop off to sleep quickly, but that night I slept fitfully with my mind full of the navigational problems I would have to confront on the voyage to Cairns. We had no radar, echo-sounding equipment or electronic aids to guide us, and I was going to need all the guidance I could get to arrive there safely.

At sunrise on 22 December I drove to St John's Church. Nothing stirred in Port Moresby's streets or around the little chapel on the hill. Its door was unlocked. I went in, knelt down, thanked God for our preservation from past dangers and prayed for continuing journeying mercies and guidance in making an accurate landfall across the Gulf of Papua. Then, having shifted some of the load on to stronger shoulders, I returned to the ship. At 8 a.m. we sailed for Cairns under gloomy skies, with an RAAF forecast of high winds and heavy rain over Torres Strait and the Cape York Peninsula in Northern Australia.

Once through the Basilisk Passage and out at sea, still worrying about our landfall, I made my last New Guinea journal entry:

> The business of making a landfall at Bramble Cay at the entrance to the Great North East Channel has been on my mind. Bramble Cay, named after HMS *Bramble*, is a small low islet about ten feet high … and the mark for which we steer across the Gulf of Papua. During the North-West Monsoon currents up to 2 knots run in this area. The monsoon is late this year and I am not certain how they are setting us now. Portlock Reefs, Anchor Cay & other dangers lie to the southward of Bramble Cay—&, to

miss it through unknown currents, poor steering, or both, could put us 20 miles off our course—miss the sight of Bramble Cay & leave us bewildered and beset by reefs and shoals, not sure of where we were. The effects of the current and wind are setting us West Sou'West at 1.5 knots so I have allowed 7 degrees for leeway & am deliberately steering for a position 20 miles to the northward of Bramble Cay, & aim to pick up the flash of its light by 4 a.m. tomorrow 23 December 1945 ... If all goes well we should be off Cape York by 1700 tomorrow. I have given strict instructions to the helmsmen to attend carefully to their steering and explained to them the consequences of missing the landfall at Bramble Cay.

At noon I took my last compass fix on New Guinea—Cape Suckling, bearing N 8° W, distant 28 miles. It suggested that we were being set south-westwards, and although I was aiming to pass just south of Bramble Cay, it supported my decision to steer as though to pass well north of it; if this worked out correctly, we should see the light dead ahead.

As this was to be a long passage out of sight of land, normally Peter or I would be continually on the bridge, working 'watch and watch', and keeping a careful eye on the steering and the weather. But Peter—a migraine sufferer—was suddenly struck down by a severe attack, and I insisted on his turning in until he was fit to stand watch.

During the afternoon, with the sky overcast, I could not take sextant altitudes of the sun to fix our position and could do no more than look at the wind and sea, try to estimate our drift, and accordingly alter our compass course at the end of each hour. As the afternoon wore on, the necessity to sight Bramble Cay sent me frequently to the wheelhouse to study the chart. Rising only about 10 feet above the sea, Bramble Cay, a resort of seabirds and turtles, was our vital signpost to Bligh Entrance and the Great North-East Channel, leading through the reefs and islands to Torres Strait and the Queensland coast. Bramble Cay was 200 miles from Port Moresby and about 40 miles from the mouth of the great Fly River, and beyond the cay the Warrior Reefs rose from deep water to bar the way to westbound shipping. From its 52-foot tower, a light, flashing twice every six seconds, was visible from 13 miles and as it would be much easier to detect in the dark, I planned to sight it before dawn. On the chart Bramble Cay was a mere speck in the ocean with a few off-lying rocks, but it was a vital land-fall and, as we ran on into the night it loomed large in my thoughts.

Darkness fell, and with it came a short rolling sea from the north. Everyone was tired and, except for the watch-keepers, below in their bunks. But there was to be no sleep for me that night. At 8 p.m. Peter, looking dreadful, emerged to relieve me on watch, but he was far too ill to stay on the bridge and I sent him back below.

With the scend of the sea pushing us off course, I had frequently to make steering corrections which, I hoped, would keep us on track. I also continually peered ahead looking for the light, although reason told me this was premature. But I could not relax: if we missed it we might blunder on to the Warrior Reefs and, if we did not sight it, daylight would find us trapped in coral waters with poor underwater visibility.

An hour passed, and then a half-hour, but nothing appeared in my binoculars' field of vision except the black outline of the waves, the deceiving flash of a white crest, and the lighter line marking the horizon. I made repeated visits to the wheelhouse to study the chart with increasingly bleary eyes and each time, as my dividers picked off the probable distance to Portlock Reefs and other dangers around Flinders Entrance and Pandora Passage, my tired mind wrestled with a stale geometrical problem which had now assumed a frightening face.

The ship's position had not been reliably fixed for sixteen hours; unknown currents might have pushed us well off track, and I did not really know where we were. My imagination began to play me tricks. What if we had been set by wind or current so far to the south that the light would be invisible below the northern horizon? Should I turn north? What if we had been pushed north into the Gulf of Papua? Should I turn south?

At 4 a.m., still with no stars to guide and no sign of the light, a chilling thought struck me—perhaps the light was out of action. Such things had happened. We might be right on track, steering straight for the reef surrounding Bramble Cay and about to hurl ourselves on to the rocks at the foot of its darkened tower. Already in my mind I could hear the crash, the sound of splintering wood and the shouts of drowning men. Already I could feel the shock of the surf breaking over the doomed ship.

Once more—now close to despair—I returned to the wheelhouse to stare at the chart and try to think. But this time something I had not noticed before caught my eye: a hydrographical 'caution' printed near the top edge of the chart. As I read it a warning voice spoke to me out of the chart:

> Owing to the proximity of Fly River the tidal streams are very
> strong and irregular especially in the N.W. Monsoon season ...[3]

This warning was for me. We were very close to the mouth of the Fly River, which was pouring all its mud and debris into the Gulf of Papua, and we were in the middle of the North-West Monsoon season.

I reached for the bridge telegraphs and rang 'Stop Engines'. The motors died and the ship, now strangely quiet, lay rolling in the hollow sea. After discussing the problem with the helmsman and the bridge lookout, 'Smiler' Evans, I decided that, as a few extra feet of height would increase the visible distance to our sea horizon and thus the chance of seeing the light, 'Smiler' should go up the mast to look for it.

Up he went and I climbed up behind him with the binoculars swinging awkwardly round my neck, and clinging to the mast above the bridge, we searched the dark horizon. 'Smiler' saw it first. He shouted and pointed. And there they were, two clear flashes every six seconds. Not where I had been looking for them, however, but far out on the starboard quarter. We had been carried off course; we were already well past Bramble Cay and heading straight for Warrior Reefs.

Weak with relief and exhaustion, I climbed down to the bridge, rang 'Full Speed Ahead' and, as the ship gathered way in the pre-dawn darkness, in the very nick of time set a new course for safety and survival. Forty-four years later, when writing a book about the debt seafarers owe to the nineteenth-century explorers who charted Australia, I touched on this incident in the preface and called the book *Mariners are Warned!*

Towards dusk on 23 December we were off the Queensland coast and once again in waters discovered by Cook in 1770. He had sailed northwards along it as I also had done, and I was familiar with his description of its hinterland, islands, capes, bays and beaches. But now, sailing south, I saw them quite differently and as we picked our way through the dangers he had confronted, I marvelled at his genius in surviving them.

Off Cape Grenville we ran into the cyclonic disturbance forecast by the Air Force in Port Moresby, and my mind was less occupied with thoughts of Christmas in Cairns than of our own safety. Under lowering clouds, drenched and buffeted by wind and spray, we punched into a steep sea. About noon on Christmas Eve, after nearly seventy-two hours without much sleep, I was exhausted. Peter's migraine had passed and we all needed a meal; having taken on no fresh bread in Port Moresby, we were still eating sandwiches made from the now-mouldy bread picked up in Langemak Bay, and I decided to pull in behind Night Island for a couple of hours so that we could have a properly cooked meal and eat it quietly at anchor.

Before stopping the engines I checked with Russell about the state of our batteries and whether he would be able to restart them. On having his assurance that the batteries were fully charged, I anchored in the lee of the island, and after eating our dinner we had a short sleep. But when we went to weigh anchor and Russell pressed the starter button, there was a deathly silence. We had developed an unidentified electrical fault, Russell told me, and he began 'working on it'.

After Russell had worked fruitlessly for more than an hour, Peter and I took stock of our situation. We were now midway between Thursday Island and Cooktown, about 250 miles from each. We were unable to move, were low in food and almost out of kerosene for the stove and refrigerators. We could only use the wireless and bilge pump while the batteries lasted and, with our anchorage behind Night Island partially obscured from the track of coastal shipping, there was little chance of attracting attention. With hopes of dinner ashore now fading, we began to consider a Christmas fare of birds, fish, or a turtle, washed down by water. But while we were contemplating this gloomy prospect Russell found the fault and the music of the Hercules once more sounded joyfully in our ears.

By sunset we were running eastwards across Princess Charlotte Bay in good weather. A moderate easterly wind scattered white horses across the darkening sea and on the bridge we were chanting carols. Apart from Yuletide joys, we had much to sing about: we had survived six years of war with barely a scratch and we were going home to our families and friends. Just before 10 p.m. Wharton Reef light blinked on the starboard bow and I went to the wheelhouse to fix our position. Our route to Cairns lay east and south, and at 11.30 p.m. we passed north of the Flinders Group, its features—Flinders, King, Stanley, Blackwood and Denham Islands, and Stokes Bay—named for men I had met in Ingleton's *Charting a Continent*. During the early minutes of Christmas morning we rounded King Island and entered waters sacred to Cook; here he had so nearly lost the *Endeavour* on the coral reef now named for her. Cook's spirit brooded here: Lookout Point, Cape Flattery, Hope Islands, Weary Bay and Cape Tribulation— the very names spoke of his troubled mind. At dawn on Christmas Day we were 3 miles off Lizard Island and, peering at it in the gathering light, I relived my climb there with Clif following Cook's footsteps to the summit.

Our course for Cairns southward of Cape Flattery would take us past the mouth of the Endeavour River, and it struck me that this was perhaps the most significant place in Australian history. Had Cook not discovered that river and been able to repair his ship there he might never have made it back to England, and Australia might well have become French. Suddenly, Cooktown became a Mecca for me and, although my orders were for Cairns, I altered course for the Endeavour River and the nineteenth-century settlement which had grown up on its banks at the spot where Cook had repaired the *Endeavour*. My act was lawless, but it was to reward me. Half a century later its recollection called me back to northern Australia researching the lives of its explorers.

As we ran in, I took compass bearings of Mount Cook and Grassy Hill and consulted the 1939 edition of *Australia Pilot*. It advised sailing vessels running for the port in strong winds to keep their 'after-canvas' set while crossing the bar. Cook would have liked that. My other guide, Admiralty Chart 1350, *Endeavour River Entrance Cooktown Harbour*, was also a mine of information. It had been published in 1893 under the superintendence of Captain W. J. L. Wharton RN, FRS, the scholarly editor of Cook's *Endeavour Journal*, after whom Wharton Reef had been named.

Australia Pilot told me that the railway wharf was in repair, that water from its hose was drinkable, and the least depth over the bar was 10 feet. The chart was a nineteenth-century traveller's guide to what had then been a booming gold rush town, showing the convent, churches, magazine, observation spot, quarry, customs house, police barracks, school of arts, post office, town hall, court house, fire brigade, cattle yards and railway station. Cooktown's large Oriental population was indicated by five small rectangles marked 'Chinese huts' and the tracing of Chinaman Creek.

Our arrival in Cooktown had some worrying moments, as I recorded later that day:

> Blowing hard at sea—a dirty, blustery windy day ... we negotiated the entrance to the harbour over the sandbar and secured safely alongside the wharf ... though the channel is twelve feet deep and we only draw five, there were steep waves five to six

feet high which raised and dropped us with considerable violence, and at times our keel must have come quite close to the bottom … In the unlikely event of us becoming stove and sunk, I wore my money belt … mostly American dollars, but some Australian pounds and Dutch gilders. We are now 150 yards from the spot where Lieutenant Cook careened HMS Endeavour in June 1770 …

I was surprised to see that the once impressive settlement had shrunk to a fraction of its former size and become something of a shanty-town. The population had dwindled to about 250 and most of the houses were dilapidated. Although its amenities could not compare with those of sixty years before, its superb stone drains and gutters still served their purpose, sluicing the wet season's torrential rains into the river. Although much of Cooktown's former architecture had crumbled into the dust or been levelled by cyclones, some handsome buildings survived and its historic sites remained intact.

I made my pilgrimage to Cook's monument and to the spot where he had careened the *Endeavour*. I gazed on Grassy Hill, from the summit of which he had scanned with anxious eyes the coral labyrinth barring his way. But while walking here in Cook's footsteps I stumbled across another explorer who had also found refuge in the Endeavour River fifty years later—while in search of Cook, I discovered Phillip Parker King, and he was Cooktown's Christmas gift to me.

But the longed-for Christmas dinner ashore in Australia did not eventuate. The streets were deserted, the pubs were shut, and we finished up back on board eating bully beef and Sao biscuits.

At dawn on Boxing Day we cleared the river's mouth and turned south for Cairns into a strong wind and steep sea. It broke over the bows, swept the fo'c's'le, and crashed into the wheelhouse, violently shaking the whole ship. One crest carried away a ventilator and sent water pouring onto the bunks below. But as morning wore on the weather eased and we were soon making good time in gentler weather.

After we had passed Cook's Cape Tribulation we had one of our own in the form of a floating mine. During the war, the Germans and Japanese had laid minefields off the Australian coast and by August 1945 thousands of Japanese mines had broken loose and were floating free.[4] During 1946, 200 of them came in on the Queensland shore, endangering shipping to such an extent that night sailings had to be restricted in some areas, and as we were running down the recommended passage for shipping south of Cape Tribulation one appeared rising and falling on the water dead ahead of us. After trying fruitlessly to sink it by gunfire, I signalled its position and estimated drift to Townsville and hurried on to Cairns.

Cairns's creature comforts compensated us for Cooktown's disappointments. We spent three days there, drying clothes and bedding, cleaning and airing the ship, fuelling, watering and provisioning. We fuelled ourselves too with as much milk, ice-cream, butter, chocolate, meat, fruit and vegetables as we could manage. And we had the joy of being able to sleep for more than three and a half hours at a time without being woken.

Then on to Townsville, which we reached at dawn next day after a night passage clouded by visions of floating mines. But after leaving Townsville for Brisbane at 4.15 a.m. on 3 January we met the worst troubles of all and the voyage became a nightmare.

Once out of harbour, Peter turned in and I stood the morning watch. We rounded Cape Cleveland at 5.35 a.m. in calm weather, and altered course to S 80° E. This, I had calculated, would take us clear of Salamander Reef, named for HMS *Salamander* which, in the nineteenth century, had found it the hard way. Soon the stars began to pale with the promise of a fine day, and what could be better than running home along such a coast in good company? Everything peaceful; I had not the slightest sense of danger, and that alone should have made me careful. I had forgotten Norman Wallis's warning on that sparkling morning in ML *823* off Coffs Harbour, that 'At sea, when all seems fair and safe, there's always danger, son.'

About 7 a.m., I went below to the heads. In such circumstances in small ships like ours watch-keepers were seldom called and I did not wake Peter. I was not below long but, as I was returning to the bridge, I glanced through the scuttle and was horrified to see a coral outcrop emerge from a gentle heave of the sea close to the ship. I raced for the deck, but before I reached the bridge the ship received a heavy shock and the port engine stalled. We had strayed too close to Salamander Reef and struck a spur.

Fortunately, we were still moving well with rudder control, and I altered course immediately away from the reef. Then, conscious that this replay of our accident at Koil Island was on this occasion the result of my own carelessness, I began to assess the damage. We were still afloat and had one good engine and although we were leaking a little in the tiller flat, its watertight bulkhead and the electric pump should keep that under control. However, we had been extremely lucky not to have torn our bottom out and sunk in deep water. Deciding, therefore, to continue the 700-mile passage on the starboard engine, I sent a signal reporting that we had hit a submerged object, damaged the port propeller, and were proceeding on to Brisbane at 9 knots.

The sea stayed calm, the barometer steady, and the wind light. But just when we needed journeying mercies, the hand that had so far liberally bestowed them became busy elsewhere. Towards midnight, in the middle of the Whitsunday Passage, our engineer, Russell, complained of severe stomach pains and nothing I could give him from the medicine chest relieved them. With his agony increasing, I altered course for Mackay, signalling port authorities there, giving my estimated time of arrival, and requesting an ambulance to be waiting for us on the wharf. We arrived at 5.15 a.m., and Russell, now nearly mad with pain, was lifted into a waiting ambulance and rushed to hospital. His lucky escape rated a journal entry:

At 0600 he was in Mackay hospital & within a few minutes was operated on for acute peritonitis & he is desperately ill. He has been given blood transfusions and is now wavering close to the shadow line. If he had developed this ten days ago in the Coral Sea, he would now be dead.

There was no replacement engineer for Russell in Mackay and, to add to our worries, a roaming cyclone was threatening the Queensland coast. Peter and I held another council of war—this time with Stoker Ken Akers. Could we press on 500 miles to Brisbane in a damaged ship without Russell when the engine room had to be manned continually while we were at sea? Akers said he could replace Russell and, if one of the seamen would volunteer to act as stoker, he would give him basic instructions about watch-keeping in the engine room and responding to orders on the bridge telegraphs. One volunteered immediately and I appointed Akers Senior Engineer. This done, we decided that if the next weather forecast was favourable we would sail at 4.15 next morning. During the night I went on deck several times to sense the weather. The omens were good: no wind and a clear sky full of stars. I decided to go. But when Akers started the engine, it made a frightful clatter and threw out clouds of smoke and unburnt fuel in the exhaust. Instead of developing 1400 revolutions per minute, it could only be coaxed up to 800, and this, he volunteered, might mean a cracked piston.

There went our last hope of getting home under our own steam. Off went yet another signal to the navy stating that we now had no power, and we settled down in Mackay to make the most of our time—fishing, reading, playing chess, and taking in the town's cinemas and cafes. The cyclone passed away and next day HMAS *Sterna*, a small General Purpose Vessel, also bound for Brisbane, arrived in Mackay with orders to tow us there.[5]

This was 'not going to be easy', her fair-haired young captain, Lieutenant Athol Johnson, told us when he came aboard to discuss arrangements. He too was almost home from a long, hazardous voyage and, after loudly lamenting his ill fortune in getting this job, he accepted it cheerfully.

Sterna had no after-winch and only a small crew which meant that, if the towline parted near our end, they would not have the strength to haul it in. It was therefore important that it be made from the best materials we had. We prepared it carefully, using 30 fathoms of 3-inch steel wire, shackled to 36 fathoms of our 3/8-inch chain anchor cable to give it the necessary weight to keep it in the water. This was the best we could do and, recalling ML *814*'s tormented tow behind the Liberty ship in 1943, I wished it had been longer and heavier.

At daybreak on 7 January 1946, we trundled out of Mackay behind *Sterna* with her big slow engine thumping quietly ahead of us. The weather was fine and watch-keeping a delight as we glided along almost as silently as a ship under sail; with no engine noises in our ears and no exhaust fumes in our noses we were all set for an easy ride to Brisbane.

That night I held the first watch. We had passed the Percy Islands and I was thinking of my bunk. When it was nearly midnight I glanced at the sky to check the visibility for the log entry. Heavy clouds were scudding up from the south, flying across the firmament and obliterating the stars and, as I watched, a cold hard wind hit me in the face.

Soon we were punching into a steep sea and shortly afterwards a savage squall struck us, the tow parted with a shock that shook the ship and *Sterna*, unconscious of our plight, disappeared into the darkness. We fired a Verey light to alert her, slowed to a stop, swung beam-on to wind and sea and lay there rolling heavily as we wrestled to haul in whatever was left of the towline.

Circling back, *Sterna* came as close as she dared and Athol and I shouted at each other through megaphones. Much of our conversation was swept away by the wind, but I gathered that the section of the towline still attached to his stern had been too heavy for his sailors to haul in by hand and, worried that it might foul his propeller, he had cut it adrift.

After much heaving, we recovered 12 of the 66 fathoms of our precious line, and it took us two and a half hours to make up another from the odd lengths of wire, chain and cordage we could find on board.

When the tow parted I had estimated that we were 7 miles to windward of an island and drifting slowly towards it; I did not need to be told what would happen if we could not pass another towline quickly, and while we were preparing one I made precautionary plans to abandon ship if we seemed likely to be wrecked on its rocks. When we estimated we were about a mile from them, I decided, we would launch our two Carley rafts, jump into the sea, swim to them and hope that Athol could find us in the darkness and pick us up.

The wind increased and the sea rose, rolling us so heavily that we had to brace ourselves on the fo'c's'le while splicing the wire and cordage for the new towline. At last it was ready and we signalled *Sterna* to come as close as she could so that we could heave her a line attached to the end of it.

Four times Athol brought *Sterna* slowly across our bows to receive it, but three times, before his sailors could catch the weighted end of the heaving line, the wind snatched it from their grasp and whirled it away into the black night. But the fourth time, as he came plunging dangerously across our bows, we were lucky. They caught it, hauled it in and soon after 3 a.m. off we went once more, lurching and stumbling in *Sterna*'s wake at a pitiful 2 knots.

The ship had taken a buffeting in the gale and we were now leaking badly, with water sloshing around the floorboards below. The batteries were too flat to work the electric pump and, as I dreaded the thought of trying to bail her out with buckets, I deferred action on that. Still the weather deteriorated and, when the wind had increased to force six, shrilling around our mast and halyards, I signalled to Athol, suggesting that we should shelter from the gale in Port Clinton. He agreed in principle, but chose the closer Pearl Bay and later that day he anchored there. With water now over our floorboards, we hauled alongside him and began bailing out with buckets and hand pumps.

The rocky country around Pearl Bay showing no sign of life, we took stock of our provisions: no bread or biscuits and, for meat, only a few tins of 'hash'—a dreary animal and vegetable concoction in watery gravy. Our efforts to supplement these provisions met with some success. Our anglers caught nothing, but three sailors who rowed off in the dinghy with hand grenades brought back sixteen good fish. A hunting party roamed the bush for hours returning weary and footsore with nothing. Two of us, armed with revolvers, chased a turtle in the skiff, but it made off to windward and left us far behind.

When at last the weather eased, we made a dash for Gladstone and arrived there late at night on 12 January. Three days later we left at dawn. The forecast for fine north-easterly weather proved wrong and we fought wind and sea all the way to Sandy Cape. When we were uncomfortably close to it, the tow parted again and it took an anxious hour and a half of work, eyes always fixed nervously on the surf, before we could be on our way once more.

At last the wind eased. We glided past the lighthouse on Caloundra Head and Tangalooma Point where we had picnicked with the WRANs, ran down Moreton Bay to the Old Pile Light and up the long fairway into Brisbane River. There at 6.15 p.m. on 17 January, Athol Johnson nudged us gently alongside the wharf at the Fairmile Base and having done so much to save our lives, he chugged on up river and out of them for ever. Our journey's end received an emotional journal entry:

> Lying there at rest from their labours were about a dozen of our sister ships nuzzling the wharf, held by their lines from the hurrying brown river. Paint-hungry and scarred, they lay there dreaming of their young days, not so many months ago, when they ran the gauntlet of enemy aircraft and ships—taking new life to beleaguered men in Timor, evacuating soldiers, escorting ships, patrolling coasts and rivers. The Solomon Islands, New Britain, New Ireland, Darwin, Torres Strait and the Arafura Sea —these were their high noons, and now, quietly in the evening of their lives, they seemed to be left alone to dream. We secured alongside these tired old horses and added to their number.

15 | ALL ASHORE

History never repeats itself exactly but events often follow simi- lar patterns. In 1815, when the Napoleonic Wars ended, the Royal Navy had over 700 ships in commission. By 1818 these had dwindled to about 200, and tens of thousands of men who had been at war since they were boys became civilians for the first time in their adult lives.

Much the same thing happened in Australia after World War II. In September 1939 the RAN had 5440 men serving under the White Ensign. By 30 June 1945 its strength had reached 39,650, the great majority of whom were volunteer reservists and many of these had enlisted straight from school. Conscious of lost opportunities in civilian life, some began agitating for release after the defeat of Germany and, following the surrender of Japan in August 1945 the trickle leaving the navy became a torrent. The rows of deserted ships I had seen in Brisbane were graphic evidence of the RAN's speedy demobilisation but, as I was about to discover, this rapid transition was causing many problems and some administrative chaos.

That January, the liquidator of small ships in Brisbane was Com- mander Arnold Green—said by some to be autocratic and eccentric. This man now controlled my immediate future and my experience quickly confirmed that opinion of him. When I reported to him the morning after our arrival he had no time for pleasantries and quickly laid down the law. ML *1347*, he pointed out abruptly, as though it was my fault, was a late arrival. Most of the MLs at the Fairmile Base were already paid off and awaiting sale, and I would have to remain in her to the last minute of her commission. She would have to be de-stored, cleaned inside and out and, in his opinion, fit for sale before she would be paid off. The families of some of my men were agitating for their sons' release and they would be quickly discharged. I would have no dockyard assistance in this work; he did not care who did it, but I had 'better get on with it'.

His tone surprised me. During my officers' training course at Flinders Naval Depot I had frequently heard the phrase 'Officers and Gentlemen' and for me those words had almost become synonymous. At Flinders it had been made clear to us that, except in emergencies, officers, petty officers and men all had their own special duties, obligations and responsibilities. But here was Commander Green turning this official wisdom on its head and ordering me—in addition to having to account for and return all the ship's weapons, ammunition, stores, charts, confidential books and other items—to become a cleaner, painter and dockyard labourer.

Now aged twenty-three, and pretty sure of myself too, I was anxious to get on with my life. Green's tirade offended me, and I pointed out that I had not been employed by the King to perform such duties in peace-time, and that, with a dwindling crew, the paying off of ML *1347* would take a very long time. At that he gave me a steely look and dismissed me with 'That argument is not worth a fart in a wicker chair.'

Peter Noad and most of the crew were quickly discharged, leaving me with only two or three hands. We were slipped and, while the damage we had received on Salamander Reef was being repaired, I laboriously balanced the account books kept by Clif and Peter before returning them together with the ship's stores, official publications and charts. Then, the last two men on board, 'Smiler' Edwards and I began the filthy job of removing the accumulated sludge and grease from the bilges. For days on end we lay on our stomachs, smeared with oil, scraping, mopping, cleaning and painting the bilges with red lead. I could not have had a more cheerful companion than 'Smiler': he may not have been an officer but he was certainly a gentleman.

Then at last, when all was done and Green's eagle eye could find no fault, he ordered me to decommission ML *1347*. On 29 April 1946 I stood on her bridge under the blue Brisbane sky and lowered the White Ensign and the commissioning pennant with its long white tail and red cross of St George, which I had raised at Sydney's Garden Island sixteen months before. A lifetime ago. That done, His Majesty's Australian Motor Launch *1347*—soon to be sold for a song—was paid off.[1]

She and I alone had been together for her entire life under the White Ensign. One by one I had farewelled my men as they had gone over the side for the last time. The handshakes were done but not the memories and, as I lingered on her deserted bridge watching the muddy river sliding out to sea, they came flooding back. And as they passed I relived them: the rows of white crosses above the bodies of the boys who had turned the Japanese back on the Kokoda Track; the pretty girls in grass skirts thronging our decks at Hula; that awful steel bow towering above us in Goodenough Bay; the stench of dying Japanese in the barge we towed down the Sepik, and the surge of relief when 'Smiler' sighted that blessed light. As I stood there with the threadbare pennant and ensign under my arm, these memories were ML *1347*'s parting gifts to me.

In 1946 the Navy still needed men to maintain her numerous ships and establishments and I was offered an eight-year commission in the RAN. I declined this, but agreed to serve until I had obtained my Arts degree through the University of Sydney's Department of External Studies.

Immediately I was appointed to command HMAS *Air Speed*, an Air Sea Rescue vessel and sister to Reg Lewis's fast little ship I had rammed in Milne Bay. I could hardly wait to get aboard her. But, during the rundown of the RAN's big fleet, planning decisions were often overtaken by circumstances. Before setting eyes on *Air Speed* I received another appointment and, instead of zooming over the waves at 40 knots with the power of 1300 horses at my fingertips, I landed ashore in Brisbane's naval depot, HMAS *Moreton*. There, comfortably quartered, I lived in style; my cabin cleaned, my bunk made up and, for the first time since I had left Flinders Naval Depot, my clothes laundered. With medical and dental services free, I had more money in my pocket and time on my hands than ever before and, while making progress with my studies, I still had time to visit restaurants, cinemas, art galleries, libraries and churches. Having kept the American dollars with which I had been paid at Hollandia, I now cashed them up and bought my first motor car for £100. This was a 1930 Triumph with a collapsible canvas hood, crest on the radiator, crank-handle to start the engine, hand-operated windscreen wiper and thin tyres on large-spoked wheels. When I subsequently tried to drive to Sydney in this machine, two of these wheels, unable to cope with the badly corrugated dirt road, fell off, leaving me stranded on a bitter night in shirt and shorts, on the New England Tablelands.

My Brisbane service over, I was appointed to command ML *1325*. She was larger and more comfortable than ML *1347* and I was keen to join her. But, as with my appointment to *Air Speed*, this came to nothing and I finished up in HMAS *Platypus*, the Sydney mothership of vessels being laid up for sale or recycling in future wars.

Now began another spell of easy living, moored in Watsons Bay. My first duty was to oversee the mothballing of the destroyer HMAS *Queenborough*, also moored at Watsons Bay wharf. Again comfortably quartered, I had ready access by double-decker bus to the city and the Fisher, Municipal, and New South Wales Public Libraries, and, for the first time since resuming my studies, I was able to attend an occasional lecture at the university.

And there was no Arnold Green on my horizon; it pleased me to think of him still stuck in Brisbane liquidating worn-out ships, but this complacency suffered a severe blow at a Government House garden party when he fairly caught me out.

The day was cool and bright. Sunlight sparkled on the harbour and yachts glided beneath the sea wall. Resplendent in my best blue uniform with its colourful new campaign ribbons, I had joined one of those small groups of strangers who cling together on such occasions, making small talk and struggling for closer acquaintance. Suddenly my day darkened: Commander Arnold Green, gleaming in white and gold, was bearing down on me like a battleship and, appalled, I realised that I had misread the orders for the official dress of the day and worn 'blues' instead of 'whites'. He halted about three paces from our group and glowered at me with profound distaste. Our conversation halted nervously. I saluted and said 'Good afternoon, Sir.' Ignoring this courtesy he eyed me coldly for a long five seconds before thundering, 'You are out of the rig of the day. I should have you arrested.' With that, he turned and strode off, leaving me to resume an awkward conversation with my fellow guests. But fortunately he no longer had the power to make my life miserable.

During this time I further developed the love of sailing gained in my childhood with my uncle in his cutter *Temptress*. Now my companion was Commissioned Warrant Officer John Homewood, Boatswain in charge of the dinghies, whalers, cutters and motor boats from the ships being placed in reserve. I liked helping John work on their hempen cordage, canvas sails and wooden hulls, and sometimes after work finished for the day, we would take one of his boats for an outing. In 1946, with little recreational sailing on the harbour during the week, we practically had it to ourselves.

Homewood had been picked to man HMAS *Wyatt Earp* on her forthcoming Antarctic voyage, designed to strengthen Australia's territorial claim there, and I envied him. When the navy had called for volunteers for this voyage I had offered to serve in any capacity except cook. But after the war the navy had many permanent servicemen requiring employment and I missed out.

I never saw the Southern Ocean's great blue bergs, or the blink of ice; but I did get a small consolation prize in an association with the expedition's leader, Commander Karl Oom. Later to become

Hydrographer of the RAN, Oom had had a distinguished career which had earned him the Order of the British Empire, United States' Legion of Merit and Bronze Star, the Polar Medal and Clasp, and the Royal Geographical Society's Gill Memorial Prize.

Born in Sydney of Swedish parents, he had begun his hydrographic work on the coast of Greenland and Labrador. He had also charted the Australian shoreline from Darwin to Mackay and, in 1942–43, surveyed sections of the New Guinea coast under the guns of the Japanese. Having also spent two summers with Sir Douglas Mawson in the Antarctic, he had learned much about boat work in the ice, and on this coming voyage south in the *Wyatt Earp* was taking two specially designed boats. He hoped they would prove more suitable than the 27-foot clinker-built Montague-rigged whalers with their cumbersome dipping lugsails, so dear to generations of seamen. These new boats were lovely creatures: 26 feet long, carvel-built—possibly to reduce the grip of newly forming ice on their planks—and Bermudan-rigged to simplify sail handling. Before accepting them, however, Oom had to test them under varying conditions, and at dinner one night in HMAS *Platypus* he asked me to help him evaluate them.

At this time he was living in some grandeur at Kirribilli House—now the waterfront home of Australia's prime minister, John Howard. The day of our first outing was blessed with a brisk sea breeze, and we walked down a flight of stone steps leading to a little dock cut into the rock face at the water's edge where the first of Oom's beautiful boats lay gently moving on the tide.

For hours we tested her on all points of sailing between North Head and Fort Denison—beating, running, reaching, tacking and gybing—with Oom frequently adjusting the canvas or rigging to improve her performance and, as the day drew in, we sailed back to Kirribilli House over a harbour which, save for a few bustling ferries and a homing tramp, we had to ourselves. We unrigged the boat, made her snug in her little dock and climbed back up the garden path to the house where, in no hurry to end the day's companionship, he proved a generous and amusing host.

This idyllic existence in HMAS *Platypus* lasted until 1947, when I graduated in Arts at the University of Sydney, was discharged from full-time service in the navy, and appointed a lieutenant in the Royal Australian Naval Reserve. Then, for the first time in my adult life, I entered the civilian world which, I was soon to discover, had its own perils and pitfalls.

So ends this account of my first twenty-five years. During the fifty-seven that have followed them there have been many misjudgements, mistakes and some successes. But journeying mercies still hovered around me, and in 1949, when in the Indian Ocean on RMS *Orion*, I met the girl who years later became my wife; that was to be the greatest journeying mercy of them all.

APPENDIX

Captain's Standing Orders
H.M.A. H.D.M.L. 1347

All members of the Ship's Company are to be certain that they fully understand these orders. Each man will be held personally responsible for knowing them.

1. The Commanding Officer will carry out the duties of Signals and Confidential Books Officer, Anti Submarine Control, Navigating and Correspondence Officer in addition to the normal duties of his Command.

2. DUTIES OF THE FIRST LIEUTENANT;
He is responsible for the discipline, organisation, efficiency and cleanliness of the ship in general and in detail.

He is also to be responsible for Censorship, Gunnery, Medical and Naval Stores, and Wardroom Mess Accounts, and he is to supervise the Coxswain's handling of the Ship's Canteen Accounts, Loan Clothing, Mess Traps and Victualling.

3. DUTIES OF THE COXSWAIN;
The Coxswain will carry out the duties of Regulating Petty Officer under the First Lieutenant, to whom he is responsible for the ship's organisation and stores.

He will compile the ship's mess accounts and see that all provisions, loan clothing, mess traps etc. are kept up to Establishment and demanded as required and that records are kept of all issues and receipts.

4. DUTIES OF THE MOTOR MECHANIC;
The M.M. is directly responsible to the Captain for the Engine Room, E.R. Equipment and personnel.

He is to see that all fire precautions are observed and to inspect ALL bilges and carry out fuel compartment inspections daily.

Water supply, stoves, refrigerators and working parts on the upper deck will be the responsibility of the E.R. Staff under the M.M.

No rating other than E.R. Staff is to use the E.R. without the permission of the M.M.

In addition the M.M. is to see that:

The E.R. Log is at all times kept accurately up to date, and submitted for the Commanding Officer's signature at 1030 every Saturday.

The Commanding Officer is to be informed if the fuel falls below 75% of total capacity. All Batteries and electrical systems are maintained. All sea cocks are efficiently working continually.

5. SIGNALS;

No signal is to be sent from the ship without reference to the Commanding Officer, or in his absence the 1st Lieutenant. All official communications arriving on board are immediately to be referred to the Captain (or 1st Lieutenant).

6. ACTION ALARMS;

Submarine or surface alarm: S.S.S. on the alarm ... ...
Aircraft Alarm: A.A.A.   ”   ”   .- .- .-
Fire: Continuous ringing of the alarm bell.

7. ROUTINES;

The ship will normally be in two watches for leave, and two watches at sea. The following harbour routines will be in force when not in tropics.

WEEK DAYS:

0630 Quartermaster call hands and report to the duty officer that this is done.
0645 Hands turn to and hose down—stow bedding.
0730 Breakfast.
0755 Q.M. report for colours.
0800 Colours.
0815 Hands turn to.
1030 Stand Easy.
1040 Out pipes.
1200 Secure for Dinner.
1315 Hands turn to.

1430 Stand Easy.
1440 Out pipes.
1530 Secure.
1600 Liberty men ashore.

Saturdays, same as for Week Days, until
0815 Hands turn to and clean ship for rounds.
1130 Captain's Rounds.
1200 Secure.
1215 Dinner, Liberty men ashore.

SUNDAYS:
0700 Q.M. call hands.
0715 Hands turn to and hose down. Stow bedding.
0745 Breakfast.
0800 Colours.
0845 Hands turn to, clean up ship and square off decks.
0930 Secure for Church.
1030 Liberty men ashore.
Where possible week end leave will be granted.

8. DUTIES OF QUARTERMASTERS;
Will be laid out in the front of the Night Order Book. All Quartermasters
are to be thoroughly acquainted with them.

9. LEAVE;
It is my wish that the men shall get the maximum amount of leave and
recreation that the service conditions permit. Before proceeding on leave
Liberty men are to leave an address (and telephone number where possible)
where they may be contacted at short notice.

Liberty men leaving or rejoining the ship are to report to the duty
officer. Liberty men must not travel such a distance from the ship that it
will not enable them to rejoin her within the time of the ship's notice
for sea.

10. DRESS OF THE DAY;
Will be as detailed for Ship's Company of parent ship, except when doing dirty work, when working rig will be worn.

11. BOOKS;
The Commanding Officer will inspect the following books, after which Rounds will be conducted each Saturday morning:
1. Deck Log
2. E.R.'s Register etc.
3. Wine and Day Books.
4. Gangway Wine Book
5. Night Rounds Book

12. ANTI-SUBMARINE;
The A/S set is to be tested daily by the H.S.D. by 0900, and its state of efficiency reported to the Commanding Officer.

13. WIRELESS TELEGRAPHY;
The telegraphist is responsible for the cleanliness and tidiness of the W/T cabin and the efficiency of its equipment. When not in use it is to be locked and no other member of the ship's company is to use it without permission of an officer.

14. WASHING;
Washed clothes may be dried on the foredeck, after 1600 on week days and 1200 on Saturdays. Clothes lines are to be rigged neatly.

15. FRESH WATER;
In view of the limited capacity, utmost economy is to be exercised in the use of fresh water. The M.M. is to see that a constant check is kept and report to the Commanding Officer when the amount falls below 50% of capacity.

16. HYGIENE, ETC;

Careful attention is to be paid to personal cleanliness, cleanliness of the ship, regular airing of bedding etc. All refuse is to be promptly disposed of and not allowed to accumulate. Care and attention is to be paid to the correct stowage of all gear, personal and otherwise, this will make for greater comfort to all aboard.

17. VISITORS;

No visitors are to be permitted aboard without the permission of the Commanding Officer, or in his absence the 1st Lieutenant.

18. GALLEY;

The cook is responsible for the cleanliness and efficiency of the galley and the galley gear.

19. LIFE BELTS;

Life belts are always to be ready for an emergency and to be continually at hand while at sea.

CONVERSIONS

Currency
1 pound = 20 shillings, 1 shilling = 12 pence and 1 dollar = 10 shillings

Temperature

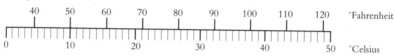

Distance

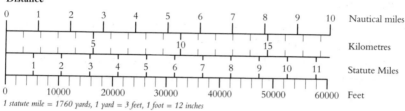

1 statute mile = 1760 yards, 1 yard = 3 feet, 1 foot = 12 inches

Depth

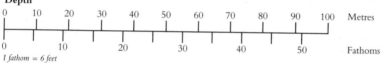

1 fathom = 6 feet

Volume

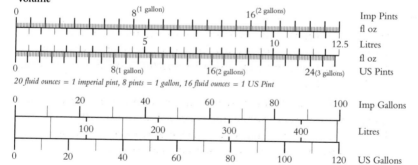

20 fluid ounces = 1 imperial pint, 8 pints = 1 gallon, 16 fluid ounces = 1 US Pint

Weight

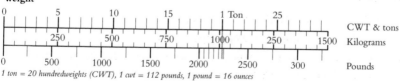

1 ton = 20 hundredweights (CWT), 1 cwt = 112 pounds, 1 pound = 16 ounces

NOTES

Preface

1 Richard Rumbold and Lady Vane-Tempest-Stewart collaborated to write *The Winged Life*, a biography of the complex French airman Antoine de Saint-Exupéry, published by Weidenfeld & Nicolson in 1953. Richard gave me a copy of it for my thirty-second birthday inscribed, 'For Marsden from Richard, in memory of our epic flight over London's rooftops.'

Being Prepared

1 Knox Grammar School Records—Vol. 1, Archives, Knox Grammar School, Wahroonga. Neil H. MacNeil, manuscript.

2 *Prize-Giving Address by Rear-Admiral E.R.G.R. Evans, CB, DSO*, Thursday 11 December 1930. Archives, Knox Grammar School, Sydney.

3 *The Australian Boy Scout Diary*, pp. 9–11.

4 Vaucluse Junior, a small-decked, watertight wooden boat, which could be righted after a capsize by standing on the fin.

5 Edmund Thomas Blacket, 1817–83, Colonial Architect, who designed or completed such notable buildings as St Andrew's Cathedral, and many others in New South Wales.

6 *The Knox Grammarian*, May 1934.

War

1 In the 1920s, when the Admiralty was considering the effect of hostile submarines on Britain's lifelines in a future war, a committee was set up called the Allied Submarine Detection Investigation Committee, and so was coined the 'Asdic'.

2 This law, propounded by Buys Ballot, concerned atmospheric pressures and the opposite rotation of winds in the north and south hemispheres. A seaman who mastered it and was caught in a cyclone or typhoon could discover where its vortex lay and steer a course to try and avoid it.

Convoys

1 Wallace, *The Secret Battle 1942–1944*, p. 51.

2 Gill, *Royal Australian Navy 1942–1945*, p. 386.

3 Correspondence 11 July 1998, from Commander A. I. Chapman RAN (Ret'd) of Burradoo, NSW, the former commanding officer of HMAS *Abraham Crijnssen*.

4   The convoy in which the *Iron Knight* had been sailing was No. OC 68. Gill, *Royal Australian Navy 1942–1945*, p. 253.

A Fairmiler

1   This method of celestial navigation was introduced about 200 years ago by Captain Marcq St Hilaire of the French navy.

2   This lightship is now moored at the Australian National Maritime Museum, Darling Harbour, Sydney.

3   On arrival in Darwin ML *814*'s crew included: Lieutenants R. R. Lewis and B. P. Wood, Sub Lieutenant M. C. Hordern, Petty Officer Motor Mechanic J. D. Livingstone, Leading Stoker J. J. Old, Stoker D. L. Ashford, Signalman D'Arcy Kelly, Telegraphist J. B. Brewer, Leading Seaman J. K. Nelson, Able Seamen G. Constable, D. W. Davey, D. Kay, R. C. Ling, Mackenzie, F. T. Morrah, G. F. Nolan, T. T. Trewick, Ordinary Seamen D. R. Partridge and R. J. Hayes, *Dits and Dahs*, Newsletter, Fairmile Association No. 29, March 2000.

Darwin's Navy

1   Later Sir Lorimer Dods.

2   On 7 October 1994, at a ceremony in Canberra, Chips, D'Arcy Kelly and the author presented this flag to the Australian War Memorial, where it is now on permanent exhibition.

Touching New Guinea

1   This medical chest is now in the Australian National Maritime Museum, Darling Harbour, Sydney.

In Command

1   The identification numbers on the American-built Harbour Defence Motor Launches originally had the prefix 'Q'. The numbers on the Australian and British-built Motor Launches bore the prefix 'ML'.

2   I was the only one to remain with the ship for her entire sixteen months' service under the White Ensign. During that time the following men served in her: Sub Lieutenants Clem McMahon, T. C. Wilkinson and Peter Noad, Motor Mechanics J. A. Page, A. W. Copeland, A. Boxer and G. J. Russell, Petty Officer W. A. Bennetts, Stokers Ken Akers and J. M. Tassell, Telegraphists J. A. Dobbs, K. T. Johnston, D. J. Kelly and Sharpe, Leading Seaman Leonard

Clarkson, Able Seamen K. A. Arkinstall, R. M. Jeffs,
E. T. Barry, C. P. Edwards, S. L. Keith, N. Whitehurst, W. T. Nye and C. A.
Wallace, and one or two others whose names I did not record and cannot
remember. All of them are now dead or old men, who nearly sixty years ago
served their country well.

3   Atkinson, *By Skill and Valour*, p. 96.

All at Sea

1   Wharton (ed.), *Captain Cook's Journal ... made in H.M. Bark 'Endeavour'*
1768–71, p. 260.

2   The Reverend Canon Boyce Rowley Horsley, BA, BD, Dip Archives Admin,
M Th, ThL, died at the age of ninety. Three former archbishops participated
in his funeral service at Sydney's St Andrew's Cathedral and Sir Marcus
Loane, former primate of Australia, also aged ninety, gave the address. Boyce
Horsley's coffin was shrouded with the White Ensign which had covered the
communion table that Whitsunday morning in 1945.

3   Dr Beaglehole, in his edition of Banks, *The Endeavour Journal of Joseph Banks*,
vol II, p. 103, states that 'No specimens of these lizards have been traced, nor
has any description of them been found. No subsequent visitor to the island
appears to have mentioned them ...' On 22 March 1968, I wrote to Dr
Beaglehole mentioning this lizard, quoting from my journal entry of 2 June
1945, and he welcomed the information.

4   On 25 July 1942 at Gorari the 39th Militia Battalion had been the first unit
of the Australian Military Forces to oppose the Japanese advance on Port
Moresby. Their average age was under nineteen, and on 5 September, when
the 39th was relieved at Efogi, it had suffered 117 battle casualties. Gash and
Whittaker, *A Pictorial History of*
New Guinea, p. 289.

Road to Hollandia

1   Dampier, *A Voyage to New Holland*, pp. 222–3.

2   Ibid. Dampier was 1° 28' out in his latitude for Manam Island.

3   *New Guinea Handbook*, published by the authority of the Prime Minister's
Department, Canberra, 1937, pp. 463–4.

Working for the Yankee Dollar

1   Rosenman, *Two Voyages to the South Seas*, p. 148.

2   Dexter, *The New Guinea Offensives*, p. 802.

3   Ibid, p. 804.

4   Dexter, *The New Guinea Offensives*, p. 815.

5   The statement that the bomb was about the size of a 'medium parcel' was deliberate misinformation to increase its horror. The bomb, codenamed 'Little Boy', dropped by the B-29 Superfortress 'Enola Gay', exploded about 2000 feet above the centre of Hiroshima. It was over 13 feet long, weighed about 5 tons, and had cost the American taxpayers $2,000,000,000. That afternoon the managing editors of the five big Tokyo newspapers were instructed to run the story in an 'obscure place in your papers and as one no different from the report of an ordinary air raid'. *Reader's Digest Illustrated Story of World War II*, p. 508.

6   'Overwhelming force delivered quickly the key to befuddling the foe', *Sydney Morning Herald*, 21 March 2003, comments on the book *Shock and Awe*.

Soldiering On

1   Wigmore, *The Japanese Thrust*, p. 113.

2   Adachi, a skilful and tenacious soldier, was found guilty of war crimes and given life imprisonment but committed suicide, leaving this message for his surviving men:

> During the past three years of operations more than 100,000 youthful and promising officers and men were lost and most of them died of malnutrition ... God knows how I felt when I saw them dying, my bosom being filled with pity for them, though it was solely for their country that they dedicated their lives. At that time I made up my mind not to set foot on my country's soil again but to remain as a clod of earth in the Southern Seas with the 100,000 officers and men, even if a time would come when I would be able to return to my country in triumph.

Gash and Whittaker, *A Pictorial History of New Guinea*, p. 280.

3   Letter from D. Monk to the author, 6 December 2000.

4   Ref. N 644/34. 'Commander (A) New Guinea, Memorandum No. 30. Transporting Japanese Prisoners—Liberated Asiatics'.

5   McCarthy, *Patrol Into Yesterday*, pp. 65–6.

6   Singh, *A Brief Sketch of the Fate of 3000 Indian P.O.W. in New Guinea*, describes his time aboard ML *1347* and his association with the author.

7   Ibid.

8   Ibid.

Sea of Troubles

1   In February 1942, when the Japanese invaded the Dutch East Indies, the 3105-ton China River steamer *Ping Wo* towed the disabled destroyer HMAS *Vendetta* from Batavia to Fremantle, where the *Ping Wo* was commissioned into the RAN. She was one of the former Chinese government ships given to the RAN in World War II, which became repair, ammunition, depot and store ships.

2   In August 1942 the 2873-ton Ammunition Issue Ship *Poyang* took part in the battle for the Solomon Islands, and on 22 September 1945 she was one of the RAN's ships present at the Japanese surrender of Ambon.

3   Admiralty Chart No. 2422.

4   *United Service* Journal, Royal United Service Institution of NSW Inc., Vol. 52, No. 1, 1999, p. 37, and *Australia Pilot*, Vol. III, 6th edn, appendix III.

5   Sixteen of these handy little vessels were built in Australia for the RAN. See specifications in Norton, *Fighting Ships of Australia and New Zealand*, pp. 92–3.

All Ashore

1   ML *431*, a Fairmile, which had cost over thirty thousand pounds, had her engines and much of her equipment removed, and was 'sold for $40 ... after towing her to Karragarra Island in Moreton Bay the remains of *431* were beached and set alight for the recovery of copper nails and brass screws'. Fairmile Association, *Dits and Dahs*, Newsletter No. 32, December 2000.

BIBLIOGRAPHY

Unpublished sources

Monthly Logbooks of H.M.A. Motor Launch 'No. 1347', 1945–6.

Hordern, Marsden, *War Journal*, 1942–6.

Hordern, Marsden, letters while serving with the Australian Military Forces and the Royal Australian Navy, 1941–1946.

Singh, Chint, *A Brief Sketch of the Fate of 3000 Indian P.O.W. in New Guinea*, November 1945, Ref. AG.940.5425/S617/1.

Publications

Alford, Bob, *Darwin's Air War 1942–1945, An Illustrated History*, The Aviation History Society of the Northern Territory, Darwin, n.d.

Atkinson, James J., *By Skill and Valour: Honours and Awards to the Royal Australian Navy for the First and Second World Wars*, Spink & Son (Australia) Pty Ltd, Sydney, 1986.

Austin, Victor (ed.), *To Kokoda and Beyond*, Melbourne University Press, Melbourne, 1988.

Bach, John, *A Maritime History of Australia*, Pan Books, Sydney, 1982.

Banks, Joseph, *The Endeavour Journal of Joseph Banks, 1768–1771*, ed. J. C. Beaglehole, Angus & Robertson, Sydney, 1962.

Buggy, Hugh, *Pacific Victory: A Short History of Australia's Part in the War against Japan*, Department of Information, Canberra, 1946.

Callinan, Bernard, *Independent Company: The Australian Army in Portuguese Timor 1941–1943*, Heinemann, Richmond, VIC., 1984.

Champion, Ivan F., *Across New Guinea from the Fly to the Sepik*, Lansdowne Press, Melbourne, 1966.

Cranswick, G. H., and Shevill, I. W. A., *A New Deal for Papua*, F. W. Cheshire, Melbourne, 1949.

Dampier, William, *A Voyage to New Holland: The English Voyage of Discovery to the South Seas in 1699*, ed. James Spencer, Alan Sutton, Gloucester, UK, 1981.

Davis, Kenneth S., *Experience of War: The United States in World War II*, Doubleday, New York, 1965.

Dawes, Allan, *Soldier Superb: The Australian Fights in New Guinea*, F. H. Johnston, Sydney, 1943.

Dexter, David, *The New Guinea Offensives*, Australian War Memorial, Canberra, 1961.

Evans, Peter (ed.), *Fairmile Ships of the Royal Australian Navy*, Vol. I, Australian Military History Publications, Sydney, 2002.

Foley, John C. H., *Reef Pilots: The History of the Queensland Coast and Torres Strait Pilot Service*, Banks Bros & Street, Sydney, 1982.

Freame, William, *A Delectable Parish: Prospect and Seven Hills, Cumberland Argus*, Parramatta, NSW, 1923.

Gash, Noel, and Whittaker, June, *A Pictorial History of New Guinea*, Jacaranda Press, Milton, QLD, 1975.

Gill, G. Hermon, *Royal Australian Navy 1942–1945*, Australian War Memorial, Canberra, 1968.

Grant, Jim, *Spitfires over Darwin 1943: No. 1 Fighter Wing*, R. J. Moore, Melbourne, 1995.

Griffiths, Owen, *Darwin Drama*, Bloxham & Chambers, Sydney, n.d.

Hides, J. G., *Beyond the Kubea*, Angus & Robertson, Sydney, 1939.

Hoffman, Carl W., *Saipan: The Beginning of the End*, Historical Division, U.S. Marine Corps, Washington D.C., 1950.

Hordern, Lesley, *Children of One Family: The Story of Anthony and Ann Hordern and their Descendants in Australia, 1825–1925*, Retford Press, Sydney, 1985.

Horton, D. C., *Ring of Fire: Australian Guerrilla Operations against the Japanese in World War II*, Macmillan, Melbourne, 1983.

Ingleton, G. C., *Charting a Continent*, Angus & Robertson, Sydney, 1944.

Inoguchi, Rikihei, and Nakajima, T., with Pineau, Roger, *The Divine Wind: Japan's Kamikaze Force in World War II*, Hutchinson, London, 1959.

Keogh, E. G., *South West Pacific 1941–45*, Grayflower Productions, Melbourne, 1965.

Laffin, John, and Badman, Peter, *Special and Secret*, Time-Life Books Australia, Sydney, 1990.

Law, Phillip, *The Antarctic Voyage of HMAS Wyatt Earp*, Allen & Unwin, Sydney, 1995.

Lewis, Tom, *Wrecks in Darwin Waters*, Turton & Armstrong, Wahroonga, NSW, 1992.

McAuley, Lex, *To the Bitter End*, Random House, Sydney, 1992.

McCarthy, J. K., *Patrol into Yesterday: My New Guinea Years*, Cheshire, Melbourne, 1967.

Mayo, Lida, *Bloody Buna: The Campaign that Halted the Japanese Invasion of Australia*, David & Charles Ltd, Newton Abbot, Devon, U.K., 1975.

Miklouho-Maclay, N., *Travels to New Guinea*, Progress Publishers, Moscow, 1982.

Murphy, John J., *The Book of Pidgin English*, Smith & Paterson, Brisbane, 1943.

Official Handbook of the Territory of New Guinea. Administered by the Commonwealth of Australia, Commonwealth Government Printer, Canberra, 1943.

No. 31 Beaufighter Squadron Album RAAF, no publication details.

Norton, Frank, *Fighting Ships of Australia and New Zealand*, Angus & Robertson, Sydney, 1953.

Odgers, George, *Air War Against Japan 1943–1945*, Australian War Memorial, Canberra, 1957.

Reader's Digest Illustrated Story of World War II, Reader's Digest Association, Sydney, 1970.

Reid, Frank, *The Romance of the Great Barrier Reef*, Angus & Robertson, Sydney, 1954.

Rosenman, Helen (trans. and ed.), *Two Voyages to the South Seas by Jules S.-C. Dumont D'Urville*, Melbourne University Press, Melbourne, 1985.

Silver, Lynette Ramsay, *The Heroes of Rimau*, Sally Milner Publishing, Sydney, 1990.

Souter, Gavin, *New Guinea, The Last Unknown*, Angus & Robertson, Sydney, 1963.

Stevens, David (ed.), *The Royal Australian Navy in World War II*, Allen & Unwin, Sydney, 1996.

The Australian Boy Scout Diary, Federal Scout Council of Australia, Melbourne, 1935.

The Knox Grammarian 1934–36, Vol VI, No. 17, May 1934.

Walker, Frank B., *HMAS Armidale, The Ship that Had to Die*, Kingfisher Press, Budgewoi, NSW, 1990.

Wallace, Robert, *The Secret Battle 1942–1944*, Lamont Publishing, Ringwood, VIC, 1995.

Warner, Denis and Peggy, with Sadao, Seno, *Kamikaze: The Sacred Warriors 1944–45*, Oxford University Press, Melbourne, 1983.

Wharton, Captain W. J. L. (ed.), *Captain Cook's Journal … made in H.M. Bark 'Endeavour' 1768–1771*, Elliot Stock, London, 1893.

Wigmore, Lionel, *The Japanese Thrust*, Australian War Memorial, Canberra, 1957.

INDEX

This book was designed by Phil Campbell Design
The text was typeset by Syarikat Seng Teik Sdn. Bhd., Malaysia
The text was set in Bembo 11.75 point with 15 points of leading
The text is printed on 100 gsm Precision Offset

This book was edited by Clare Coney

Three thousand copies of this edition were printed in Australia by
BPA Print Group

THE
MIEGUNYAH
PRESS

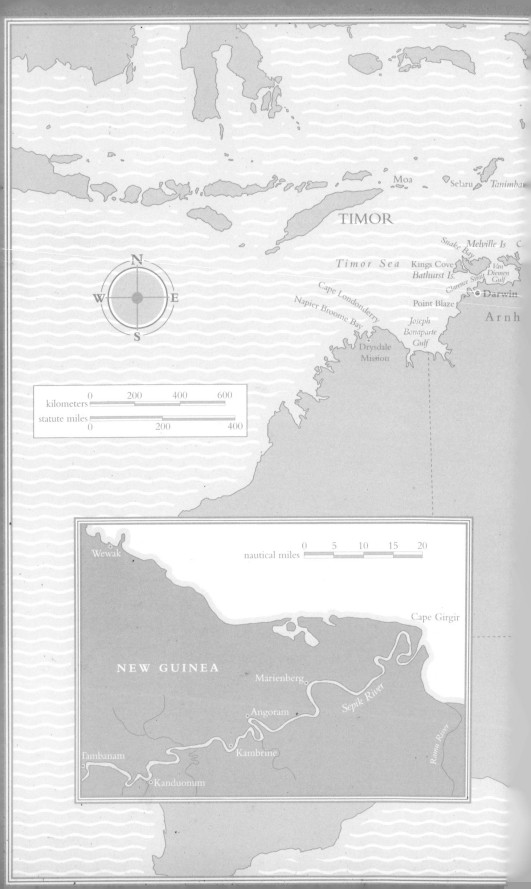